Being

Japanese

American

Being Japanese American

A JA SOURCEBOOK FOR NIKKEI, HAPA . . . & THEIR FRIENDS

Gil Asakawa

Stone Bridge Press | Berkeley, California

Published by
Stone Bridge Press
P.O. Box 8208
Berkeley, CA 94707
TEL 510-524-8732 • sbp@stonebridge.com • www.stonebridge.com

The translations of the nursery rhymes appearing on page 43, "Rabbit" ("Usagi") and "A Rolling Acorn" ("Donguri korokoro"), words by Nagayoshi Aoki and music by Tadashi Yanada, appear courtesy Ayako Egawa. These rhymes and others can be found on Lisa Yannucci's Web site, Mama Lisa's World (www.mamalisa.com).

All photos supplied by the author except where noted.

Cover and text design by Linda Ronan.

Second edition, 2015.

Printed in the United States of America.

LIBRARY OF CONGRESS CATALOGING-IN-PUBLICATION DATA AVAILABLE.

P-ISBN 978-1-61172-0-228
E-ISBN 978-1-61172-9-146

Contents

Preface to the Second Edition 7

Introduction 9

Part I: JAs Yesterday

CHAPTER 1 Where Did We Come From? 19

Paving the way 21 • Here to stay 24 • The camps 27 • Fighting for a place in society 30 • Speaking out 31 • Redress 33

CHAPTER 2 Memories of Home 35

Games 36 • Crafting a culture 38 • Musical roots 42 • Spiritual roots 45

CHAPTER 3 Customs 47

Turning Japanese 50 • The gift of giving 51 • Celebrations 52 • The rules of death 54 • Rules of etiquette 56 • Values—good and bad 57

CHAPTER 4 Food 59

What's "authentic" Japanese food? 62 • Ramen 64 • Rice 65 • JA specialties 67 • Mochi and the special foods of New Year 68 • Mochi madness 70 • Recipes you can try 71

CHAPTER 5 Language 73

Typically Japanese—and therefore JA 74 • Growing up in a bilingual household 75 • It's my name; please don't mangle it 76 • Learning Japanese 77

Part II: JAs Today

CHAPTER 6 It's Hip to Be Japanese! 83

The power of anime 85 • The man in the lizard suit 89 • Ameri-kana 91 • Hai! Karate 93 • The sporting life 94 • JAs online 95 • J-pop and the sound of young Japan 98 • On the silver screen 102 • On the small screen 104 • JA lit 106 • On the cutting edge 111

CHAPTER 7 JA Communities 113

Japantowns 113 • Community organizations 115 • Community without J-towns 117 • Church life, newspapers, and the Wonder Years 120 • Nikkei, not just JA 122 • Japanese Canadians, eh 124

CHAPTER 8 Scrapbooking Your History 125

Photos, postcards, and other memorabilia 126 • Climbing the Japanese family tree 127 • Immigration records 129 • Researching internment history 129 • Recording your family history 130 • Preserving your family's legacy 133

CHAPTER 9 Homeward Bound 137

Strangers in a familiar land 138 • Ways to go 139 • Getting young people to Japan 143 • Tips for your trip 144

Part III: JAs Tomorrow

CHAPTER 10 AAPI, Not Just JA 149

Pan-Asian, not pan-Oriental 151 • Rugs are Oriental; we're Asian 152 • The rise of Yellow Power 153 • A better tomorrow for AAPIs on screen 155 • An apology at last 156 • Our work's not done 157 • Building bridges in a post-9/11 world 158

Staying Informed, Staying Connected

The Internet 163 • Newspapers 165 • Magazines 165 • Blogs 166 • Social media 166 • Organizations 166 • Sites about Japan 168 • Japanese culture 169 • Genealogy 172 • Hapa issues 172 • Internment resources 173 • JA/Nikkei/AAPI sites & Blogs 174 • Shopping 175 • Travel to Japan 176 • Books 177 • Films and videos 182

Afterword 185

Index 187

Preface to the Second Edition

Since the first edition of this book was released in 2004, I've been to Japan four times, and I've become much more involved in the pan-Asian community, both in Colorado where I live, and nationally. That means that I'm becoming both more Japanese and more Asian American simultaneously. I think that's how many Asian Americans and Pacific Islanders (AAPI) feel: proudly rooted in the culture of their families' origins and at the same time aware of the growing combined presence of the many AAPI communities that are thriving throughout the United States.

For this second edition of *Being Japanese American*, I've added content (to use the parlance of the digital world, in which I make my living) that focuses on JAs and AAPIs online, especially through social media, which was just being invented when *Being JA* was originally published. I've also written a section on how to keep up with news about Japan, which is also something that's greatly enabled by the Internet.

Because of my recent trips to Japan with my wife Erin Yoshimura (we weren't married when the book was published), I feel more pas-sionately than ever that Japanese Americans should visit Japan at least once. It can be a life-changing, identity-affirming journey to discover your roots. You don't even have to visit family if you're nervous about meeting a bunch of foreign relatives. But just going to Japan and being surrounded by, well, Japanese people, will give you a renewed perspective on who you are in America. And I hope you'll find that you feel an almost indescribable sense of coming home when you land in Japan and see that so much of that country's culture and traditions are familiar to you, even through filters of generations and assimilation into American society.

The past decade has been one long coming-out party for Asian Americans as a whole, if not quite so for Japanese Americans as a group. It's as if we've found our collective voice and made cultural impacts everywhere, from Hollywood to social media, from K-pop (yes, so J-pop got overtaken as the "next big thing" in the past decade) to the explosion of popularity in almost all Asian cuisines in the U.S., including not just sushi for Japanese food but, these days, hipster ramen. Anime continues to influence new generations of American *otaku*, or animation fans, who ultimately want to visit or study in Japan.

Social media have exploded within the past decade, and Asian Americans have rocked the online world. Social media have made it easier to solicit input from JAs across the U.S. and Canada to include as marginalia—I simply put an online survey form on my blog for readers to fill out, and I got the word out on Twitter and Facebook.

But the most important fact of the past ten years for the AAPI community is that, as a group, we have become the fastest-growing segment of the population in the United States. The media have made a lot of noise about Hispanics and how important they are to elections, but AAPIs will soon be an equally important and even more influential demographic for politicians to pay attention to. According to a 2013 Nielsen report on Asian American consumers, "The Asian American community continues to be the fastest-growing multicultural segment in the U.S., with a current population of nearly 19 million. This represents a growth rate of almost 58% from 2000 to 2013, mainly spurred by immigration."

No wonder that newspapers before and after the 2014 election began running stories about how Asian Americans vote.

Although it wasn't a JA news story, the March 11, 2011 earthquake and tsunami in northeast Japan stirred up negative emotions that affected Japanese Americans. The disaster even sparked an anti-Japanese backlash that claimed the earthquake and tsunami and the meltdown at the Fukushima nuclear power plant were somehow revenge for the Japanese attack on Pearl Harbor that drew the United States into World War II. But these ignorant, racist messages brought out many more people who defended Japan.

Some other things have changed since 2004 in my own language.

For one, I've chosen to no longer use the term *hapa* for mixed-race people. Although the term is more commonly used than ever, its origins are as a racial slur, and I've met too many mixed-race people of different ethnicities who find the term offensive. I believe that impact is ultimately more important that intent, and though I would certainly never intend *hapa* as a racist term, I'm fine with just saying "mixed race."

The subtitle of this book, as well as my earlier text and any stories submitted by mixed-race JAs who use *hapa* will remain as-is, but for now, I'm using "mixed race" in new text. I use "mixed race" in my blog too, and in a February 2015 post titled "What Are Words Worth: Hapa, Hafu or Mixed-Race?" I explained why. That post has generated a long and thoughtful conversation with readers on my blog and on Facebook, so the topic resonates. My guess is that in the future the use of *hapa* will become so commonplace that negative perceptions will fade. But for now, "mixed race" feels right to me.

And although there still is no consensus among Asian Americans, I now use "Asian Americans and Pacific Islanders" or "Asian American Pacific Islanders" or just "AAPI" to describe our multifaceted community. Back in 2004 I used "Asian Pacific Americans" or "APA." Some people and organizations still do, but many now use AAPI, including President Obama and his White House Initiative on AAPIs. That's good enough for me.

Gil Asakawa
Spring 2015

Introduction

DEDICATION
This book is dedicated to my Nisei dad, George H. Asakawa, who started me on my journey of self-discovery when he told me he wasn't in Honolulu the day Pearl Harbor was bombed.

I was a banana.

That's what I've been told by people who know—Japanese Americans who've been involved in community activism all their lives. Even though I was born in Japan, I haven't studied my roots in Japanese culture or even the history of Japanese Americans all my life. I didn't know who Vincent Chin was, or about the No-No Boys. Because I didn't know about the history, I was told I was a banana: Yellow on the outside, white on the inside.

It's true that I grew up among Caucasian friends—especially after my family moved to the States—and I wasn't involved politically or socially with Asians or Asian causes. But I like to think of myself as more than just a fruit. I'm really a dessert. I'm a banana split, with both my "yellow" and "white" sides sharing equal attention.

I know more about Japan than some other Japanese Americans, for one thing. Since I lived there as a kid, I have vivid memories of Japan (albeit the Japan of thirty-five years ago, before the first McDonald's or KFC stormed the Yamato shores), and feel at home—sort of—when I visit. I've also immersed myself in Japanese history and pop culture in recent years, and I feel I'm as much a Japanese as I am an American.

My Japanese-language skills are still pretty wretched, I'll admit. But that's not uncommon for Japanese Americans. My mother tried to teach my brother and me to read and write Japanese after our family moved to the States, but we refused. Instead, I learned every American obscenity I could and went around the summer of 1966 proudly enunciating some of the foulest language on Earth, even though my eight-year-old mind had no idea what any of those words meant. My idea of a cool four-letter word wasn't *"kana,"* and my vocabulary didn't include any Japanese alphabets.

Still, I can understand a fair amount of *Nihongo*, and if I say so myself, my accent on the few words I know is pretty authentic. I'd never "pass" for a Japanese in Japan, but I can surprise an employee in a Japanese restaurant by sounding first-generation, at least on a limited scale. When I'm not cursing loudly in English, anyway.

It's my appearance that's more American: rumpled jeans, baggy clothes, loud colors, the loping way I walk (as if I'm moving to the beat

9

Living in two worlds: The author in Tokyo in the early 1960s, living out his cowboy dreams like any American kid, except he was in the land of the samurai.

Even while I was attending art school, it didn't occur to me that I might be a banana—or any ethnic flavor, for that matter. My work followed the paths of centuries of white Euro-centric artists from Leonardo da Vinci to Andy Warhol. I learned about Japanese art, including the *ukiyo-e* woodcut prints that influenced the French Impressionists I loved so well, yet I never felt the urge to make "Japanese-inspired" art.

All my life, though, I was Japanese in all sorts of very visible ways—not the least of which was my skin. The banana peel, I guess. I loved all kinds of Japanese food, I usually took off my shoes even in my friends' homes, I was polite to seniors. I respected authority. Well, sort of.

And slowly, as I got older and began to feel the need to get involved in the community around me, I began to realize that the part of me that was the banana peel wanted to reach below the surface. I wanted to be around others who looked like me (whether or not they were also bananas didn't matter). I became involved in the local Japanese and Asian Pacific Islander communities, joining nonprofit organizations and participating in Asian Pacific American events. These outlets helped me connect my internal and external selves and make sense of my self-image. Ultimately, the interaction with others has helped me accept my split personality and feel comfortable in my own skin.

Sure, there are millions of people who are more Japanese than me. Good for them. I've also met JAs who are even more banana-like than me: people who can't speak any Japanese without fumbling over the syllables, who've never dined on *Nihon meshi* (Japanese food) and prefer hamburgers and fries, people who mangle their own name, saying it American-style, people who've never had Asian friends, and people who just have no clue that they

of rock music in my head) with my head up and making eye contact with others. And my tastes: brightly painted car, loud music, and colorful language.

Since I didn't have Asian friends in grade school and high school, I eventually forgot that I was Asian. I thought of myself as white, and I hung around with my white friends and acted like any American kid, at least while I was away from home. I was only reminded of my different face and skin color (why do they call it "yellow" anyway? I'm not yellow . . .) when racism periodically raised its ugly head and confronted me.

have a wonderfully rich culture that's deeply rooted in their DNA. It's taken me a while, but I feel more aware of political issues and the pervasive racism that surrounds all people of color in our culture. I now know who Vincent Chin was, and why the No-No Boys deserve some respect.

In a way, I am a born-again Japanese American. I'm aware of both sides of my culture, the inside and the outside of the banana. I am a Nikkei—someone of Japanese descent living outside Japan.

To be specific, I am a Sansei, or third-generation JA, but I used to tell people I'm a Nihan-sei, or "second-and-a-half generation," because I was born in Japan to a Nisei father from Hawaii and an Issei mother from Hokkaido.

I was eight years old when my family moved to the States and I became aware of being Japanese American. Until then, I was just a Japanese kid who went to American schools. I grew up in a bicultural world where I spoke English and attended American schools on U.S. military bases in Tokyo and Iwakuni, but my family always lived off-base so I played after school with Japanese pals. The language at home was a mish-mash of Japanese and English, and it all made sense to me.

Once we arrived in a Washington, D.C., suburb, I embraced the American side of my culture wholeheartedly. I ate my first McDonald's hamburger (I had lived in pre-fast-food Japan), and I became enchanted with *The Man from U.N.C.L.E.,* the Beatles, and all of Western popular culture. I also forgot my Japanese. I never learned to read or write despite my mom's valiant efforts to get my older brother and me to study the grade school *hiragana* and *katakana* primers she'd brought across the Pacific. I was too busy learning those English cuss words, I guess.

But—and here's the part I think is consistent with many, if not most, JAs—even though I stopped thinking in Japanese, I still lived with Japanese all around me. Japanese-ness permeated my life. It was in the décor of my parents' house. It was in the rice that we ate with our meals virtually every day of our lives, along with the steak, hamburgers, fried chicken, and other all-American foods that mom served with it. It was in the smelly things my mother sometimes cooked, so stinky that I was embarrassed to bring my friends over. It was in the ritual of taking our shoes off at the front door. It was the fact that my mother would speak to my brothers and me mostly in Japanese and we would reply mostly in English. Our brains had settled into a groove that allowed Japanese and American stuff to live side by side.

In college, I had a tiny rice cooker my mom had given me, and I learned some of my mom's recipes for authentic Japanese cooking. But I also cherished learning to cook authentic Italian food from my roommate and dined on every kind of ethnic food available in New York City, where I went to college. It never occurred to me that I was performing an internal balancing act. On the campus radio station, where I had a weekly show playing country-rock music for the mostly East Coast students, I gave myself a nickname that unwittingly reflected this duality: I would go on the air in my best "laidback FM disc jockey" impersonation, purring, "Hello everyone, I'm Gil Asakawa, the 'Teriyaki Cosmic Cowboy.'" I wince when I think back on those days, because even without realizing it, I was searching for my identity.

Sometimes I felt like an imposter, like a phony Japanese. When my grandmother in Hokkaido called me in the middle of the night to wish me a happy birthday, I couldn't reply in Japanese, although I understood enough to know that she was berating me for not speaking

Nihongo back to her. After the phone call, I went back to bed feeling like a complete loser, and a bit irritated that I had to be reminded that I had become "too American" and was losing touch with my own past.

The fact is, I had been a banana for many years. It took the death of my father in the early 1990s to jolt me into being curious about my heritage. When he was diagnosed with cancer (he had smoked all his life), it finally occurred to me to ask what life was like for him and his family to live in Honolulu when Pearl Harbor was bombed. "I don't know," he responded. What? He was born and raised in Hawaii with his seven brothers and sisters. How could he not know? It turns out my grandfather had decided in 1940 to take his family back to Japan, where they lived in his hometown of Fukui on the west coast for the duration of the war. This revelation sparked a fascination with wartime and postwar Japan for me, as well as with the Japan of my early childhood.

And it also initiated my interest in how I've evolved, not as a *Japanese*, but as a *Japanese American*.

My Japanese isn't much better today, but at least now I appreciate my duality more than when I was a punk kid. I'm involved in both Japanese and Japanese American organizations and events, and thanks to my Yonsei partner, Erin, there is more of a Japanese presence infusing all aspects of my life. Nowadays I cherish my Japanese heritage and value my American spirit. I am Japanese American. Still, I really wish I'd paid attention to those damn *Nihongo* primers–the "Dick and Jane" versions of Japanese language books. I would love to have a job that sends me to Japan once or twice a year, but there's no chance without the ability to communicate in Japanese. That's one of the basic facts I've learned to accept as a Japanese American—I'm simply not Japanese.

When I was approached to write this book, I figured it would be a piece of cake—*mochi* cake. Since I spend an awful lot of my time thinking about my heritage and have written a column about pop culture and politics from my JA perspective since 1998, I thought all the words for the book were already swimming around in my head. But when it came time to actually write it, I found that defining Japanese American culture is a lot more complicated than just looking Japanese and living in North America, or living in the West and celebrating the traditions of the East.

The problem is Japanese Americans don't necessarily have a lot in common with each other, let alone with Japan.

I've come to realize that there is a huge range in the amount of Japanese culture we incorporate into our lives. The variety inherent in the JA community means that anything and everything counts, whether we speak lots of Japanese or can't even pronounce our family name "correctly." We may share roots across the Pacific, but our family experiences can be wildly divergent.

The one common theme that is in many accounts woven throughout the JA experience—the internment of 120,000 people of Japanese ancestry in the United States during World War II (along with the internment of Japanese Canadians and the expulsion and imprisonment in this country of Japanese Latin Americans)—can't even be applied universally. My family wasn't affected by internment. During World War II, my mom was growing up in fear of American bombers over her hometown; my dad's family, who had just moved back to Japan from Hawaii, were being heckled as "American spies" by Japanese kids. Only the JA population along the western United States suffered the imprisonment that Congress in 1988 declared had been unconstitutional and based on nothing more than racial prejudice and war hysteria.

The fact of internment is a dividing line between JAs whose families date back to the prewar decades and those who've arrived in the States since World War II. The JAs—especially the younger ones—with internment in their family past often want to explore that time, lest the country forget the injustice. But any Japanese who came to America after the war is loathe to relive the era because Japan's loss and brutal conduct brought such shame to the entire society (although the Japanese government is still coming to terms with its wartime military atrocities).

Still, the scars of internment have affected the JA community at large. Even if they themselves weren't interned, many JAs know someone in their family, or another JA family, who was. I was spared because on both sides my parents' families were in Japan during the war, and we moved to the States decades later. On the other hand, I've met lots of people who have internment in their family history, including my partner Erin, whose great-grandparents, grandparents, and parents were all interned.

Because of the enormous injustice of internment, a significant number of Japanese Americans are often overlooked who arrived long after World War II. The Shin Issei (New Issei), who have immigrated recently to the United States for work or school, are also Japanese American. Some have become naturalized citizens and many have had children here who are American citizens by birth. These new JAs live with the same duality as those who have been in this country for generations—the duality of being Japanese to whatever extent in America. This book needs to include these newer JAs, too.

For the most part, though, Japanese Americans are Sansei, Yonsei, Gosei, and now

The author's father was in the U.S. Army during the Korean War, when he met the author's mother in Hokkaido.

even Rokusei—third, fourth, fifth, and even sixth generations descended from mothers, fathers, grandparents, and great-grandparents who came to America to start a new life. The pioneering immigrants were the Issei, or first generation. Their children were the Nisei, or second generation, the first who could truly be called Japanese Americans because they were American citizens by birth and because they were raised with very traditional values and Japanese culture at home, while absorbing the American culture around them.

One of the ironies of immigrant communities maintaining their heritage is that the culture that's kept alive and handed down through the generations becomes preserved as if it were in a time capsule. For many JA families, the Japanese traditions they keep may be outdated and harken back to the Japan of the late 1800s or the early 1900s. Even the language has changed in a century; some of the words commonly used by JAs are hopelessly old-fashioned, like *benjo* for bathroom (Japanese today say *otearai* or *toire*).

We're both Japanese and American, but the amount of each side that enriches our lives is as varied and dynamic as the American landscape. Some of us look very Japanese and act very American, while others look less and less Asian, thanks to increasing numbers of JAs who marry non-Japanese. We can't be pigeonholed as a group that shares the same cultural values and interest in our heritage. Some Japanese Americans can speak perfect Japanese while others speak only enough to get by at family gatherings. Many don't speak a word. Some have Japanese food often, while others have never eaten sushi.

The purpose of this book is to explore those things that make us Japanese Americans: to celebrate the traditions that keep us connected as Japanese and also to note how we're *not* Japanese. This isn't a comprehensive manual by any means. Consider it a starting point for exploration of our (sometimes distant) collective Japanese roots, and how we've adapted them to our Western upbringing. The history of our community is rich and can't be squeezed into a few chapters. So let the resources at the back of the book guide you to further discoveries. Many of them have inspired me in recent years.

As much as I can within these pages, I'll take a loving look at our roots in Japan and at how Japanese culture still colors our day-to-day lives—from the pearls of wisdom of our grandmothers (*obaachan*), the words we grew up hearing (*urusai* for "noisy" and *gambatte* for "work hard"), and the constant presence of rice in our lives.

For many of us, these cultural echoes of Japan have started to fade, and it's important to keep them vivid if we are to appreciate our heritage. For others who may have lost touch with our common culture or have grown up without Japanese accents in your lives, I hope this book will be a worthy introduction to your roots and a starting point for your own journey.

Like the Nisei who first faced the dilemma of living within two cultures, we're still doing a balancing act, even generations down the line. Even if we think we're not very Japanese, in America we aren't always accepted as Americans. So why deny it? One of the great things about being JA is that we can be proud of both our American and Japanese sides. So we champion George Takei's role as Sulu in *Star Trek* but we're also proud as hell of the accomplishments of Ichiro Suzuki.

There's still time to hold onto the best of what it means to be Japanese even as we strive to find our place as Americans.

A note about the marginalia

In the margins I have collected photos and anecdotes that depict the diversity of the JA experience from a wide range of people, some recent immigrants and some whose families have been here for generations. I've also gathered some Japanese words and phrases that JAs probably grew up hearing, with definitions and examples filtered through my JA perspective. Some of the words aren't very nice and probably show our coarser roots in farmer stock.

Acknowledgments

This book is my view of my place in the world as a Japanese American; much of this territory has been covered in my online column Nikkei View (http://nikkeiview.com). But *Being Japanese American* couldn't have been written without the pioneering efforts of people like Bill Hosokawa, whose *Nisei: The Quiet*

Americans (University Press of Colorado, revised edition 2002) I read in high school in the mid-'70s.

Other writers and filmmakers to whom I owe debts of inspiration and knowledge include Ronald Takaki, Michi Weglyn, Satsuki Ina, Emiko Omori, Yuji Ichioka, Brian Komei Dempster, Brian Niiya, John Tateishi, T.R. Reid, Gary Okihiro, Ken Mochizuki, Ben Fong-Torres, Joyce Hirohata, Karen Ishizuka, and Robert Nakamura for the important work they're doing for JANM's media arts center. Also a tip of my beret to everyone on the Internet who maintains Web sites about Japan, Japanese culture, Japanese Americans, and Internment. For me, the Internet is the most wonderful invention since the printing press. I also am thankful to those who helped me research this book, including Marie Masumoto at the Japanese American National Museum's Hirasaki National Resource Center; Wataru Ebihara, who took a bunch of helpful photographs in Little Tokyo on short notice; Tom Ikeda of Densho.com, Lane Hirabayashi of UC-Riverside; Bill Watanabe of the Little Tokyo Service Center; and Stewart Ikeda of IMDiversity.com's Asian American Village.

I also want to thank many people in the Denver JA community who have taught me about our history from their experiences. They are: Helen Nitta, Marian and Rex Yoshimura, Carolyn Takeshita, Mariagnes Medrud, Jim Hada, Derek Okubo and Aiko Jane Okubo, True Yasui, and John Hopper in Granada, Colorado, who has led students' efforts to preserve nearby Camp Amache. I'll always be grateful to Yoriko and Eiichi Imada, Naomi Horii, and Miho Shida for asking me to write a regular column for the *Rocky Mountain Jiho* newspaper.

And I can't forget the people who so generously loaned me their photographs and wrote the many snippets of their lives that bring this book to life: Alisa Sanada, Angela Uyeda, Barbara Horiuchi, Bill Imada, Brian Tanaka, Bruce Alan Johnson, Carol Nichol, Caroline Tu Farley, Cindy Yoshida-Moromisato, Craig Hirokawa, Emily Chapman, Emily Porter, Eri Izawa, Erin Yoshimura, Frances Kakugawa, George Yoshida, Glenn Asakawa, Harusami Pickrell, Ian Ferguson, Jack Kunio Miyasaki, JANM, Jenna Nakagawa, Jill Nakawatase, John Tateishi, June Inuzuka, Kathy Ajisaka, Kota Mizutani, Kristin Fukushima, Lisa Imamura, Lisa Sasaki, Lois Hashimoto, Loryce Hashimoto, Mariko Yamashiro, Marty Davies, Masaye Okano Nakagawa, Michael Itamura, Midori Yenari, Miku Maeda Rager, Myleen Hollero, Pam Yoshida, Peggy Seo Oba, Peggy Smith, Phil Yu, Randy Kirihara, Rodger Hara, Ron Mori, Scot Kamimae, Scott Takeda, Shizue Seigel, Stann Nakazono, Steve Nitta, Stone Bridge Press, Susan Hamaker, Tadaaki Hiruki, Tamiko Wong, Toshiko Kikuta, Traci Kato-Kiriyama, Wataru Ebihara, Yayoi Lena Winfrey, and Tak Toyoshima for his always-thoughtful "Secret Asian Man" comic.

Thanks, too, to those who taught me about JA life through conversations, e-mails, and other documents. James Ohashi, in particular, generously sent me two manuscripts of his family's story.

To the folks at Stone Bridge Press, my eternal thanks for the opportunity to write this book. When publisher Peter Goodman contacted me, I promised to be on time with everything. But my life was complicated by a new job. My editor, Barry Harris, has been incredibly patient at every stage of this project.

Thanks to my family, with whom I've become closer with a strengthening bond of JA-ness. Thanks to the extended Yoshimura/Nitta family, which has made me feel alive to my JA core since I met Erin. Thanks, too, to Jared, a feisty Gosei who helps me better understand younger JAs, and to my beautiful nieces Sage, McKenna, and Joann, who are terrific examples of *hapa* as the hope for our future. And of course, my most heartfelt thanks and hugs and kisses go to my partner in life, spirit, and fun, Erin Yoshimura. I love the journey we're on together! Her unflagging support, coaching, ideas, cooking, knowledge, and *itazura* spirit kept me going through this project, and the book is as much hers as it is mine.

G.A.

Where Did We Come From?

"You speak such good English!"

Most Japanese Americans have probably heard this backhanded compliment, and then suffered through a variation of this conversation.

"Really, your English is so good, what nationality are you?"

"American."

"No, really where are you *from*?"

"California."

"Oh, you know what I mean. Where's your *family* from?"

"California."

Then the other person walks away thinking you're a jerk who's just being difficult. In actuality, what's difficult is the inescapable feeling that you were not being taken seriously as an American, not just as an American citizen, but as a person who is *American*.

Non-Asian Americans seem to always think of us as foreigners, even if we happen to be third-, fourth-, fifth-, or even sixth-generation Japanese Americans. Not even *hapa*, or mixed-race JAs, are exempt. I've heard of *hapa* who get this version of the conversation: "Oh, you're half Japanese? Which parent is American?"

The fact is, almost all Americans, Asian or otherwise, came from someplace else. In the case of the majority of Japanese Americans, our ancestors—our great-grandparents, grandparents, or parents—came from Japan, or like me, we've arrived recently from Japan. The flipside of the assumption that we're FOB—"fresh off the boat"—is that to Japanese speakers, we may as well be from another planet. Sure, some of us can speak Japanese fluently, and a lucky few may even work in Japan and eventually "pass" for a *Nihonjin*. But in most cases, we either speak just a few typical words of Japanese (the ones our parents

Being different

I've always realized I was Japanese. I remember wanting to be beautiful and thinking that I could never be beautiful because I wasn't white. I remember really wanting to be white.

Jill Nakawatase, postwar Nisei

Second-and-a-half generation

My paternal grandfather and grandmother emigrated in 1919. I am Nisei-han, since my father is Nisei and mother is Issei. My mother came to the United States with my father when he returned from a tour as a Staff Sergeant in the Army during the Korean conflict.

Scot Kamimae, Nisei-han

19

Family portraits like this were sent back to Japan to show how successful the Issei were.

The right look

Growing up with Japanese traditions and culture here in the U.S. is totally different than in Japan. We learn it's our heritage, but over there it's a way of life. I remember once while in Japan, on an exchange program, I was introduced to a neighbor of my host family. Her comment was (in Japanese) "She really looks Japanese." What???

Loryce Hashimoto, Sansei

WORDS & PHRASES

iranai

It's not needed, no thanks. This can be used to answer when someone asks if you need something (although Japanese also use *iie* to decline or say no), or by parents when they're telling their kids, "What do we want a new fancy car for? *Iranai*."

and grandparents used to yell at us when we did something bad), or we don't speak any Japanese at all.

There are Japanese Americans who have come in recent years to the United States who are much more connected to contemporary Japan. But it's the JAs whose families arrived in the United States in the early part of the twentieth century who have set the image of Japanese Americans in this country. They're the ones whose lives—whose language, food, and traditions—define Japanese American culture. It's Japanese culture of a century ago, kept alive through oral traditions, annual festivals, family picnics, and even funerals.

Things were much simpler all over the world a hundred years ago, when the first Japanese immigrants—the Issei generation—came to Hawaii and the West Coast in search of work.

The agriculture-based Japanese economy, still freshly absorbing Western ways after several hundred years of enforced isolation, had been battered by a drought, and, especially in rural parts of the country, an already hard life had become downright harsh, with no relief in sight. When the Japanese government agreed to allow a limited number of citizens to go to Hawaii in search of work, the bulk of the first plantation laborers came from the rural provinces of Hiroshima, Yamaguchi, Fukuoka, and Kumamoto prefectures.

Signed up by labor contractors (a less scrupulous precursor to today's employment agencies), laborers left their homes beginning in 1885 and took the long journey to Hawaii, with some continuing on to the U.S. mainland.

The key word here is "laborers." Some of the first to arrive from Japan were students—often ones who were not qualified to enter the more prestigious universities in their homeland—who came to learn English and continue their studies. These students found themselves working as household servants or day laborers to earn their keep while pursuing their studies. The vast majority of Japanese, who were almost all men, were hired as laborers for plantations in Hawaii and farms along the U.S. west coast. They were called *dekaseginin*, or sojourners (literally, economic nomads working away from home), and they still considered Japan their home. They perceived their time in Hawaii or the United States to be a temporary necessity, a way for them to make money to send to their struggling families back home. In fact, many of the earliest Japanese did go back, some after squandering their money on gambling or other vices, and others after becoming quite wealthy by Japanese standards. The success of this latter group led to more and more Japanese heading across the Pacific in search of riches.

Early on, women also emigrated from Japan. In Hawaii they joined their husbands to work side-by-side on the plantations and raise a family; the Caucasian plantation owners had discovered that having entire families on the payroll helped the men settle down, work harder, and avoid some of the vices that distracted the workforce. Other women were either tricked, induced, or just plain kidnapped and taken to America to serve as prostitutes for the laborers in their racially segregated camps and in the bustling Nihonmachi or Japantowns that had sprung up to serve the immigrant population.

Paving the way

The seeds of these Japanese enclaves in America were sown in previous decades by the first Asians to arrive in great numbers, the Chinese. Like European immigrants who came to America and made their way west to California, the Chinese were attracted by the promises of riches: the California Gold Rush that began in 1849 at Sutter's Mill in the Sierra foothills east of San Francisco. They called the United States *Gum Saan* or "Gold Mountain."

Many Chinese men left behind their wives and families to seek their fortune and return home wealthy, but only a few accomplished that goal. Conditions were difficult for the Chinese miners. They mostly worked abandoned mines because they were excluded from active mines by the whites who had settled in northern California. The U.S. government required the Chinese to pay an extra tax on any gold they found because they weren't citizens (and weren't even eligible to apply for that status). As they were forced out of mining, most Chinese ended up as laborers, working on the railroads, as migrant farm workers, as servants, or as business owners, taking much the same path as the Japanese immigrants to come. Those businesses were either within their own tightly knit ethnic communities, or in the few menial industries (like laundry and shoemaking) that the whites allowed them to work in. Anti-Chinese sentiment started the moment they arrived and followed them everywhere. They were dropped off at Angel Island in San Francisco Bay and forced to wait out weeks of questioning and examinations before they were allowed to officially set foot in the United States. Many were refused entry and sent back to China.

Along with personal prejudice, institutionalized racism continued

Early Issei immigrants looking suave in their Western finery.

WORDS & PHRASES

chotto matte

Hold on; wait a moment. The more polite (or sarcastic) version is *chotto matte kudasai.* "*Chotto matte,* I gotta go to the *benjo.*"

to plague the Chinese once they arrived on American soil. They weren't allowed to testify against Caucasians in court, they were blocked from working in certain jobs, and Chinese children weren't allowed in San Francisco's public schools. They lived in Chinese enclaves or in itinerant work camps. If they owned businesses, they were usually restaurants or shops that catered only to other Chinese.

The exception was laundry, which was such a menial task that Caucasians were happy to allow the Chinese to take over. And take over they did, so much so that even today the Chinese laundry is still an evocative image—despite the fact that the Chinese didn't use laundries or irons in their homeland.

The anti-Chinese movement culminated in the Chinese Exclusion Act of 1882, which shut the door on further immigration of Chinese and their families. Ironically, however, it opened the door for Japanese immigration under the twisted logic that Japanese people would be better workers than the Chinese. We were just the next wave of cheap labor for America.

The first Japanese visitor to America hadn't planned on coming to this country. Manjiro Nakahama was a fourteen-year-old fisherman who was stranded in the Pacific in 1841 when his ship was disabled in a storm. He was rescued by William Whitfield, a whaling captain from New England. Whitfield took Manjiro under his protection, gave him a "proper" Western name of John Mung, and took him back to Fairhaven, New Hampshire, to raise and educate. After adventures in America, including a stint as a Forty-Niner during the Gold Rush in California, Nakahama returned to Japan and later served in the Japanese government when the Americans arrived in 1853.

U.S.-Japan relations began when Commodore Matthew Perry sailed across the Pacific with his "black ships" (*kurofune* in Japanese) and forced the country to open to trade and, coincidentally, to Western ways. During the forty-four-year reign of the Meiji Emperor, who ruled Japan during the late 1800s and early 1900s, Western styles were all the rage. The country had been isolated for over two hundred years, barring trade with most of the world, and killing or imprisoning any foreigner who dared to land on its shores. Commodore Perry brought a symbol of modern industrialization—a miniature locomotive—that so captured the Japanese imagination that the rush was on to modernize, an instinct that has been a hallmark of Japanese society ever since.

At the time of the Chinese Exclusion Act in the United States, Japan was suffering an economic depression that hit farmers especially hard. Between the need for cheap laborers in America and the Japanese government's newfound interest in having some of its citizens go overseas instead of add to the growing social instability, Japan agreed to allow workers to go to Hawaii and the United States. When it was announced in 1884 that the government was looking for workers to go to Hawaii, 28,000 Japanese submitted applications. The first group of 943 government-sponsored immigrants began working in the plantations of Hawaii in February 1885. Japanese have since been a mainstay of the Hawaiian economy, where they fit in with the native population and the other Asian immigrants from China, and later Korea and the Philippines.

Some of the farmers and laborers leaving Japan had their sights set on the U.S. mainland. Those Japanese began arriving in 1885. According to the 1890 census, 2,039 Japanese were already living in the United States, almost all of them in California. The major port of embarkation was San Francisco, where the Japanese immigrants had to suffer through the same entry procedures as the Chinese, funneled through Angel Island. It didn't take long before the Caucasian majority in the United States showed the same intolerance toward the Japanese that they had shown the Chinese in previous decades.

The California-based Hearst chain of newspapers owned by William Randolph Hearst (the man who inspired Orson Welles's celebrated film *Citizen Kane*) was particularly noted for its "Yellow Journalism," giving the phrase a new and more literal meaning. Yellow Journalism was first used to describe the Hearst and the Pulitzer newspaper chains; both ran the first popular comic strip, "The Yellow Kid," featuring a character who wears a yellow nightshirt. As the chains competed for readers with increasingly sensational reporting (they even began making up stories), Yellow Journalism came to describe their style. But the phrase also fit the Hearst chain's virulent anti-Asian editorial attitudes, first smearing the Chinese and then the Japanese, and inciting racial hatred and paranoia.

There were attacks against Japanese workers in rural areas, where groups of vigilantes threatened the laborers unless they moved on.

Courtesy Erin Yoshimura.

Images of home: Issei immigrants kept photos of family in Japan and also sent back photos of themselves in the New World.

Racism from an official

I was once told by a Los Angeles City Councilmember that he preferred speaking with Asian Americans because "you" are not as radical as Latinos and African Americans. He said we are more reasonable, quiet people who don't speak up inappropriately. I have also been told to go back where I came from (in arguments).

Bill Imada, Sansei

Courtesy Erin Yoshimura.

Nisei schoolgirls of the 1930s.

Signs reading "No Japs Allowed" were a common sight in businesses' windows. The climate of prejudice led to the dehumanization of Japanese immigrants, and eventually, as with the Chinese in earlier decades, many of the Issei were deliberately forced out of the various fields of labor they had undertaken. Restrictive laws based on race pushed Japanese out of farming, fishing, and railroad labor. Legislatures enacted alien land laws, the sole purpose of which was to prevent Japanese from owning property and settling as permanent immigrants—as full-fledged Americans.

First brush with prejudice

When I was in kindergarten, a white boy called me a "Jap." I had to ask my Dad what he meant. The next time he called me that I kicked his ass. Never called me that again.

Scot Kamimae, Nisei-han

Here to stay

But stay they did. With the arrival of women came a change in how the Japanese immigrants saw themselves. They were no longer *dekaseginin* working temporarily outside Japan. They now considered themselves settlers, pioneers who were committed to new lives in a new land. They would start families in this new world, investing their children with the Japanese culture that was still fresh in their hearts and minds. But those children would be raised as American citizens.

To create families, the immigrant population, which at the turn of the nineteenth century was still mostly made up of men, needed Japanese women. The practice of marrying picture brides was commonly used because most men working in America couldn't afford to travel to Japan to choose a wife. Families provided photographs of the women in Japan. The men in America sent portraits of themselves back to their villages and towns to entice women to join them; the pictures often showed them looking much more spruced up, and younger, than they would be in real life.

In 1907, President Teddy Roosevelt signed the "Gentleman's Agreement" with Japan promising that the United States wouldn't ban outright the immigration of Japanese laborers in exchange for Japan limiting the emigration of laborers. This left the door open for women and children to come to America, and that's what they did—almost 67,000 of them—for more than fifteen years, until the Immigration Act of 1924 stopped any more Japanese from entering the country.

The prejudice that ultimately led to the internment of people of

WORDS & PHRASES

dorobo

Common thief, as in "Wash your face and hands, you look like a *dorobo.*"

Japanese heritage during World War II was at the heart of every one of the laws designed to stem the flow of Japanese immigrants. It also drove efforts to prevent the immigrants already in the States from owning property, and put in place other obstacles that attempted to prevent the Japanese from settling in this country. Alien land laws such as the one passed in California in 1913 made it difficult for Japanese farmers to commit to long-term crops because they couldn't own their land or even lease it in their own names.

With the Immigration Act of 1924, the Japanese who had already settled in America were isolated. Without hope for other Issei to join them—not even family members—and without the ability to own property in the country they had adopted as their own, the first generation placed their hopes for the future of their community in their American-born children, the Nisei, or second generation, who were American citizens by birth.

Courtesy Erin Yoshimura.

Early Issei women with their Nisei children.

Imagine yourself in this position: you've come from a far-off land and worked hard for decades to make a living in America despite numerous obstacles. You've finally earned enough money to marry and raise children, and you've written to friends and family members back in your home village to come to the United States because, even with the hardships and prejudice, life is better here than the poverty back in Japan. But suddenly you're cut off from your roots in Japan. No more Japanese will be allowed into the country, and if you travel to Japan you won't be readmitted to America. What would this mean to your sense of being Japanese? It means that you would hold onto your heritage as if it could blow away in the slightest breeze. You would bestow it unto the next generation—the first born in the United States—knowing that if you didn't pass down your culture it would surely be lost.

After 1924, the only individuals who could go to Japan and return were American-born citizens, the Nisei. The thousands of Japanese Americans who were sent back to Japan by their Issei parents to study Japanese and soak up their traditional culture were called Kibei, and because they were bilingual and bicultural they played an important role in the United States military during World War II—once their loyalty was accepted.

The Nisei generation bore an incredible burden. They had to be perfectly Japanese for their parents' sake and preserve the heritage

Cowgirl

I never felt deprived as I was growing up. The only thing I really wanted and never got was a guitar. Gene Autry was my first movie idol and I wanted to become a yodeling cowgirl. Seriously.

Lois Hashimoto, Nisei

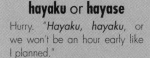

WORDS & PHRASES

hayaku or hayase

Hurry. "*Hayaku, hayaku,* or we won't be an hour early like I planned."

Culture clash

My mom arrived in the United States married to a Black soldier with my two-year-old self in tow. She landed in the Jim Crow south—Richmond, Texas—where she was invited to sit at the front of the bus while my dad's family could not.

Yayoi Lena Winfrey, *hapa* Issei

Effects of internment

The internment still affects me because there's so much of my family experience that I don't know about. I continually feel the urge to seek more understanding. Silence doesn't guarantee that the next generation is free from the experience. Personally, I constantly battle feelings of fear and vulnerability.

Erin Yoshimura, Yonsei

foo-foo

Onomatopoeic word for blowing on something to cool it off, used especially with kids. "The ramen's still hot, why don't you sit there and *foo-foo* it for a little while."

their families had brought with them, but they also had to be perfectly American to prove that Japanese Americans could be good citizens able to fit into the Caucasian mainstream. This was an internal tightrope that they passed down to their children, and to their children's children. Many Japanese Americans today are acutely aware of a deep-rooted responsibility to be as Japanese as possible and as American as possible at the same time.

That balancing act was severely tested when the Nisei generation was imprisoned along with their immigrant parents during World War II. And the question of identity as a group wasn't really settled—if indeed it has been—until four decades later, when then-President Reagan formally apologized to Japanese Americans as a group and signed into law the Civil Liberties Act of 1988, which established reparation payments for JAs who had been interned and their descendants.

In between, the federal government had loosened the rules regarding immigration of Asians into the country. The Immigration and Naturalization Act of 1952 finally allowed the Issei to become naturalized U.S. citizens. But it wasn't until 1965 that the Immigration and Nationality Act opened up quotas that had been in place since 1924, the year Japanese immigration was completely stemmed. For those decades, the number of immigrants entering the United States was restricted by national origin—and Asian countries were, unsurprisingly, the ones with the most severe limits. But now America welcomed immigrants from Japan and other Asian countries (notably Korea and, especially in the 1970s, Vietnam) with the same open arms she held out for immigrants from northern Europe.

The Immigration and Nationality Act established a new quota system of 20,000 from all countries, with a total of 170,000 immigrants allowed each year and exceptions for families that were being reunited. The new law also established a preference for immigrants with professional skills that were needed in the United States—a critical passage that opened the door for a dramatic rise in the number of immigrants from all over Asia to work in high-tech industries.

For Japanese Americans who had settled in the United States for two or three generations, the relaxed immigration laws meant more chances for Japanese culture to continue and thrive, with younger Issei finally arriving to revitalize their traditions. However, during the long decades of restricted immigration, Japan had changed considerably. The overall values might have been similar, and many of the traditions may have stayed the same, but much else, even the Japanese language, had changed.

The JAs had turned into their own island of culture, with a unique group personality. And they could speak English very well.

The camps

It's impossible to overstate the effect that the internment camps had on the JA community. Certainly not everyone was affected directly by it. Members of my family, and many other JA families, were not interned, or they've come to the United States in the decades since World War II.

Nevertheless, the scars are indelible on the whole Japanese American community because the majority of Japanese Americans lived on the West Coast before the war. California, Oregon, and Washington were deemed sensitive military zones. America's most racist policymakers were afraid that Japan, having brazenly attacked Pearl Harbor, would launch a similar attack on the U.S. mainland, starting with the West Coast. And, they figured, Japanese Americans were more loyal to Japan than to the United States and would somehow aid in such an attack. This line of thinking isn't surprising, given the decades of prejudice heaped on the Japanese for two generations by citizens, media, and lawmakers. And, there were economic motivations behind removing the Japanese from the West Coast—so that others could take over their businesses, including the truck farms and floral industries developed by the JAs.

Internment only targeted JAs living on the United States' West Coast. In Hawaii, some JAs were rounded up and sent to internment camps on the mainland (most went to Rohwer, in Arkansas), but the vast majority of JAs in Hawaii lived the war years just like any other American in Hawaii—under strict rationing and blackouts—but not subject to the bald-faced prejudice directed at JAs on the mainland. In California, Oregon, Washington, and parts of Arizona, thanks to Army Lt. General John DeWitt, everyone of Japanese descent—over half Nisei, or American-born citizens, and two-thirds of those just children—were forced to leave their homes, farms, and businesses and live in hastily erected camps scattered inland away from the coast, some as far east as Colorado and Arkansas. Most sold off their possessions at pennies on the dollar, or buried or destroyed family heirlooms such as photos and samurai swords handed down through generations.

At the time, most JAs shrugged their shoulders and accepted their

Courtesy Erin Yoshimura.

Marian Yoshimura spent some of her formative years in internment camps. This photo is from around 1943.

Passing on the internment experience
I relate [to my Japanese American heritage] when I read about the internment camps. My mom and her family were all interned in WWII. I read a lot about it and make sure my daughter understands what an injustice was done to grandma's family. Actually, my mom talked a lot to my daughter about it.

Caroline Tu Farley, Japanese Taiwanese mixed-race Sansei

Courtesy Erin Yoshimura.

In the internment camps, families were determined to make the best of their situation, and even dressed up for formal portraits.

Life during wartime in Hawaii

My father's family in Hawaii were never interned or arrested. Since they lived in rural Kona at the time, my father doesn't remember anything unusual other than normal wartime rationing and restrictions.

Lisa Sasaki, Yonsei

Nihongo

Japanese language. "Can you speak any *Nihongo?*"

imprisonment with two Japanese phrases, *shikataga-nai*, or "it can't be helped," and *gaman*, or "endure." They figured the best course of action was to accept internment as a way of actually showing their patriotism. The Japanese American Citizens League (JACL), a civil rights organization founded in 1929, helped cement this mentality, and has suffered ever since from accusations of "selling out" their membership and aiding the U.S. government in the unconstitutional imprisonment.

The internees lived in barracks, families sharing one-room spaces with a hanging light bulb and a wood stove. Bathroom facilities served each block of barracks and offered no privacy. They ate their meals every day at the ringing of a bell in huge open cafeterias that made it easy for children to ditch their families and eat with friends. The adults whiled away their days, the men scrounged the camp for scrap wood to make furniture, and the women did laundry and battled the constant invasion of dust that sneaked in through knotholes and gaps in the tar-paper-and-pine buildings. The kids went to school and were taught by Caucasian teachers. They joined Scout troops established within the camp boundaries, played on Little League baseball teams against other teams within the camp, and sensed but never discussed their parents' distress.

In all, about 120,000 people of Japanese ancestry were affected by internment. Some of the imprisoned JAs were able to leave camp with work or school permits, but always to jobs or schools away from the West Coast. For some—especially children, who found internment an opportunity to explore freedom beyond their strict upbringing at home—the internment years might even be described as fun. Some families were able to leave the camps with the sponsorship of religious groups or employers but ended up in midwestern or eastern locales where they were the only Asians and faced prejudice and racism in addition to isolation.

For most internees, the experience was humiliating. The feeling of being imprisoned without having done anything wrong, on the pretext of their heritage, has affected families ever since World War II. According to observers such as therapist Satsuki Ina, the Sacramento-based maker of the documentary *Children of the Camps*, internment has had the long-lasting effect of holding back many Japanese Americans in their personal and professional lives, and of crippling their ability to express emotions. As if that internal sense of reserve due to our

Japaneseness wasn't enough, an additional legacy of the camps is a deep-rooted fear of drawing attention to ourselves. Sansei, Yonsei, and even Gosei have felt the subtle (and sometimes not-so-subtle) family pressure to excel at school and work, to "grin and bear it," to work hard and not do anything to bring shame, embarrassment, or attention to ourselves or our families.

Not everyone was interned, but those who weren't still faced prejudice in their communities. One man I know remembers seeing his mother knocked down in Colorado during the war by a Caucasian man, her groceries scattered, just because she was Japanese American. Inland JAs also had to live by rules that restricted their freedom. They had to give up their radios, cameras, and anything else that the government perceived could be used for espionage or sabotage. They had to register with the local authorities and were restricted to staying within a five-mile radius of their home unless they received special permission. One Denver Nisei remembers having to get permission to drive all day down to southeast Colorado to the one internment camp in the state, Granada Relocation Center (better known as Camp Amache), so he could visit his mother. She had divorced his father and moved to California before the war, and, along with every other Japanese American in California, she had been interned and by chance sent to Colorado.

Japanese Americans weren't the only ones incarcerated during World War II. Over 2,200 Latin Americans of Japanese descent were taken from twelve different countries at the insistence of the U.S. government and placed in twenty-seven smaller Justice Department camps in states including Texas, New Mexico, and Montana. Most of those Japanese Latin Americans were Peruvians; over 900 were summarily deported back to Japan. North of the border, Japanese had been living and working in Canada since 1887, not long after the first immigrants arrived in the United States. Not surprisingly, most lived in British Columbia, the westernmost province. After the bombing of Pearl Harbor, 22,000 Japanese Canadians were given twenty-four hours to pack and were sent to temporary assembly centers before being dispersed to internment camps. Unlike in the United States, where families were generally kept together unless the father was a leader within the JA community (like the head of a club or a martial arts teacher), in Canada the men were sent to work camps separate from those for the women and children.

Internment years

Both sides of the family were interned in Tule Lake (although they did not know each other). My mom's dad was very angry about the internment and was maybe one of the "no-no boys." The family lost their grocery store. I have three aunts and an uncle, and they were very young when they entered the camp. I assume my dad's family was angry about the internment as well, because they left for Japan once they were released. My grandmother was pregnant with my dad in the camps. My parents met at a dance party in Santa Cruz (in the early 1970s). I'm not sure about my grandparents except that my dad's mom was a picture bride.

Jill Nakawatase, postwar Nisei

Getting pigeonholed

If you have to be pigeonholed, I suppose it is better to have generalizations like doing well in school and being honest. Often, Asians are viewed as quiet and unassuming. Asian females are often viewed as submissive. This became more of a problem during college years.

Midori Yenari, Sansei

WORDS & PHRASES
doko?

Where? "You saw him the other day? *Doko?*"

Courtesy Erin Yoshimura

Helen Nitta holding her daughter Marian in front of tar-paper barracks at Jerome internment camp.

Identification

Basically, I don't consider myself very Japanese. There are some Japanesey things I do that I didn't realize until friends called it out. But I generally consider myself very Japanese American, and identify with the wonderful/ hilarious hybridity that comes from that.

Kristin Fukushima, Japanese Caucasian mixed-race Yonsei

WORDS & PHRASES

takusan

A lot. "Eat, eat, there's *takusan* left in the kitchen still."

Fighting for a place in society

Back in the United States, some of the JA men found a way to show their patriotism beyond quietly accepting imprisonment. After the attack on Pearl Harbor, Japanese Americans in the U.S. Army and Navy were discharged because they were classified, along with all JAs, as "enemy aliens." Even though they were already in uniform and ready to prove their loyalty, they weren't allowed to fight for the United States.

But in 1942, Nisei soldiers in Hawaii were assigned to the 100th Battalion. Beginning in 1943, the mainland Nisei were allowed to join the U.S. military and formed the 442nd Regimental Combat Team. In 1944, the 100th Battalion was attached to the 442nd in Europe. As a group the Nisei earned more medals and honors than any other comparably sized unit in the history of the U.S. military. They were involved in key battles in Italy and France, including the fabled rescue of the "Lost Battalion," a unit from Texas that was trapped in the Vosges Forest in France. The Nisei in the 442nd suffered eight hundred casualties saving the two hundred men of the Lost Battalion. They were the most highly decorated combat unit in U.S. history, with 18,000 individual awards.

Meanwhile in the Pacific, the Nisei proved they could fight against the Japanese as well as they could against the Germans and Italians. Just before the start of the war, some Nisei and Kibei—American-born Japanese who were sent to Japan for part of their education—were recruited for the Army's Military Intelligence Service (MIS) to become Japanese-language translators, interpreters, and instructors. The school was originally based at the Presidio in San Francisco, but after the start of the war the school was moved to Minnesota—not exactly a center of Japanese culture.

There the Nisei were trained for their mission to fight the Japanese. But unlike in Europe, where the Japanese American soldiers fought as a group and received medals, commendations, and media coverage (which eventually led to a 1951 feature film about the 442nd, *Go for Broke!*, starring Van Johnson as a Caucasian lieutenant who leads a Nisei platoon), the MIS served in small units, with several men assigned to various units scattered throughout the Pacific theater from India and Burma to the Philippines. Their work was classified for decades after the war, denying these men the chance to receive the accolades of their counterparts in Europe. Yet they served just as heroically, and under trying circumstances: They were assigned Caucasian GIs as escorts so American soldiers wouldn't fire at them, thinking they were the enemy. They performed an invaluable service, translating captured enemy documents and interrogating enemy prisoners. According to General Douglas MacArthur, the commander of U.S. forces in the Pacific, the Nisei soldiers helped shorten the war by many months and saved hundreds of thousands of lives in the process. After the war, many stayed in Japan and served as interpreters and key administrators within the U.S.-led Occupation Forces from 1945 to 1951.

Denver's JA community makes an annual pilgrimage to the Amache internment camp. Similar pilgrimages are made to most of the camp sites.

Speaking out

Not all Nisei were so eager to fight for the United States. Not surprisingly, some Japanese Americans were bitter and angry at their internment, and stated so publicly. Some also chose to protest the evacuation and imprisonment. Gordon Hirabayashi, Minoru Yasui, and Fred Korematsu all fought the evacuation at the start but were imprisoned, their convictions for violating the exclusion order upheld by the Supreme Court during the war. Yasui, who went on to become a pioneering Asian American civil rights attorney, marched up and down the streets of Portland in violation of the curfew placed on JAs. When the police refused to arrest him, he turned himself in at a police station and insisted that he be jailed.

A JA woman, Mitsuye Endo, also played a part in fighting the internment. A California state employee who was questioned about her ties to Japan and fired along with other JA employees after the bombing of Pearl Harbor, Endo challenged the evacuation on behalf of all JA employees with a petition filed by the Japanese American Citizens League. Endo was a Nisei who couldn't speak Japanese and who had never visited Japan, yet her treatment was upheld on a technicality even though the Supreme Court's decision admitted that the justices felt she "should be given her liberty." By this time, of course, she'd been in an internment camp for two years.

While in the internment camps, other Japanese Americans protested a loyalty questionnaire handed out in 1943. The survey was an initial step in gauging the feasibility of recruiting Nisei into the military

Positives and negatives

In California, the assumption was Japanese Americans were all good, hardworking students and well behaved. It's easier to have someone make a positive assumption about you if they are going to make any stereotypical assumptions at all. The negatives: To do things outside the expectations—be assertive or especially creative—was not associated with JAs so there were inner barriers I had to get over. I don't feel I ever suffered discrimination in school, work, etc. In fact, I am someone who benefited from affirmative action in graduate school.

June Inuzuka, Sansei

Courtesy Yayoi Winfrey.

The years following World War II saw American soldiers returning from Japan with Japanese wives. Yayoi Lena Winfrey, shown here in Japan with her mother, is the daughter of an African American GI who identifies more as black than Japanese.

and in identifying loyal JAs who could be granted off-camp passes for work or school. Two questions in particular created a stir within the camps, and those who answered "no" to both were dubbed the "No-No Boys" and ostracized by many JAs. One asked if the respondent would foreswear allegiance to the emperor of Japan, which assumed that they were already loyal to Japan. The other asked if the respondent would be willing to fight for the U.S. military. Later in the war, JAs who protested the draft of Nisei into the Army were again ostracized as not only war resisters but traitors. They were imprisoned for two years and, although they were pardoned by President Eisenhower in the 1950s, the JA community is still emotionally split over the issue of whether the community should have supported the government during World War II or protested the injustices of evacuation and internment. In the end, both sides expressed their patriotism in their own ways.

These days, there's a concerted effort to preserve the memory of the internment and the heroism of Japanese Americans who fought in the war. There was even an acknowledgment, finally, of those who protested the war. The Japanese American Citizens League, which some JAs have long accused of helping the government implement the internment and which led the criticism of the No-No Boys and draft resisters in the decades after the war, offered an official apology in 2003.

There is also an ongoing effort to preserve the camps themselves, or what remains of them. Manzanar, in California, has been given national historic status. Groups led by survivors are trying to get historic status and raise funds to rebuild portions of several other camps and create memorials and museums where tens of thousands of Japanese Americans were once imprisoned. The state of Arkansas is undertaking a massive project to commemorate the two camps there, Rohwer and Jerome. The Japanese American National Museum in Los Angeles, which has a permanent exhibit about internment, hosted an All Camp Summit in 2002 where survivors of the camps, their families, and others shared their memories and attended workshops on how to obtain their family's records from the U.S. government.

All the camp sites still exist—although the ones in Arizona are on Indian tribal land and are not open to the public—and some groups make annual commemorative pilgrimages to many of them. February

19—the day Franklin D. Roosevelt signed Executive Order 9066—has become an annual Day of Remembrance for the Japanese American community nationwide.

Redress

In the 1970s, as the civil rights and antiwar movement brought a loud and proud voice to Americans, "Yellow Power" flowered alongside the gay-rights and feminist movements. The first pilgrimage by JAs to the internment camp at Manzanar in California led to survivors from other camps mounting similar annual pilgrimages. That sense of self-identity eventually led to a renewed anger toward a government that had imprisoned the JA community. From within the community leaders such as Edison Uno and Michi Weglyn emerged who campaigned for redress for the injustice of internment. Uno pushed the JACL in 1970 to approve a national resolution seeking compensation from the government for internment. Weglyn's exhaustively researched book *Years of Infamy* was published in 1976.

In the early 1980s, the three men who first fought internment—Minoru Yasui, Gordon Hirabayashi, and Fred Korematsu—were cleared of any wrongdoing by an appeals court after a team led by JA attorneys filed a legal petition claiming there were errors in the original wartime Supreme Court decisions that upheld their conviction. The team used newly released government records to prove that the Justice Department had suppressed evidence in the original cases against the men for violating the Army's exclusion order in 1942, and that the Supreme Court's decision to uphold was based on an unjust conviction.

It took many years and a lot of work at the highest levels of the U.S. government by grassroots organizers and pioneering JA politicians such as Sen. Daniel Inouye of Hawaii and California Congressmen Bob Matsui and Norm Mineta (now Secretary of Transportation under President George W. Bush) before the Civil Liberties Act of 1988 was signed by then-President Ronald Reagan. Ultimately, $20,000 in reparations was approved for each person who was interned.

After the war, many internees settled far from the West Coast—one of the largest JA populations is now in Chicago—but many returned to their former homes and faced more prejudice.

But as a community, JAs not only persevered, we prospered. We succeeded in relative anonymity, however. The decades after World War II found the JA community keeping a decidedly low profile. As a group, JAs seemed to not want to bring any attention to themselves,

Being the good student

I got picked on a lot for being one of the only Asian students in the school and also because I was a good student. I was also good at sports, which gave me some respect at school. Yes, I was definitely a "good student." My parents did drive me to do well. I knew it was expected of me and I never challenged it. School was always really easy for me so my parents continually expected perfect grades. I never let them down.

Jill Nakawatase, postwar Nisei

Proud to be JA

I've always loved being Japanese American, although sometimes it was painful when racial slurs were flung at me. It made me feel special to have another life filled with different foods and cultural traditions. We celebrated all the traditional American holidays like Christmas, Halloween, and Thanksgiving because it was an excuse to get together with family. New Year's Day *oshogatsu* was the most important, though, and my family would cook many wonderful foods. Dancing *obon* was important, especially if a family member had recently died. And forget traveling on Memorial Day—you have to go to all the cemeteries and services.

Erin Yoshimura, Yonsei

WORDS & PHRASES
konnichiwa

Hello. "*Konnichiwa*, I'm here to see Mr. Asakawa."

Facing prejudice

When I was around six years old riding home one day on the school bus, I remember an older girl telling me to "go home." I can vividly recall my confusion when I told her that I was going home since that was the whole purpose of me being on the bus in the first place. In hindsight, though, I think it was really the adults in my life, especially teachers, who made me realize that I was different somehow. I think they just naturally assumed that I was aware that I was Japanese rather than exactly like all of the other white students around me. I can't tell you how many times a teacher said something like "Why would you want to do a report on European castles or the Civil War? Wouldn't you be more interested in doing a project on Japan/the internment camps/origami?"

Lisa Sasaki, Yonsei

and endeavored only to be good, if quiet, Americans. Many Nisei parents raised their Sansei children in an entirely American environment, in some cases even forbidding the use of Japanese even at home.

Even more than before the war, the watchwords for the following decades were good grades, hard work, and citizenship for young Sansei. These are the values that more and more of the fourth and fifth generations now seem to be rebelling against.

Looming in our community's collective memory, whether our families were affected at the time or not, is the fact of internment. Like Americans who had grandparents who lived through the Depression and were raised to be especially protective of their money, many JAs can be paranoid, fearful of sticking out, and thrifty to the point of saving and reusing everything from shoeboxes and Tupperware to plastic bags and rubber bands. Thriftiness can be a good thing, of course, but not the need to be invisible. Why do you think there are so few JAs in politics? Or even in show business? It may be partly the fault of "the system" which denies opportunities to Asians. But what if Japanese Americans have been internally wired to not be outgoing?

With the rise of younger generations and the passing of the internment generation (very few Issei are still left, and many of the Nisei are elderly), there's been a resurgence of interest in not just the history of internment, but its still-lingering effects. I have already mentioned Dr. Satsuki Ina's excellent documentary, "Children of the Camps," which explored the trauma that still haunts the Nisei who were mere children in the camps. And Erin Yoshimura, a Denver-based life coach, thinks that the trauma has been handed down to the Sansei, Yonsei, and even Gosei.

It's up to us all to break those bonds and become more vocal, more assertive, and more willing to be involved in mainstream America.

Memories of Home

Anyone who's ever moved knows the trauma of being dislocated—the nostalgia you feel for your old home and the alienation you feel in your new surroundings.

Imagine how much worse this feeling might be if you moved not just across town, or to another city, but across thousands of miles of ocean. Not just any ocean, but the Pacific Ocean, which is by far the largest on the planet. The Pacific covers almost a third of the Earth, an area approximately 64 million square miles. In comparison, the land area of the United States, including Alaska and Hawaii, covers less than 4 million square miles. And imagine making that move at a time before transpacific telephone lines, radios, satellites, or—god forbid—cell phones.

What's more, in that age the move was made not by airplane, but by sea. The journey via ship took more than two weeks, and letters back and forth were sent and received at a snail's pace. Lives and situations could change drastically in the time it took for news to travel from the new world, to the old, and back.

Although most of the people who waved goodbye as they left ports such as Yokohama meant to return, many did not. They simply got caught up in living new lives in their new homes. But they kept much of what they knew of their old country in their hearts, and kept alive many of the traditional customs right down to regional festivals and games to while away the time, as a way of staying connected to Japan. Memories were all that was left them of the land they'd left behind, and they cherished those memories, and handed them down as the heritage of Japanese Americans. Many cultural touchstones of Japan have endured over the generations in America.

Parenting

My family did not express emotion very much. As children, we knew we were loved. We were aware of the sacrifices our parents made for us. But we never talked about anything, i.e., sex, drugs, love, relationships. In America, parents are expected to talk to their kids about this stuff if they are "good parents." I make more of an effort to talk to my kids about these kinds of issues and tell them I love them. Also, my family was not physically demonstrative, and I try to hug my kids as much as I can.

June Inuzuka, Sansei

Games

Some of the simplest traditions to maintain were games, some meant for children, but most meant for adults. Remember, the first wave of immigrants arriving on the West Coast was almost all men, not women or children. Women and children—families—came later. The familiar children's game we know today as *jan ken pon* (better known in the West as "Rock Paper Scissors") crossed the ocean as an easy-to-play, adult pastime used for gambling.

Almost all Asian cultures seem to know how to play the game, probably because it's easy: two players make a fist and simultaneously bring down their arms and make a scissors shape with their first two fingers, a piece of paper represented by the flat palm, or a rock symbolized by keeping the hand clenched. Each player must guess what shape the other will make with his fist and try to beat it. A rock can break scissors, the scissors can cut paper, and paper can wrap up the rock. Japanese men in boarding houses and work camps on farms and along the railroads could gather together and spend hours betting on the game. *Jan ken pon* is so universal—what appears to be Rock-Paper-Scissors was played in ancient Greece—that its origins can't be traced, but variations on the theme were played in China centuries ago, and the same game seems to have spontaneously evolved in many countries including Thailand and Korea.

Jan ken pon was the easiest game in the world because no pieces or complicated rules were needed, and you could start the game anywhere at a moment's notice. Other games, such as *hanafuda*, required a set of cards. Luckily, the cards were easy to carry—thicker than American playing cards but much smaller—so they could be pulled out almost anywhere. The game is sometimes called "The Flower Game" because each suit is represented by a different type of flower, such as wisteria, cherry blossom, iris, or plum blossom. The game is played in Korea with slight variations in the cards and scoring, but no matter where it's played it's a game of chance and bluff—again, perfect for gambling away your hard-earned money.

Another game popular with gamblers, *mah jong*, originated in China but has always been popular in Japan. I have a vivid childhood memory of falling asleep during one of my parents' many house parties, the smell of cigarette smoke in the air amidst the mumbled chatter and occasional raised voices and loud laughter, the clink of ice in glasses, and the popping of beer cans. Beneath these typical party noises was the soothing sound of the game that brought the grownups to our house: the clatter of bamboo-backed ivory tiles and small ivory sticks being thrown on the table.

Mah jong is an ancient game that some speculate was created by the philosopher and teacher Confucius, but was more likely an evolution of several ancient games played in China. It spread centuries ago throughout Asia, with variants developing in each country. In 1893, a *mah jong* set was brought to the United States for an exposition in Chicago. The same year the Smithsonian Institution wrote a paper describing the game and calling it "Chinese Dominoes."

In 1920, a simplified set of rules was published in English and game sets were imported with Roman numerals on the tiles. The game caught on as a fad during the decade under various names, including *mah jongg, mah junk, mah chang, man-chu, ma cheuk,* and *pung chow.* Played for money, it's an enticing gambler's game.

If you've seen the terrific movie *The Joy Luck Club* or read Amy Tan's novel, you've been introduced to *mah jong* and the way it can bring friends together.

A more refined game, and one probably not often played among the mining shacks and railroad tracks, is *go*, a game of strategy developed in China as *wei ch'i* and known as *baduk* in Korea. Along with backgammon, *go* is one of the oldest games still played in its original form.

Teaching the art of brush writing at a cultural festival.

Buddhist priests brought the game to Japan centuries ago, where it was refined and embraced by the samurai class during the time of the Tokugawa shogunate. By the 1800s, the game had filtered down to the general population and has remained popular ever since. There are annual national tournaments, and Japanese newspapers run columns on the game.

To play *go*, however, you need a game board that in its original form looked like an extra-thick chopping block (you can now get portable versions that fold up). The playing pieces are small black and white stones, but the heavy game board made *go* impractical for sojourners who saw themselves as "just passing through" on the way to riches before returning to Japan. *Go* was a pastime of the settlers, the immigrants who came to stay. As a game of the samurai class, *go* would not even have been available to the earliest immigrants, who were poor farmers and workers.

This brings up an important point that was brought to my attention when I shared a panel discussion with Japanese American writer Bill Hosokawa, whose *Nisei: The Quiet Americans* (University of Colorado

WORDS & PHRASES
becha becha
Soaking wet. "I can't believe it rained like that. Here's a towel; you're all *becha becha.*"

Courtesy Lisa Sasaki.

Bonsai is one of many traditional arts and crafts that Japanese Americans have kept alive over the generations.

Press, revised edition, 2002) is one of the must-read histories of Japanese Americans. Bill noted that it's generally a positive thing that so many Americans are interested in traditional Japanese culture and assume that Japanese Americans are steeped in such well-known Japanese traditions as flower arranging and tea ceremony. In actuality, most early Japanese immigrants didn't grow up learning the crafts that are so identified with Japan today. These were reserved for the higher classes, the samurai families and diplomats, not the farmers and merchants. The pioneering Issei brought with them their earthier traditions of harvest festivals and *obon* dances, songs, and simple pastimes like *jan ken pon* as a way of evoking memories of the homes they had left behind.

Crafting a culture

As another way of holding on to their culture, immigrants practiced the arts and crafts of Japan. Some of these crafts, such as songs and festival dances, were available to the earliest immigrants. Others became part of Japanese American culture with later arrivals or were taught to the Nisei children of the first immigrants by the community organizations (the *kenjinkai*, usually formed around the home prefectures of members, such as the Hiroshima Kenjinkai) and Buddhist churches that sprang up to serve the increasing number of Japanese families settling in America. Today, these traditions are the hallmarks of Japanese culture in the West, and many such crafts are enthusiastically enjoyed by JAs across the generations.

Origami is one of the first things that come to mind when Americans think about Japanese culture. It's commonplace because it's inexpensive and relatively easy to learn. It doesn't take traditional Japanese paper, although it's prettier when colorful origami paper is used instead of, say, pieces of newsprint or sheets of notebook paper.

These days every kid in America learns origami in school or day care. It's the easiest of Japanese crafts to enjoy. All it takes are squares of paper, some patience, and the discipline necessary to fold the paper with care and precision (that's why it's a great exercise for young children).

Like almost everything else in Asia, origami, literally "folded paper," probably has its origins in China, although the written record places it as a Japanese invention. Paper, at any rate, was invented in China about two thousand years ago as a cheaper, easier-to-make writing surface than rolls of silk. It's easy to assume that someone soon figured out how to fold the newfangled sheets into geometric shapes. Papermaking reportedly came to Japan in the seventh century via the usual route of Buddhist monks traveling from China through Korea. The Japanese studied the books the monks brought and began making paper of their own by about A.D. 610. Wherever it was invented, origami was fine-tuned by and has become associated with the Japanese.

Records in Japan of folded paper as an art or craft show up during the Heian period (794–1185) as a tradition of the noble classes at a time when paper was a rare commodity. Samurai exchanged gifts with *noshi*, a good-luck charm made of paper folded with a strip of dried abalone or meat, and the upper classes celebrated weddings by wrapping sake bottles in butterfly forms representing the bride and groom.

The first written origami instructions were published in a fifty-nine-page manuscript called *Senbazuru Orikata* ("Thousand Crane Folding") in 1797. The *Kayaragusa*, an encyclopedia of Japanese culture dating back to 1845, included origami instructions, too. The word origami originally referred to formal folded paper certificates that accompanied gifts and valuable objects, but it became associated in the late nineteenth and early twentieth centuries with the playful kind of folding we know today.

Many of those same American school kids who learn to create cool origami balls, samurai helmets, and other ornaments also learn the story of Sadako and the thousand cranes, which has come to symbolize Japan's antinuclear sentiments. Sadako Sasaki was two years old when Hiroshima was destroyed by an atomic bomb in 1945. When she was twelve she was diagnosed with leukemia. According to a Japanese legend, if someone makes 1,000 origami cranes he or she is granted a wish. Sadly, Sadako was only able to make 644 cranes before she died. Her family and friends made the remainder in her memory. In tribute, thousands of children the world over send origami cranes to adorn the statue of Sadako in Hiroshima's Peace Park.

Japanese Americans learn about Sadako in school, too, but by the time they're shown origami during craft hour, they've most likely already been introduced to the discipline of folding paper. Especially within Japanese American communities, origami is taught to kids in community centers and churches by the older generation. In addition to cranes, colorful balls, hats, samurai helmets, shirts, frogs, and many

Wartime in Japan

Mom has no knowledge of the internment and hates talking about the war. In Tokyo, she suffered greatly from the bombing and lost her job and her home. She eventually worked on military bases including as a dance partner to American GIs. Sometimes, she would tell us about some horrific war scene like the little girl in the train station who was trying to eat a leather wallet. She used to make us cry with her tales of inhumanity. We became antiwar activists because of Mom.

Yayoi Lena Winfrey, *hapa* Issei

Buddhist church

The Buddhist church was very central growing up—most times I'd be there four times a week. I recall my high school friends asking me to do things with them and telling them I couldn't because I had to go "to church." That probably made me sound very religious but it wasn't about religion at all—it was about hanging out, playing volleyball, basketball, going to dances, Youth Buddhist Association events. I remember how we kids couldn't wait to be old enough to be "YBA" because that's when we could hang out with the older group and do more exciting things. There was a great feeling of belonging and kinship at church and that was something I couldn't get from school groups.

Erin Yoshimura, Yonsei

Living in Colorado, not being interned

As far as discrimination during the war in our area, it wasn't too bad. We had to turn in all our cameras and guns to the county but those Issei with children got them back after the war. When the war started, the Issei were not allowed to own property, so father had to transfer the title of the farm to my name. After the war started my father stopped at a bar in Longmont, Colorado, to get a beer to drink, but they wouldn't serve him. He said the bartender pointed to a sign that said "White Trade Only," but he couldn't read English. Besides being called "Japs," it wasn't too bad. We stayed pretty much within our own ethnic group.

Jack Kunio Miyasaki, Nisei

suppai

Sour. "There's too much vinegar in that dressing, the cucumber salad is too *suppai*."

more complex creations have helped generations of Japanese-American kids stay connected with their heritage.

Much more difficult is the craft of Japanese doll-making, with its variety of established forms from child-like *kimekomi* dolls and *hago-ita* (flattened "dolls" created on the backs of shuttlecock paddles) to realistic adult dolls in full kimono-clad splendor.

Growing up, I watched my mom working on the fanciest dolls, their graceful forms made of gauzy white fabric stuffed with thin shreds of wood. She meticulously assembled and sewed together beautiful silk fabric in layers just like those for real kimono, except in miniature, and draped them on the doll's waiting figure. She topped them off with tiny, elaborate wigs made of real hair decorated with miniature combs.

Someone in every Japanese American community—often a recent Issei immigrant or an older Nisei who learned the art as a child—teaches the crafts to anyone who's interested. And at every community's *obon* dance or Cherry Blossom festival, someone will be selling a variety of handmade dolls at a booth. There are several types of Japanese dolls, starting with the most basic made of folded paper to more elaborate ones with clothing made of real kimono fabric. My mother continued to make some of the fancier dolls until she was no longer able to order the forms made of wood shavings stuffed in a cotton body. Now, doll bodies are made of plastic.

Dolls in Japan aren't just for Barbie-style make-believe playtime. They're an expression of artistry and can be exquisitely detailed, intended solely for display in glass cases. They're also celebrated in an annual girl's holiday called Hina Matsuri on March 3. The centerpiece of the holiday is a group of dolls representing the Japanese imperial court placed on a multi-tiered stand with the emperor and empress in Heian-period court dress sitting at the top. Today, doll displays of the entire court are much more common in Japan than among Japanese Americans. Maybe in America Barbie has turned the concept of a doll into just a plaything, not a symbolic, ceremonial object. Hina Matsuri began in the Edo period (the 1600s to the 1800s) as a way of warding off evil spirits. Some Japanese today float paper dolls down rivers following Hina Matsuri, praying that the dolls will carry away sickness and bad fortune. But over the centuries the holiday has also become a celebration of the girls in a family. In fact, in Japan some families still believe that if they don't quickly put away the dolls after Hina Matsuri, their daughters will have a difficult time finding a husband. Many Japanese American communities celebrate Hina Matsuri with doll displays, often at the local Japanese church.

As with other crafts in Japan, doll making is taken seriously, and there are even certified master doll makers. Within the United States, doll making is less structured, although serious classes are available in some cities. (The Japanese Doll School in Washington, D.C., is headed by a master instructor.)

A related craft, *bunka shishu*, is a Japanese form of embroidery most commonly created with prepackaged kits imported from Japan. The kits produce intricate artworks that, from a few feet away, look like paintings. *"Bunka"* means "culture" and *"shishu"* means "to stitch"—so the art form is literally "stitching culture," an indication of the high regard in which it is held. The exacting patterns are usually of Japanese subjects such as cherry or plum blossoms, swallows, and landscapes, including the ubiquitous Mount Fuji. Chances are someone in your JA community does *bunka shishu* and is willing to teach others. You can consider it the JA version of an old-fashioned, all-American quilting circle!

Bunka shishu is a relatively obscure art in JA communities. When Americans think of the cultural practices of Japanese living in the United States, the most familiar are the high-culture forms that have been practiced for centuries in Japan: *shodo* or calligraphy, *ikebana* or flower arranging, and the rarefied aesthetic reflection of the tea ceremony.

Many JAs of all ages study *shodo* and *ikebana* as a way of connecting with their cultural roots—every Japanese Buddhist church has a group of respected leaders who teach these disciplines, or people who are happy to demonstrate them at festivals and cultural events. My mom, who used to teach calligraphy, often volunteers at events and in classrooms to write American names in *katakana*, the Japanese alphabet that's used for non-Japanese words. Learning *shodo* is not like learning to write the English alphabet—imagine having to learn thousands of Chinese characters (many are complex, and Japanese need to know several thousand just to read a newspaper), and then having to learn how to write them beautifully, with fluid but steady precision, using ink and brush. It brings renewed appreciation for the penmanship lessons you had in grade school. And you thought learning to write in cursive was hard. . . .

Likewise with *ikebana*, arranging flowers is more than just a matter of dropping a bouquet into a vase and fluffing them out for display.

Courtesy Erin Yoshimura.

An Issei couple and their award-winning garden.

Japanese culture is still fresh in the family

As a Shin Nisei, I was raised in a Japanese-speaking environment with Japanese traditions all around me. Everything from deep Japanese-style baths right in my Northern California home to *bento* school lunches were integral parts of my childhood. Even in college, I preferred to cook with my own rice cooker than eat at the cafeterias!

Kota Mizutani, Shin Nisei (child of recent immigrants)

WORDS & PHRASES

zannen deshita

Too bad, bad luck. "Well you tried hard and did your best but you didn't win, *zannen deshita.*"

Photo by Glenn Asakawa.

Denver Taiko is one of the oldest taiko drum groups in the United States. It was formed in 1976 and comprises Sansei and Yonsei Japanese Americans.

Regrets

I was a child right after Pearl Harbor, when it was not good to be Japanese. As kids, we tried to look white. My grandma used to praise me for my Haole nose or my white complexion. I worked hard to be non-Japanese to pursue my dreams of being a writer. (I speak of this in one of my books: *Kapoho: Memoir of a Modern Pompeii*.)

Frances Kakugawa, Sansei

WORDS & PHRASES

omedeto

Congratulations, on an auspicious occasion. "*Omedeto* for graduating first in your class. We knew you could do it." *Akemashite omedeto gozaimasu* is the formal greeting for "Happy New Year."

Over centuries, *ikebana* has evolved into an art form that values the space around each flower or plant as much as it does the flower or plant itself. And, as in an intricate miniature living sculpture, you might see various elements included in an arrangement, such as a twisted willow branch, simply for their compositional effect.

All of the above arts can be learned, enjoyed, and expressed by anyone Japanese, Japanese American, or non-Japanese. But the tea ceremony is something that takes extra effort and a committed interest in multiple Japanese disciplines—including traditional dress, cooking, and a depth of knowledge of the ritual itself.

To perform a tea ceremony, or *chanoyu*, to traditional standards requires a space dedicated to the ritual, whether it's a tea house in a garden or a cleared-out space in a basement room with tatami mats arranged to facilitate the proper clarity of mind. The ceremony is a slow, deliberate way of making and serving green tea, along with a prescribed menu of sweet snacks and other foods, that is designed to focus the mind and spirit of those in attendance on the pure aesthetics of the ritual itself. Even the way the food is served, and the way the ladle that pours the tea is held, has been determined for centuries. All participants should be dressed in kimono and sit in the traditional way on the floor. There's a lot of bowing and quiet meditation, and the tea doesn't even taste very good (it's frothy and bitter). There is no "new wave" in tea ceremony—at least none that's accepted as anything connected to Japanese culture.

But, as with many other traditional arts of Japan, someone in every Japanese American community knows how to do it right and is available to teach the next generation how to conduct a proper tea ceremony.

Musical roots

Many of us can remember snatches of Japanese songs from our childhood—and I don't mean just the *Speed Racer* or *Astro Boy* theme tunes. Deep in our memories are embedded the sound of nursery sing-alongs and lullabies—songs that serve as evocative reminders of our cultural past. Japanese Americans are fortunate, because along with the American nursery rhymes and children's songs we learned in preschool, we heard the songs of another culture, either sung to us by our mothers or grandmothers, or in weekend Japanese school or Dharma school at the Buddhist church. We sang "Old MacDonald Had a Farm" and "Yankee Doodle Dandy" on weekdays and then found ourselves phonetically singing along on Saturdays, "*Chee-chee pah-pah chee pah-pah, suzume no gakko no sensei wa . . .*," a song about a school for young sparrows.

We might recall a song about frogs that go *"kero, kero, kero"* (the Japanese way of describing the American "ribbit" sound), "Kaeru no Uta" ("The Frog's Song"), or the lilting melody of "Donguri Koro-koro" ("Rolling Acorn"):

A ROLLING ACORN

An acorn rolled down and down,
He suddenly fell into a pond.
Then came the loaches,*
Hi boy! Come play with us!

The acorn enjoyed playing with them.
But he soon began to cry,
I want to go back to the mountain.
The loaches didn't know what to do.

どんぐりころころ

どんぐり　ころころ　どんぶりこ
おいけに　はまって　さあ　たいへん
どじょうが　でてきて
こんにちは　ぼっちゃん　いっしょに　あそびましょう

どんぐり　ころころ　よろこんで
しばらく　いっしょに　あそんだが
やっぱり　おやまが
こいしいと　ないては　どじょうを　こまらせた

The most haunting melody, "Akatombo," is a mournful-sounding song about a dragonfly. Many songs are short, sweet poems, such as "Usagi" ("Rabbit"), which was sung during Jugo-ya, or the celebration of the full moon.

RABBIT

Pretty rabbit, what do you watch
while hopping around?
I watch *jugo-ya* moon
while hopping around.

うさぎ

うさぎ　うさぎ
なに見て　はねる
十五夜　お月さま
見てはねる

And of course, even fourth and fifth generation JAs will recognize "Sakura, Sakura," the simple but unforgettable folk melody that has come to represent Japan musically because it's so often played with traditional instruments such as the thirteen-stringed koto (which I like to describe as a musical surfboard), the shamisen (a three-stringed

_____
*Loach is the name for various Eurasian and African freshwater fish of the carp family.

A 1952 Denver Post article headlines "Orientals Plan Buddhist Fete Sunday," showing a photograph of a drum group rehearsing for the Bon Odori festival.

Spirituality

I am more into Jodo Shinshu, as that is the religion of my family, but I study Zen Buddhism as it applies to *chado* (tea ceremony).

Masaye Okano Nakagawa, Sansei

gaijin

Foreigner. "You speak very good *Nihongo* for a *gaijin*."

lute that has the timbre of an American banjo and might fit right in with a bluegrass band), and the shakuhachi (a bamboo flute with a haunting sound).

There's a healthy and growing interest in such traditional Japanese instruments, and as with the arts of tea ceremony, *ikebana*, and *shodo*, most JA communities have resources on hand in the form of a teacher who has been trained and can introduce students to the music. However, obtaining the instruments themselves can be a major undertaking, since your typical guitar shop or musical instrument retailer probably won't have them. A private teacher will have sources and can give advice on what to buy for your degree of serious interest in the music. For the shakuhachi, an enterprising public school teacher in Denver, Colorado, has figured out how to make a passable Japanese flute out of PVC pipes used in plumbing. After drilling holes and sanding down the mouthpiece, his students stain and paint the white pipes so they look like bamboo!

The most exciting of all Japanese musical instruments, and one that has caught on with young Japanese Americans, is the *taiko* drum. *Taiko* is Japanese for drum, and it applies to a variety of percussion instruments, from small snappy drums to the thunderous *o-daiko*, or giant drums, used by internationally acclaimed groups such as Kodo.

Although *taiko* music is ancient—it has been around since the feudal era in Japan when it was used for village activities such as blessing crops and in village festivals, as an essential element in religious ceremonies and in formal court music called *gagaku*, and to rally samurai for battle and scare off enemy forces—it wasn't a major part of Japanese musical culture. Traditionally, *taiko* drums were played singly or in pairs but never in groups. In fact, the ensemble, or *kumi-daiko*, format that we think of today when we think of *taiko* drumming, didn't emerge until the 1950s in Japan. The style didn't crystallize into an American movement, that is, with JAs along the West Coast, until the 1970s. The contemporary style can be traced to one musician, jazz drummer Daihachi Oguchi, who arranged a traditional piece of music in a jazzy setting and played it with *taiko* drums of varying sizes to obtain a range of tones and textures. That's the sound we hear today from Japan's Ondekoza and Kodo, two world-renowned *taiko* groups, and from the numerous regional groups such as San Francisco Taiko Dojo, the first America-based group, which was founded by Sensei Seiichi Tanaka in 1968, and Denver Taiko, which formed in 1977.

The physical impact of *taiko* music, along with the sheer visual poetry of a choreographed ensemble presenting its music in perfect synchrony, is so powerful and inviting that *taiko* is beginning to catch on as Japan's most influential and lasting gift to world music.

Spiritual roots

Long before they became hip, *taiko* drums were brought over by immigrants during the early part of the twentieth century, not for concerts, but for use in simple Buddhist ceremonies and for the participatory *matsuri*, or festival dances, that kept their homeland's culture alive in America. One of the most important ways the Issei and the Nisei held onto their culture was through a network of Japanese community churches, primarily the Jodo Shinshu Buddhist sect and the United Methodist Christian church.

The Jodo Shinshu Buddhist church is based on the teachings of Shinran Shonin (1173–1262), who preached that the "pure land way" was to put total faith in Amida Buddha. It's one of the main branches of Buddhism in Japan. In the United States the sect evolved to include some Westernized practices, including Japanese-language schools for children on Saturdays and Dharma School, or Sunday School, after services on Sundays. Dharma schools were modeled on Christian Sunday schools, so that Nisei children could attend Buddhist church and have an experience similar to that of their non-Japanese playmates.

Jodo Shinshu churches in America feature both an English service and a Japanese service, sometimes with two separate ministers to serve the congregations. From the start, the churches fostered cultural life in the JA community and served as a bridge between Japan and America by sponsoring such celebrations as Hana Matsuri (Buddha's birthday), various Sakura Matsuri (Cherry Blossom festivals), and *obon* street dances to pay tribute to the ancestors. Today they hold classes on everything from language to *ikebana* and martial arts like judo, karate, and aikido. They usually have their own gymnasiums and sponsor athletics for young JAs, such as basketball and softball teams. The church's annual Japanese American National Bowling Association Tournament is held in different cities and attracts bowlers from Hawaii and all over the mainland.

Photo by Glenn Asakawa.

The local Minyo Kai traditional dance group leads the obon street dance by the light of paper lanterns at Denver's Cherry Blossom festival.

Roots run deep

I believe the consideration of others that especially comes from being a Japanese female is deeply engrained in me. I dislike being late, will always consider the thoughts of others (to a fault sometimes), retain a connection to my elders and honor them. I am very connected to my family of origin as well.

Angela Uyeda, Sansei Japanese Canadian

moshi-moshi

"Hello," but only used over the phone with other Japanese, as in "*Moshi-moshi*, is this the Asakawa residence?"

Internment in the family
My mother went to Pinedale Assembly Center, where she married her first husband and moved with him to Chicago. My father was arrested and held for some time before being sent to Poston. My uncle was both a ham radio operator and an amateur photographer, so both his brothers who had come to the mainland were arrested and interrogated. One of my uncles and his family were sent to Heart Mountain. My uncle, who was a ham radio/amateur photographer, went to Tule Lake. *Otosan* did not talk about his experience much except to say that when they arrested him, he fought very hard and gunshots were fired. Then he was imprisoned for maybe six months before being put in Poston. After he had been there for some time, they asked him to help teach the others how to raise vegetables, as he had been a farmer in the Imperial Valley (in California). He told them he wanted to be paid the same as if he were outside. They told him it was his civic duty to help his people out and he would not be paid. As they had confiscated his crops when he was put in jail, he told them to ——— off and went back to playing *Hana*.

Masaye Okano Nakagawa, Sansei

The Buddhist church also supplies troops of tireless volunteers—often the little old Nisei ladies of each church's *fujinkai,* or the church's women's association—to cook and prepare for events and festivals, including bake sales (an adaptation of the Christian church practice) and Japanese food bazaars. The Buddhist churches are also important because they perform Buddhist funerals as well as memorial services on certain important anniversaries of a loved one's death.

Christianity in Japan has a long history that began with the Spanish Jesuit priest Francis Xavier, who introduced the Western religion to Japan when he landed in Kagoshima in 1549. Christians were persecuted during much of the country's history, but in the 1870s the first Christian university, Doshisha University, was established in Kyoto by Jo Niijima, a former stowaway who had been inspired to go to America by a friend's Chinese Bible. Niijima, renamed Joseph Hardy Neesima, became the first Japanese ordained evangelical minister. In 1872, four Japanese students who were studying in San Francisco began attending the Chinese Methodist Mission because "orientals" weren't allowed to go to white churches. These students could speak a little English but no Chinese, so within a few years a movement grew to establish Japanese Congregational Churches. Over the next century, the Japanese Christian community mainly worshipped within the Congregational Christian Churches, which in 1957 merged with United Church of Christ and the United Methodist Churches because both were willing to include Japanese-language services. In JA communities, these Christian churches hold Japanese cultural events such as Hina Matsuri festivals and food bazaars, and sponsor sports teams and leagues, such as softball, bowling, and basketball, for their JA members.

Like the Jodo Shinshu Buddhist churches, these Christian churches have been important oases for Japanese culture, even as that culture has evolved into a uniquely Japanese American form of community.

CHAPTER 3

Customs

Along with the cultural arts, customs and traditions are an enduring reflection of who we are and where we came from. And as we drift away from the customs that our ancestors lived by, who we're becoming. We often take for granted some of the things we do, and give little thought to why we do them. In the case of some Japanese customs, it's simply because we were taught to do them by our parents, who learned from their parents.Customs

As Japanese Americans, we don't all take off our shoes inside our homes anymore. But many of us still do; after all, it's a pretty practical ritual, because our shoes track dirt and mud all over the floor (I'm starting to sound like my mother!).

The custom came about centuries ago in Japan from the upper classes who lived in lavishly appointed homes and castles that had tatami mats throughout for flooring. By the time of the Meiji Restoration, when Japan opened up from over two centuries of isolation and was trying to catch up with Western technology and society, even farmers had tatami mats. Typical tatami are about three feet by six feet, and Japanese homes and rooms are measured by the number of mats it takes to cover the floor—the Japanese equivalent of square footage in a home. Because tatami was woven out of rush (an aquatic grassy plant), it would wear out quickly if walked upon with shoes—or in ancient Japan, *geta* or wooden sandals. That, and the need to keep the tatami clean, meant you left your *geta* at the door.

Modern Japanese homes today might have only one special room with tatami flooring dedicated to old-fashioned family get-togethers, but they still have a *genkan*, or entranceway, just inside the door where you can take your shoes off. Slippers are *de rigueur* even for guests

Oshogatsu and mochitsuki

Oshogatsu is one tradition we have celebrated since I was born . . . we have continued the family tradition to this day! We also periodically host *mochitsuki* with our families . . . we use the equipment my grandparents brought over from Japan. Even though they are no longer with us, we feel their presence.

Cindy Yoshida-Moromisato, Yonsei

47

Courtesy Erin Yoshimura.

Flower arranging is a popular Japanese tradition across the United States.

The next generation

I tried to be a much better, more caring parent. I tried to teach my children the difference between being Nikkei and being Japanese. I tried to give them the strong principles of my father, the culture of my stepmother, and tried to show them how hard it was being female, a single parent, and Nikkei. They seem to have taken those lessons in and are very compassionate, kind, caring men. I tried to be harder on them to do well in school. Other than that, I pretty much followed my father's example.

Masaye Okano Nakagawa, Sansei

dame

(Pronounced "da meh") Bad; Stop it, or don't do that. "*Dame,* you're going to get in trouble if you keep that up."

(but in the tatami room, even the slippers come off and it's bare feet or socks).

In early Japanese American homes, especially in those of the first immigrants who were farm laborers and whose accommodations were not much better than shacks for families and bunkhouses for single men, taking off shoes was often an exercise in futility. And today's younger generation may be less willing to continue the tradition when their American friends don't take off their shoes in their homes or when they're in a hurry to live their lives. But I have always thought that taking your shoes off was a thoughtful consideration, even when I visit someone else's home where it wasn't required.

Traditional Japanese footwear reflects this custom of removing shoes—the *geta* and *zori* of the past, still often worn in Japan, are open-toed and easy to slip off in a *genkan*. Even the most common modern shoe of Japanese children, slip-on sneakers with an elastic front where American kids would have laces to tie, are designed for ease of use in a culture that takes off its shoes.

The *zori* has become a Western staple in the form of the flip-flop. Traditional *zori* are made of rush straw with a rubber sole and cloth straps. During World War II, it was common to see *zori* made of a piece of tire with makeshift straps. American soldiers brought back *zori* after the war, and the simple sandal evolved into the ubiquitous summertime gear of today.

Another Japanese custom, one so established that Westerners still think of it as the quintessential Japanese costume, is the kimono. There are formal kimono of great beauty that are only brought out for occasions such as weddings, and more casual *yukata* for informal events such as summertime *obon* street dances. There are kimono and *yukata* for both men and women. There are also the shorter *happi* coats, which are often used for summer festivals and are popular with Westerners because they can be worn over shirts and pants as a jacket. At JA community events, performances, and festivals you'll always see men and women in traditional garb, demonstrating a tea ceremony, or perhaps performing in a *minyo*, or folk-dance group, and keeping alive the traditions of Japan even now, well over a century after the original immigrants came to America.

The first immigrants to America worked hard to fit in—they came dressed in formal Western clothing, often paid for with cash advances from the contractors who hired them as laborers. Unlike the Chinese laborers before them, many of whom wore traditional Chinese clothes and kept their queues, the long ponytail that was part of their tradition, the Issei didn't want to set themselves apart from other Americans. Of course, other Americans did that for them anyway because no amount of fashion sense could hide the Issei's features or their lack of language skills.

Courtesy Stone Bridge Press.

The Four Immigrants Manga, an illustrated chronicle of Issei life by Henry Yoshitaka Kiyama, humorously shows some of the cultural and linguistic barriers that early Japanese immigrants had to overcome.

As with the Chinese, prejudice and racism forced the Issei to stay within tightly knit communities, which made it easier to hold onto traditions. Within the confines of the Nihonmachi, the Japantowns that sprang up along the West Coast, you could see women shuffling along the sidewalk in kimono and *geta* and men bowing respectfully to each other as they went about their day. In those early, isolated Japantowns, the culture of Japan remained undiluted. The process of becoming Americanized was inevitable because the immigrants worked within American society for American bosses even though they may have gone home at night to purely Japanese communities. Gradually, they learned the language and the lifestyle of Americans.

The language barrier was the hardest hurdle for the early Issei. Many of the very first immigrants were students who came to America and were hired as servants for wealthy Caucasian families, and they were thrown into a culture and society that was as foreign to them as Japan was to their employers. Henry Yoshitake Kiyama, a Japanese artist who immigrated to San Francisco in 1904 and eventually moved back to Japan, drew a series of journalistic comic strips about the lives of the Issei. His observations reveal the humor—and often the pathos—of their adventures. These comics are collected and translated in *The Four Immigrants Manga* (Stone Bridge Press, 1999). In one scene about Japanese versus American traditions, a Japanese who's hired by a woman as a houseboy wants to please his employer so much that when she takes a bath he grabs a brush and prepares to help clean her, something that would be perfectly acceptable in Japan for a servant to do.

Many Japanese customs were no longer necessary in America, but within families and tight-knit ethnic enclaves like the Nihonmachi, such shows of respect as bowing continued, at least for the Issei and, early on, the Nisei generation.

Depth of culture

My thinking is apparently very Japanese. I was instilled with the absolute importance of automatically considering the needs of others, to minimize stress or distress. I was also saturated with the admiration of delving into the deepest aspects of any field of study or work, the same drive that produces the Japanese craftspeople who take their work to dizzying heights of mastery, in form, function, and philosophy. (That said, I'm not necessarily good at applying these things in most aspects of my life. I like to think, however, that this has enriched my spirit and my appreciation of the good aspects of humanity.)

Eri Izawa, Nisei

WORDS & PHRASES

ofuro

Bath. "I'm going to go *ofuro* and then go to bed."

Turning Japanese

I've tried to learn to bow when I meet Japanese, especially in business situations, but try as I might, I can't hide the fact that I'm American, a *gaijin*, a foreigner. My immediate compulsion is to reach out to shake hands, whereas a Japanese businessman would never do that with another Japanese. Japanese bow by degrees, depending on how much respect needs to be shown the person you're greeting. If you're meeting an older person or someone of a higher rank, you must bow lower and stay bowed longer. For *gaijin*, just a slight dip of the head will do—followed by the extended hand for the handshake. Japanese understand that foreigners just don't have the same level of courtesy, I guess.

The same goes when you're sitting on the floor Japanese-style, *seiza*, and you're introduced to someone. For anyone who's taken aikido or other Japanese martial arts, the sitting position on your knees with your feet under you is a little less excruciating. Most non-Japanese will simply slide their legs out to the side, or sit cross-legged on the floor. But if you're bowing, you need to do it correctly. I was taught in an aikido class that when kneeling I had to show the utmost respect for the *sensei*—the teacher—and bow my head almost to the ground, with my arms first on my thighs and then on the floor in front of my knees as I bow my head. I was taught to be aware of what others around me were doing even when I had my head bowed, and when straightening back up, my right hand came to my thigh first, like a samurai who might at any moment have to reach for his sword.

This protocol only matters if you're a JA interested in visiting or doing business in Japan or with Japanese people. It can be especially embarrassing for Japanese Americans not to know the proper customs in Japan, since we look like we ought to.

When I traveled to Japan in the 1990s, I became cocky after a week because I could speak fairly well—albeit with a child's vocabulary—and my accent was good. I could hold conversations with taxi drivers about the beauty of the Rocky Mountains or the coming flood of Japanese baseball players into the American Major Leagues (the cabbie was right—at the time, only Hideo Nomo had been signed from Japan, but now more and more Japanese players are becoming MLB stars). So when I approached a chestnut cart at Asakusa Temple in Tokyo, I felt confident in my Japaneseness. I asked for the 200-yen bag of chestnuts and gave the vendor my money. I thanked him in Japanese, but as I walked away he replied in English: "You're welcome."

Astounded, I turned back and asked him how he could tell I wasn't Japanese. "Hmmm, feeling," he said simply. I couldn't hide my American side no matter how hard I tried. It was in the way I dressed—

too loud, too loose, and too comfortable. It was in the way I walked—too jaunty, bouncy, and confident. It was even in the way I looked at the world around me. I wasn't walking with my head down, avoiding eye contact with others. I was curious about my surroundings and all too eager to connect with people around me. I was American.

I've had the same thing happen in Japanese-owned stores in the United States. I once walked into a Japanese video store in Colorado Springs to see if they had documentaries about postwar Japan. I bowed slightly to the shopkeeper, a middle-aged Japanese woman, when I entered the store and started to explore the titles. Several customers came in after me. I noticed in each case the shopkeeper greeted them in Japanese when they entered; she didn't call them by name, so I don't think they were regular customers that she recognized. She hadn't spoken to me at all when I came in. I finally asked her—in English—why she hadn't greeted me in Japanese. She told me it was because she could tell I was American and didn't need to be greeted formally. She said she could tell by the way I walked up to the door.

So, a word of advice: if you're Japanese American and interested in being more Japanese, or in doing business with Japanese, be sure to leave your American habits at home. It's ironic that after more than a century of trying to fit in as Americans and raising the younger generation to be as American as possible, some of us are now trying to be as Japanese as we can.

There are other Japanese customs to be aware of if you're a JA wanting to be more Japanese. For more tips for visiting Japan, see Chapter 9.

The gift of giving

There are lots of Japanese ways that have been passed down to us by our parents and grandparents. Many of us are keenly aware of the practice of taking *omiyage*, a small gift, whenever we visit someone. It could be just a bag of *osembei*, rice crackers, or other snacks, a pen, a CD, or it might be something more formal and parent-like such as a hand towel or handkerchief. We have been taught to offer something as a small token of respect when we visit someone. But the gift

Courtesy Lisa Sasaki

Santa Claus brought toys to JA kids just like every other kid in the United States.

Culture in the house
We observed some special days like girl's day and *obon*. We'd celebrate New Year in the Japanese-style and basically got raised with Japanese ethics.

Jill Nakawatase, postwar Nisei

WORDS & PHRASES
shoppai
Salty. "That's so *shoppai*, you used too much *shoyu*."

Japanese Americans in many cities celebrate their culture with annual Sakura Matsuri, or Cherry Blossom Festivals, like this one in Denver.

Photo by Glenn Asakawa.

shouldn't be extravagant because the recipient might feel obligated to match the gift.

And like the Japanese, when we give our *omiyage*, many of us take the extra step of wrapping the present nicely, in paper or perhaps bundled in a silk *furoshiki*, or placed in a nice box or container. If you've ever been to Japan, you'll know that Japanese are almost obsessive about their packaging and wrapping. Even manufactured goods such as snacks and candies can be beautifully and individually wrapped within the outer package.

There are rules about receiving and opening gifts. They're always presented and received with humility and respect. The giver hands over the gift with both hands, bows, and says demurely, "It's just a little thing" or "This is nothing." The recipient takes the gift with both hands and bows. Japanese usually don't open the gift right away, but if you want to do so, you should just ask if it's okay to open it, but don't tear into it like you're an eight-year-old on Christmas morning. In fact, if you do open the gift, don't tear and crumple the wrapping paper. Fold it up nicely while in the company of the giver.

In the same vein as obligatory gift giving, many JAs will offer to pay for the meal at a restaurant, and even fight over the bill if necessary. Also, while dining at other peoples' homes or at a restaurant, JAs will often try not to pig out, and leave the last serving for someone else—that's the Japanese concept of *enryo*, or self-control. We were steeped in such traditions as children.

Celebrations

We were also taught that certain occasions are more important than others—specifically some birthdays and holidays—and therefore were important for gift giving.

Children's third, fifth, and seventh birthdays are thought to be lucky ones, and Japanese kids participate in the Shichi-Go-San, or Seven-Five-Three, festival, celebrated on November 15 every year. During the festival, families visit a shrine, temple, or church to give thanks for good health and ask for continued well-being in the future. Other important birthdays for Japanese include the official beginning of adulthood at twenty, and auspicious celebrations at ages sixty, seventy, seventy-seven, eighty-eight, and ninety-nine.

While JA families may not pay attention to birthdays that are traditionally marked in Japan, JA communities almost always celebrate various noteworthy dates throughout the year. Whether the celebrations are led by a community organization, a church, or temple, Japanese Americans are nothing if not ready for a festival.

Earlier, I mentioned Hina Matsuri, or the Doll Festival, which is a celebration of girls on March 3. On May 5 is Tango no Sekku, or Boys Day, when families fly carp-shaped wind socks for their sons (the carp is a traditional symbol for bravery and determination) and decorate the house with armor and warrior dolls (no, GI Joe doesn't count) as a way of wishing for health and success for boys. In Japan, the festivities also include iris leaves placed under the eaves to fend off evil and special rice cakes wrapped in oak leaves for the boys to eat.

Hana Matsuri, or Flower Festival, is the festival of Buddha's birthday, which obviously is celebrated by the Buddhist community. At the Denver Tri-State Buddhist Church, the annual celebration includes a full afternoon of performances by the Dharma School students including dances and skits, and a set by Denver Taiko. (Buddha's birthday is actually in May but Hana Matsuri is celebrated on April 8.) If you haven't figured it out by now, the word *matsuri* means "festival" in Japanese, and the one that's most visible every year in many JA communities is Sakura Matsuri, or the Cherry Blossom Festival.

One of the most popular family pastimes when the cherry blossoms bloom in the spring is viewing these beautiful, fragrant trees with a picnic lunch or dinner in parks all over Japan. These much-anticipated parties are called *hanami*, or flower-viewing. The Japan Meteorological Agency issues an official "Cherry Blossom Flowering Forecast" predicting the peak blooming dates for regions of the nation. In America, *hanami* isn't quite as organized or widespread. For one thing, cherry trees themselves aren't terribly common and don't even grow in some parts of the country.

One place that does take cherry blossom viewing seriously is Washington, D.C., where there's the well-known National Cherry Blossom Festival. In 1912, the Japanese government gave the United States a gift of 3,000 cherry trees. The trees were planted around the Tidal Basin where the Jefferson Memorial sits and make for a spectacular sight when they're in bloom. For the National Cherry Blossom Festival, which happens in late March and early April each spring, the National Park Service offers a "Bloom Watch," much like the forecasts in Japan. Across the United States, though, cherry blossom festivals

Courtesy Micahel Itamura.

JAs also took part in traditional American celebrations, like Halloween (early 1930s).

Life after internment

My mother's family (Oikawa) left Heart Mountain a few years early. This is because my mother was able to enter college at Earlham in Indiana. She managed to secure jobs as domestics for her parents in Cincinnati. Her father worked as a butler, and her mother as a maid to an eccentric old woman, who allowed my mother to board at her estate while she attended college. My uncle started at the same college, but had to interrupt his studies as he was drafted into the 442nd. The Oikawas remained in Cincinnati, where they still live today.

Midori Yenari, Sansei

WORDS & PHRASES

nan desu ka?

What is it? Huh? "You wanted to see me? *Nan desu ka?*"

Connected to culture

I have been studying Japanese history and culture all my life. My spoken Japanese is pretty good. Some of my Japanese friends/ acquaintances thought I was a Japanese national until they got to know me better. I make a lot of errors in colloquial jargon, or complicated language/formal language, but in general conversation I get along quite nicely. I have studied Japanese history quite extensively on my own since I was a child and some at the University of Washington where my major was Japan Regional Studies, a part of the Henry M. Jackson School of International Studies. I've also studied *chado* (tea ceremony) for twenty-two years. I will be receiving my Tea Name this year. I also teach *taiko* drumming and related to that, I teach my group members various points of Japanese history, traditions, vocabulary, and so forth to expand their knowledge of and appreciation for *taiko* and *chado* as it applies to our group's use in *taiko*.

Masaye Okano Nakagawa, Sansei

WORDS & PHRASES

enryo

Restraint, reserve. A Japanese trait. "Since Uncle Joe is buying dinner, *enryo* a little bit, don't order the most expensive thing on the menu."

are more about celebrating Japanese and Japanese American culture than they are about celebrating the blooming trees. In fact, Denver's Sakura Matsuri started over thirty years ago in the springtime, but over the decades has shifted to midsummer to accommodate Colorado's unpredictable climate, Denver's busy outdoor festival season, and even the city's baseball team schedule (because the Colorado Rockies' stadium was built just two blocks from Sakura Square, where the festival takes place). Each of these cherry blossom festivals includes performances of traditional culture, vendors, art exhibits, and of course lots of Japanese food as a way of introducing non-Japanese to—and remind Japanese Americans about—our heritage.

The rules of death

Other, more somber traditions within the JA community include those for deaths and funerals. One of the most persistent traditions is that of the *okoden*, the practice of giving a monetary condolence gift in an envelope to the bereaved family when you attend a funeral. *Okoden* can be given at Buddhist or Christian funerals. The amount depends on how close you were to the deceased. The money is placed in an envelope (special envelopes are used in Japan but mailing envelopes are used by JAs). Even the kind of money is dictated: It must be in clean but worn bills; the money should not be brand new because that might indicate the giver was expecting the death. Japanese Americans send a return gift of a handful of stamps with a thank-you note to those who gave *okoden*; this tradition seems to have evolved only with JAs over the past century.

Many JA families, like Japanese ones, care about gathering together for certain anniversaries of a loved one's death, and hold a brief *hoji* ceremony followed by a festive dinner—often, in the case of Japanese Americans, at a Chinese restaurant. They also honor deceased relatives every Memorial Day with brief services and a family meal.

The spirits of the deceased are celebrated at home altars called *kamidana* and *obutsudan*. Both are small shrines used in the home for prayer and to honor deceased loved ones. The *kamidana* is Shinto in origin (the word means "shelf of spirits" or "shelf of gods") and is meant to be a place to make food offerings and to instill a sense of wonder in the world and in nature. The *obutsudan* is a Buddhist altar where you can *gassho*, or pray, light a candle and incense to the Buddha, leave the first helping of freshly made *gohan* rice for deceased family members in front of a photograph and icon with their Buddhist name, and tell the Buddha and your family what's happening in the physical world. Like a cross in a Christian home, both *kamidana* and *obutsudan* are a sign of a devout household, and though they're much more common in Japanese homes, Japanese Americans might have them too.

JA families have held onto many superstitions about death imported with their Japanese ancestors. For instance, the number four is avoided in every way possible. The number four, *shi*, is pronounced the same as the word for death. In Japan, nothing is packaged in sets of four. When a well-known American golf company tried to sell balls in Japan packaged in sets of four, the promotion failed miserably. Likewise, gifts are never given in sets of four or with items lined up in foursomes. Buildings such as offices, hospitals, or hotels sometimes strike the fourth floor altogether (much like American hotels leaving off the thirteenth floor).

The numbers game can get complicated: Not only is 4 avoided, so are variations such as: 14, 24, 42, and even 420. The number 42 can be pronounced *shi-ni*, which means "to die," while 420 is pronounced *shi-ni-rei*, which means "a dead spirit." The number 24 is *ni-shi*, or "double death," and some hospital maternity wards avoid using 43, *shi-zan*, because as pronounced it means "stillbirth."

Other common superstitions connected to death among Japanese American families include:

- Never clip your nails at night or you won't be with your parents when you die.

- Never sleep with your head to the north. That's how bodies are placed during Buddhist funerals.

- Hide your thumb if you see a hearse drive by.

- Never stick chopsticks into your rice standing up. This is only done at funerals where rice is placed on the altar. When eating, chopsticks should be laid across your *chawan*, or rice bowl.

- Likewise, never pass food directly from chopsticks to chopsticks. The only time chopsticks are used to pass anything

Courtesy Erin Yoshimura.

Hundreds turn out to dance during obon, *even in Denver.*

Japanese customs

Mom always sat on her knees even in a straight-back chair. She would never let us take a photo with four people in it. We had to take gifts to anyone who ever invited us anywhere.

Yayoi Lena Winfrey, *hapa* Issei

Old-fashioned in Japan

I feel like things are familiar; the houses smell like my grandmother's. But my attitude is what my father-in-law calls Taisho. He says I am a very old-fashioned girl, and upon occasion he even calls me "Meiji Woman."

Peggy Seo Oba, Sansei

WORDS & PHRASES

abunai

Dangerous, as in "Don't play over there; it's *abunai!*" or "Hey, *abunai!* Put that knife down!" The JA way of saying "You'll poke your eye out, kid!"

Every JA business needs the good luck that is promised by the maneki neko, a cat with the upraised paw (with the other paw holding onto gold coins).

Turning American

When my parents were with other Nisei, they celebrated New Year's and cooked chicken teriyaki. Once they moved away from other Nisei, they seldom spoke Japanese or cooked any Japanese food.

Peggy Seo Oba, Sansei

Photo by Wataru Ebihara.

irasshai or irasshaimase

"Welcome, come on in." A familiar phrase of greeting at sushi restaurants throughout the West. In Japan *irasshai* is also used to greet those who enter any shop or as an invitation to enter a home.

from person to person is when family members move the bones that remain after a cremation into the urn. Instead, put your food on a plate for the other person to pick up.

As you can see, the Japanese and Japanese Americans can be very superstitious. Just ask some of your older relatives and you'll find that they know all of the above superstitions. Plus, JAs are just as likely as the Japanese to buy any number of good luck charms to dangle from their car rearview mirrors, their key chains, or their travel luggage. Certain animals such as turtles and frogs are said to be imbued with good luck, prosperity, or long life and are often seen dangling from good luck charms on sale in shops in any Japantown.

Rules of etiquette

One superstitious symbol you'll see in almost every Japanese restaurant is the *maneki neko*, or beckoning cat. *Maneki neko* can be found in several varieties—cartoonish cats, black cats, spotted cats—but the typical cat is a wide-eyed, tri-color creature sitting with one paw held in the air, Buddha-like, beckoning customers (and money) to enter a business or home. Because they look so cool, *maneki neko* appeal to Japanese Americans and non-Japanese alike. The raised paw reflects the Japanese way of beckoning to someone, with the hand swinging down.

Once you're in the door of a restaurant, or sitting at a table in a home and ready to eat, there are many traditions that are carryovers of Japanese etiquette:

- JAs who are more Japanese always serve tea or alcoholic drinks for others and let others pour drinks for them.

- Most JAs know that when you're drinking miso soup or other Japanese soup, you can lift the bowl to your lips and sip right out of it instead of using a spoon.

- Likewise, rice is eaten with the bowl lifted to the mouth, not Western-style where bowls and plates stay glued to the table.

- The back ends of the chopsticks are used to pick food from communal serving bowls or platters to place onto your own plate.

- Don't point with your chopsticks. (There are a lot of rules about chopsticks, but aren't they the greatest eating utensil ever invented by humankind?)

- It's okay to slurp ramen or other Asian noodle dishes. In fact, the louder your slurp the more you show your appreciation of the flavor and compliment the chef.

- You shouldn't rub your chopsticks together—even if they're the break-apart type—because it indicates that you think the chopsticks you've been given are cheap.

- Japanese (especially women) traditionally cover their mouths when they laugh. It's not just the poor dental health of many Japanese; there's an old Buddhist belief that showing bones is unclean.

- If you use a toothpick at the table (they're always available in Japanese homes and eateries, often at the table), be sure to cover your mouth.

- Also, don't blow your nose, bite your nails, or in other ways groom at the table or in public.

- If you're like me, you grew up with a mother or grandmother who yelled at you every time you drizzled a little soy sauce on your rice. That's offensive to Japanese (although a lot of Japanese do it anyway) because it implies the food is boring.

Values—good and bad

Japanese culture is reflected in more fundamental ways in JA families than by just observing the rules of etiquette. These behaviors have become part of Japanese American values, ingrained as if they've been hard-coded into our DNA.

These values can be innocuous, such as the need to be early to appointments, never late. If a traveler is supposed to be at the airport an hour ahead of his flight, JAs will be at the gate at least two hours

Traditions
I still celebrate many Japanese traditions, like New Year celebrations, including *otoshidama* (packets of money for children). I also observe funerals and funeral-related events such as *hoji* (memorial services marking certain anniversaries of a death), and place a fresh bowl of rice and a cup of tea every day in front of the *obutsudan* altar.
Miku Maeda Rager, Shin Issei

Feeling connected
Dressing up in kimono and dancing *odori*. My most fond memories are of attending Nisei Week Parade dance practice in the JACCC Plaza on cool summer evenings, dressed in *yukata*. The combination of the music, being dressed up in traditional *yukata*, and dancing in the cool summer air next to other *yukata*-clad dancers in J-town always made me feel especially connected to my Japanese roots.
Mariko Yamashiro, Yonsei

WORDS & PHRASES
obaachan or **obaasan**
Grandmother or elderly woman. "Over the river and through the woods to *Obaachan*'s house we go." *Obaasan* is the more honorific form. *Baachan* is even more casual.

Grandparents
My grandfather had immigrated to the United States in 1914 to work with his father on a farm in Colorado. In fact, they had found a bride, but that got nixed after the marriage to my grandmother was arranged back in the villages. So my grandfather and grandmother both exchanged photos and "did the right thing" by consenting to marriage. My grandmother once told the story of how she waited on the docks to meet her future husband. She saw all these handsome Japanese men get off the ship and kept asking herself, "Is that man my future husband? Or is that man?" My grandfather was one of the last men to get off the ship, and my grandmother said she broke down crying after seeing how short and dark he was.

Scott Takeda, Yonsei

beforehand. If a group is to meet someplace at 6 P.M. for dinner, you can be sure that the JAs will be at the restaurant at 5:30. You can imagine this can cause consternation when you're busy preparing for a huge family gathering and your JA in-laws show up an hour early.

Other Japanese values may be detrimental to JAs. Perhaps in the conservative, homogenous society of Japan these values are helpful, but in the States they can be used to hold us back. Take, for instance, the value of extreme modesty. We've been told time and time again not to brag about, or bring attention to ourselves. The old Japanese saying "The nail that sticks up will be hammered down" was one that was, well, pounded into me by my parents whenever I acted excessively rebellious and individualistic—that is, when I chose to go to art school, when I wore clothes that I liked, or when I busked with friends and played guitar in public.

The main values that have held Japanese American communities in check (and in the process made them practically invisible to the American mainstream) can be encapsulated with two phrases: *gaman* and *shikataganai*. Both helped people of Japanese descent through the injustice of the forced evacuation and internment during World War II. And both still have a powerful hold over many of us.

Gaman, or endure, is invoked when you are required to bite the bullet and quietly accept a hardship, such as the forced evacuation and internment, with very few (if any) protests. *Shikataganai*, which means "it can't be helped," was used to keep the anger, especially of the younger JAs, in check during the internment years. It helped prevent mass community upheaval against what was clearly an injustice. Even today some JAs live by the mentality that it's better not to make waves but accept things as they are, even if they're not right.

The process of becoming Japanese American has meant that, by definition, we as a people have changed some aspects of being Japanese. By varying degrees, we have added on American culture and, in some ways, lost touch with our Japanese culture. But there's no denying that for many of us, Japanese traditions and values have served as guideposts for living our lives. Our ancestors have passed down to us so many strange, wonderful, sensible, and wacky (as well as ill-advised) ways of doing things that often we simply take them for granted. We might fail to even notice that by following some of our rules, we're showing our cultural diversity and serving as living bridges between our two cultures.

Food

CHAPTER 4

Like many clichés, "you are what you eat" has an element of truth at its core.

As a Japanese American, I was raised on a combination of cuisines, and it reflected my bicultural roots. I remember eating plenty of "American" food as a kid—steaks, burgers, and spaghetti, with Jell-O and ice cream for dessert. But those dinners usually had a Japanese twist. We always had rice with our meals instead of bread or potatoes (except for the spaghetti, of course, which didn't need an additional starch). And we would often have little servings of Japanese *tsukemono* side dishes with our meals.

Even if we had something familiar to Americans, like spinach, we didn't eat it like my friends, boiled into a drab olive-colored mush. We had it Japanese-style, boiled just enough to wilt the leaves and served cold with shaved dried bonito fish and drizzled (or in my case, drowned) with soy sauce. For Thanksgiving, we always had turkey—with some *futomaki* sushi rolls on the side. And our weekly steak dinners were cooked with garlic, soy sauce, and butter, never the plain way Americans eat it. (No wonder Americans rely so much on bottled sauces like A-1 to add much-needed flavor to the meat!)

And since my mom would often sit down to a traditional meal after serving the rest of us, the smell of grilled salmon mingled in the kitchen air with the aroma of our American dishes. It never occurred to me that our family dinners might be unconventional. I was used to the international variety of cuisine, a mix-and-match mentality that has stuck with me in everything from fashion and design to pop culture and, of course, food. Yet I know some Japanese Americans who consciously avoid anything overtly Japanese, including food. I

Cooking

I don't cook much in general but about half of what I can cook is Japanese food. My favorite dishes include *misoshiru* (as a side) and *kitsune udon*. These are what I would eat mostly when I would eat Japanese food when I was younger other than Japanese snacks. They make me very nostalgic. I also think that just about everything is better with *shoyu*. And Japanese rice is always my favorite. It's hard for me when I'm at school and can't have *gohan* for a long time.

Emily Porter, Japanese Caucasian mixed-race Yonsei

Both sides

I definitely feel very American. But I also feel half Japanese. My friends and coworkers recognize that I'm Japanese (when we're talking about food, etc.) in our everyday discussions. Today I was sharing some rice crackers with the seaweed wrapped around them.

Peggy Smith, *hapa* Nisei

Courtesy Lisa Sasaki.

Many JA families still fondly remember their Issei ancestors, the "Baachans" and "Jiichans" who served as the link to Japan.

have a Sansei friend in Texas who until a few years ago had never eaten one piece of sushi and would sooner go to a Mexican or Italian restaurant than to a Japanese joint for a meal out.

These days it's harder to avoid at least trying some Japanese cuisine. There are Japanese restaurants seemingly sprouting like *shiitake* mushrooms, touting tempura, teriyaki, noodles, and other healthy, fast, and tasty fare. There's more than just sushi on the menu, and let's face it, Japanese cuisine isn't limited to sushi any more than Italian cuisine is to pasta.

Originally, Japanese restaurants were opened by immigrants to serve other immigrants who missed the food of their homeland. They clustered around the Nihonmachi, where other Japanese-owned businesses catered to the immigrant population, usually with inexpensive, hearty fare like noodle dishes, dumplings, and rice, not the fancy sushi we see so often today.

Japanese restaurants serving American customers increased over the decades, but it wasn't until 1964, when former Olympic wrestler Hiroaki "Rocky" Aoki opened his first Benihana of Tokyo restaurant in New York, that Japanese food began attracting the attention of mainstream American diners. Aoki had been raised during the post-war years in a Tokyo coffee shop run by his parents. The shop was called Benihana, or Red Flower. Aoki's father had been an entertainer before the war, and Aoki obviously inherited his father's penchant for showbiz. Aoki's idea—to bring the showmanship of knife-juggling chefs tableside in a *teppan-yaki*, or grill top, setting with the diners sitting around the "stage"—relied as much on the flashy entertainment value as it did on the food.

Then again, no one has ever accused Benihana and other *teppan-yaki* restaurants of being particularly authentic. There are certainly *teppan-yaki* restaurants, including Benihana, in Japan these days, but I don't know if the showbiz concept existed before Aoki's creation. Even the idea of eating meat is relatively new in Japan. The Japanese ate a mostly vegetarian and seafood diet for centuries until the Americans arrived in Tokyo Bay in the mid-1800s. I've always assumed *teppan-yaki* was a Japanese-American invention, an adaptation of a traditional idea.

The renamed "Rocky" Aoki—easier for Americans to pronounce—came to the United States in 1960, selling ice cream by day and studying restaurant management by night. He opened his first four-table Benihana Restaurant in 1964 near Times Square in New York City, featuring chefs who entertained the diners as they cooked. The restaurant took off after a rave review in a New York newspaper, and the Benihana chain was off and running. Rocky eventually sold his interest in the chain, and by the 1980s was more famous for speedboat racing than as a restaurateur. The chain now has many rivals—in the Denver area Japanese steakhouses have come and gone over the years using the same *teppan-yaki* concept.

Japanese cuisine has become a part of the American dining mainstream—Japanese restaurants are no longer exotic oddities. The trend has certainly been boosted in recent decades by the explosion in the popularity of sushi. When I was a kid, sushi was something only Japanese and Japanese Americans ate. Some Japanese restaurants had a sushi bar and my family was more than happy to place our orders. At that time, the thought of eating raw fish draped over balls of vinegared rice was enough to make Americans green—and not with envy. But beginning in the 1970s and accelerating in the 1980s and 1990s (thanks in part to the emergence of the yuppies, baby boomers who saw themselves as worldly, sophisticated, and willing to try new things), Americans began to see sushi as a food worth going out for.

In the 1990s many new Japanese restaurants sprang up, and they emphasized their sushi bars over the traditional mainstays of the Japanese restaurant, teriyaki and tempura. Now there are such cosmopolitan, pan-Pacific chains as Roy's, started in Hawaii by Roy Yamaguchi, a Japanese American chef trained in haute French cuisine who incorporates the Hawaiian flavors and ingredients of his childhood into Japanese and European recipes.

When my family first moved to Denver, there were only a few Japanese restaurants, and we only went to them for major family celebrations. Now, smaller Japanese restaurants are squeezing into strip malls everywhere, even though I can't vouch for the quality of all of them (some definitely don't seem "authentic," whatever *that* means). And, the menus in these new Japanese restaurants reflect the growing awareness and appreciation for the cuisine. It's not just teriyaki chicken and beef or tempura that's served anymore. Every Japanese restaurant serves *edamame*, boiled and salted soybeans. Almost every Japanese restaurant now serves *tonkatsu*, traditional breaded pork cutlet, and sushi restaurants serve *chirashi zushi*, which translates as "scattered sushi" and means a variety of sashimi served on top of a bowl of sushi rice. Even in the Midwest you can find Japanese restaurants that serve *chawan mushi*, a steaming-hot custard of eggs, vegetables,

---

Japanese Canadian food

My mother (an early sixties immigrant) made white bread jam sandwiches for my father and me when I was growing up in Alberta, Canada. We weren't rich back then, and Japanese groceries were next to impossible to come by in Edmonton at that time. I never saw a Japanese *bento* (box lunch) in North America until I worked in a research lab during postgraduate studies in Toronto, where the personnel came from all over the world (England, India, China, Iran). There was a visiting scientist from Japan who had brought his family with him for the year, and every day his wife prepared a beautiful *bento* box. Everybody marveled at it, and at the time (they thought) it must have taken to make.

Today, I am married to a Japanese woman, but she is not a morning person and so doesn't get up early enough to make a *bento*. I'm not a morning person either, so I make my own lunches the night before—still sandwiches, though I have graduated from jam on white to (a bit of) meat and cheese with (lots of) lettuce on whole wheat.

Tadaaki Hiruki, postwar Nisei

karai

Spicy hot. "Those jalapenos are super *karai*."

Food

Rice curry (curried stew served with rice) was a big favorite of mine. Bread and butter with sugar sprinkled on it was a great afterschool snack. Bologna sandwiches with mustard were made elegant if you added lettuce leaves. Fried potatoes with bacon bits and onions with *shoyu* as a condiment—mmmm—and served with rice, would that be considered Western? We usually had rice and *miso* soup for breakfast. We didn't acquire a toaster till we were in the internment camp at Slocan, B.C, but this is probably because we lived in a houseboat, which floated up and down with the tide (I learned to row a boat before I learned to ride a bike!) and didn't have electricity. We made toast on a wire rack on top of the wood-burning stove.

Lois Hashimoto, Canadian Nisei

Japanese food

When we were growing up, we ate typical Japanese food. *Miso* soup in the morning and rice with every meal. Today, we still like to eat Japanese food, so we go Japanese food shopping in Denver whenever we need rice.

Jack Kunio Miyasaki, Nisei

WORDS & PHRASES

Eigo

English. As in, "Pardon me, but do you know any *Eigo?* I can't speak *Nihongo*."

chicken, and seafood. And the most adventurous restaurants serve *natto*, fermented soybeans, which even many Japanese in Japan shy away from because of its smell and slimy texture. You can really get a complete taste of Japan when you dine out nowadays.

I figure this is a good development, because anything that spreads Japanese culture to Americans helps break down racial and cultural barriers. And having all these restaurants to choose from keeps me fat and happy with the flavors of my childhood. Even as an adult, I love my burgers, steaks, and spaghetti, but I still mix and match my food.

What's "authentic" Japanese food?

The word "authentic" is often used in the description of ethnic restaurants, but signs outside restaurants proclaiming "authentic Italian/Mexican/choose-your-country food" are just silly hype. Who would ever claim that their restaurant served "unauthentic" food?

Authenticity in food is an issue, though, as it should be in the appreciation of any cultural experience. It's trickier to judge the authenticity of food than, say, a folk costume or traditional dance. It's easy to just use elements of a style to give food the flavor of another country without being true to the roots of the style. Plus, the authenticity of food is partly a matter of the diner's knowledge. Until I moved west when I was a kid, I thought tacos were all supposed to taste like the ones I ate at Jack in the Box in Virginia. Wrong. I know better now.

Even when the culture is authentic, there can be wide differences in taste. My mom makes great Japanese food, no doubt about it, and I measure restaurants by her cooking—the flavors and textures I've grown up with. It would never occur to me that her cooking might not be authentic. She's Japanese, right? Yet, her *norimaki* sushi rolls can taste different from her friends' versions, and her teriyaki or *gyoza* can vary from the same dishes served in my favorite restaurants. Is that bad? Does that mean my mom's cooking isn't truly Japanese? No. It just means there isn't a definitive measure, beyond certain basic principles, that makes a cuisine authentic.

For example, the popular "California rolls" that are served in sushi restaurants throughout the United States were not invented in Japan. In fact, most Japanese from Japan would look at a California roll and wonder why there's rice on the outside of a *norimaki*, which is technically supposed to have *nori* seaweed on the outside, not rice. Personally, I don't care for California rolls and still feel that they aren't authentic. An avocado just isn't an ingredient you'd find in sushi in Japan. But after a while, the variations become so persistent that they're given the aura of authenticity simply because they're everywhere and everyone eats them.

Another way to judge ethnic restaurants is by looking at the diners. It's reassuring to see Asian faces at the tables of Asian restaurants and Hispanic faces in Mexican restaurants. Does this reasoning bear a tinge of racism? Maybe. The more overt version of this theory reasons that a good ethnic restaurant will have only ethnic cooks and servers. But there's no reason to believe that a non-Japanese can't make a great piece of sushi. All across America, in fact, Japanese restaurants are staffed by non-Japanese. It's not just the servers that are Caucasian, Hispanic, and African American, but the sushi chefs and cooks as well. Many times when you see an Asian face behind the sushi counter, that chef may be Korean, Chinese, or Southeast Asian. Restaurants hire from their pool of applicants, and if few Japanese apply, well, there you go.

Does that impact the authenticity of the cuisine served at the restaurant? I guess it might, but I'll reserve judgment until I dine there. Certainly in Japan you'll find a range of quality among Japanese restaurants from wonderful to just awful—and they're usually run by Japanese. The same variation in quality exists everywhere.

The one thing I've found, though, when non-Japanese make sushi (varieties of which are increasingly showing up in non-Japanese restaurants as side dishes, appetizers, or part of an all-you-can-eat buffet), is that the rice isn't flavored correctly with rice vinegar, and it's either undercooked and too hard or overcooked and too mushy. Some JAs wouldn't know a bad Japanese dish if they ate one, anyway. If you've never experienced sushi made by, say, your mother, how would you know that the mushy sushi you were served by a proud Latino chef at the ritzy Hotel Bellagio in Las Vegas was awful? Believe me, it has happened.

Then again, I return to the question: What's "authentic" food, anyway? Her Japanese dishes might be the real thing, but my mom's spaghetti and pizza sure aren't. Yet, I grew up tasting her way of cooking them, and though I know a great Italian restaurant when I taste one, I still count my mom's pizza and spaghetti among my favorites.

I guess authenticity is in the taste buds of the beholder.

Courtesy Erin Yoshimura.

A JA picnic, probably in Northern California, circa 1920s.

A Chinese dish as a JA favorite

Ham Yu is ground pork topped with salted fish and chopped ginger and steamed, then sprinkled with sliced green onions or fresh coriander before serving. The fish has a pungent flavor that permeates the pork. Ten or fifteen years ago, the handful of Nikkei in the advertising business in San Francisco used to get together every couple of months to eat Ham Yu. We all grew up with it, but none of our families would tolerate us ordering the stinky stuff for a family dinner.

Shizue Seigel, Sansei

tsukareta
Tired. "Ah, all that yardwork made me *tsukareta*."

Courtesy Midori Yenari.

Nisei kids enjoying watermelon in Yakima, Washington, around the 1920s.

Dining Japanese

Probably about once every couple months we'll eat Japanese. My husband (who is Caucasian) was afraid to try sushi at first because of the seaweed, but now is disappointed if I don't bring it home from my mom's house.

Peggy Smith, *hapa* Nisei

jozu

Skillful, good job. "You're going to grow up to be a famous artist—that's such a *jozu* painting."

Ramen

Long before sushi, there was another, more profound Japanese food invasion in the United States. Since the mid-1970s, instant ramen has been the cheap meal of choice among college students, bringing Asian culinary subtlety (OK, so it's not exactly subtle) to young American palates for mere pennies a bowl. Ramen has also been a staple within JA families, though in many cities along the West Coast JAs can get the stuff fresh in their Japantowns.

Instant ramen may be a ubiquitous presence in U.S. grocery stores today, but it was only introduced to America in 1972. It took several years, and some marketing savvy, before ramen caught on as a dorm room staple. The inexpensive packages of fried-and-dried, boil-and-serve noodles didn't catch on until they were sold in the soup aisle of the supermarket.

Although ramen is a relatively young food product in America, it has a long and distinguished history in Asia. According to the *Book of Ramen* (Turtleback Books, Friday Harbor, Washington, 1993), ramen is the Japanese pronunciation of the *kanji* characters for *lau mein* or *lo mein*, a boiled noodle dish invented by the Chinese centuries ago and imported into Japan. Types of noodles native to Japan include *soba* (buckwheat noodles) and *udon* (a thicker style of noodle served in fish-based stock), but ramen is far and away the best-known Japanese noodle export today. A host of Internet Web sites extol ramen in all its varieties and add additional history and more recipes to the noodle culture. In Yokohama, the official Ramen Museum even recreates the first recorded instance in the seventeenth century of a samurai, Mito Komon, eating a bowl of ramen.

Today, ramen shops are everywhere in Japan. The terrific 1986 film by director Juzo Itami, *Tampopo*, celebrated the culture of the ramen shop, with its unique secret soup stocks and bar-like ambience. I recall when I was a child in Japan, how ramen shops all had delivery boys on bicycles who would skitter through the alleyways and crowded streets of Tokyo precariously balancing a huge tray of steaming ramen bowls to their destination. It's an image that's an indelible reminder of Japan for me.

The world can thank Momofuku Ando for instant ramen. The founder of Nissin, the maker of Top Ramen and the ubiquitous Cup Noodle brand of instant noodles that comes in its own Styrofoam cup,

Ando invented chicken-flavored instant ramen in 1958. He reportedly got the idea for the product during the postwar years when he witnessed long lines of hungry Japanese waiting to pay top dollar for fresh hot ramen meals on the black market.

In creating the dried noodles and powdered soup stock to feed his own country's hungry, Ando made a product that would feed the world. I grew up with Nissin's Top Ramen (it had the silly name "Oodles of Noodles" for the first couple of years stateside) as well as brands such as Maruchan and Sapporo Ichiban (Sapporo was one of the first places in Japan to embrace Chinese *lo mein*, and thinks of ramen as its own local specialty). These days ramen is commonplace in American supermarkets, but if you visit a Japanese grocery, you can find a bewildering array of other instant noodle dishes, from exotic kinds of *udon* to *yakisoba*, a pan-fried style of ramen. Many are sold in their own Styrofoam bowls, borrowing yet again from Ando's ingenuity. Ando reportedly got the idea for Cup Noodle on a visit to the United States where he saw someone pour his ramen into a cup to eat with a fork. The concept took the convenience of instant ramen to new heights, and reduced cooking time from several minutes down to almost nothing.

The many sites for ramen on the Internet boast of its healthful qualities. Now, I'm not a nutritionist, but I can't imagine it's good for you to eat nothing but ramen. Maybe your body can get away with it in college, but mine won't today. There's too much fat and salt, even if I do like the flavor.

There are plenty of flavors to choose from, and Nissin tailors its many offerings to suit its various markets in Asia, Europe, and the Americas. The recipes are spicier in some countries than others. The United States gets the blandest flavorings while South Korea's ramen is hot hot hot. Other flavors include Cajun Chicken, Chili, Mushroom, Picante Beef, and the original "Oriental." It looks like Nissin will do well for many years to come, even if noodle shops in the United States do serve the real thing.

We should note again that ramen originated in China, and that the native noodles of Japan are the fat *udon* noodles and the thin strands called *soba*. Ramen is a popular dish in Japan, but purists would contend that it's not Japanese. But this is another topic to add to the authenticity discussion.

Rice

More than noodles, the one Japanese staple that has remained constant in the diets of Japanese Americans is rice, or *gohan*. As I mentioned,

JA food specialties

As a Yonsei, I was exposed to all types of food growing up. Our meals would vary between American and Japanese. One night we'd have chicken *katsu* and the next would be tri-tip beef. The one constant in every meal was rice. Obviously with the Japanese meals there would be rice, but we would also have it with steak, tri-tip, chicken cacciatore, and pork chops. Some of the best meals were chili and rice, *shoyu* wieners and rice, tuna and rice, and spaghetti with Portuguese sausage. Not good for the body, but oh so yummy!

We ate a few Japanese meals, but the best was *shabu-shabu*. Preparing it took a long time and I couldn't wait to eat so I would help my mom. Anything to get the food into my mouth faster! So, there I was grating the *daikon*, cutting the *napa* and *kamaboko*. My brother and I really didn't eat all the healthy stuff though. All we wanted was the meat.

Now that I'm living on my own, I've made a few dishes that I learned from my mom. Since I have diabetes and high blood pressure, the chili and rice and Portuguese sausage are out. And I've had to train myself to reach for the green-topped low-sodium Kikkoman bottle. I eat more sashimi now than I did growing up. It was too slimy back then.

If I had to name my favorite food, though, it would be pizza. What a typical American answer!

Brian Tanaka, Yonsei

we always had rice for meals in my family, even when we had American entrees. I rarely recall having mashed or baked potatoes, and the only time I had french fries was at McDonald's. Instead of mashed potatoes with gravy next to my turkey at Thanksgiving, I had rice with gravy, a combination that still makes my mouth water.

The most common rice is, of course, white rice, although brown rice is becoming more popular with Americans in general, not just with JAs, because of its healthier properties. Japanese—and JAs—don't buy Uncle Ben's instant rice or the rice that supermarkets sell in plastic bags. Those kinds of Americanized rice cook up dry and fluffy so the grains don't stick together. Television commercials for Uncle Ben's even used to promote its texture—it wasn't sticky, the announcer said proudly. Don't they know that rice is *supposed* to be sticky? Otherwise, it's almost impossible to pick up with chopsticks! My mom used to watch those TV commercials with disdain, making a disgusted Japanese sound. "Shyaaaah," she'd sneer, calling the American stuff *poro-poro* rice because it fell apart, *poro-poro*.

The ritual of washing rice correctly is passed down through the generations even within the JA community. You must buy rice by the gigantic sackful even if you don't have space for it at home. Then you must measure out the amount you wish to cook into the rice cooker and rinse off the starch with cold water. I was taught to pour running water in and loosely stir the rice with my hand, pouring out the milky water until it ran clear. Then I was told to stop pouring in water, and vigorously stir the wet rice with my hand, then rinse again several times until most of the starch is washed off. Next, I was supposed to add water according to the rice cooker's measuring lines. Other JAs were taught to add 1½ cups of water for each cup of rice or, more commonly, to use the knuckle method—measuring the depth of water with your finger. The water should be one full knuckle above the level of rice, with the finger pointing straight down to the bottom of the cooker.

I have no idea if the process is as ritualized in Japan. My guess is that with the fancy computerized rice cookers that do all the thinking for you these days it isn't anymore.

Rice is a versatile staple. Japanese have found many ways of serving it other than as just a mound in a bowl. The lightly vinegared sushi rice is probably the variation best-known in the West. A common JA take on fried rice is to make it using bacon as the meat and then frying the rice in the leftover grease instead of using vegetable oil. It adds a deeply satisfying flavor that's different from any fried rice you'd get in an Asian restaurant.

My mom also made fried rice (without the bacon), and something she called "chicken rice," which was fried rice made with small chunks of chicken and flavored with a dollop or two of catsup, of all things. As it turns out, this red rice is popular in Japan (sans chicken) as *omuraisu* served inside omelets.

Another common way to serve rice, especially in the fall, is *mazegohan*, or rice cooked with *matsutake* mushrooms.

Another rice variation that many JAs are familiar with is *omusubi* or *onigiri* rice balls. Made with rice formed into balls (or triangles) with a little bit of salty water on your hands for flavor, they're a simple way of eating rice on the go. You can include a sour pickled plum or a bit of salty salmon in the middle as an extra treat. Often the rice balls are wrapped on the outside with a strip of *nori*, or seaweed. Variations abound, like sprinkling the outside of the *omusubi* with *furikake*, a packaged mixture of spices and flakes of seaweed. A *yaki onigiri* is a rice ball that's been lightly grilled.

I always considered *omusubi* to be the Japanese version of the peanut butter and jelly sandwich—easy to make and carry, and tasty to eat. In Japan rice balls are mass-manufactured and sold individually wrapped in convenience stores everywhere—a quick, cheap bite for busy people at work. In the United States, for the JA community, *omusubi* are more of a special treat. They are made for family gatherings, holiday get-togethers, picnics, road trips, and hiking adventures like *matsutake* hunting (if you are lucky enough to live where the pine mushroom, an expensive delicacy in Japan, grows wild).

Eric Hayashi, a Sansei arts administrator and film producer, has breakfast at May's in San Francisco's Japantown. The JA menu includes hamburger with rice and gravy, Portuguese sausage, and Spam musubi.

JA specialties

Japanese Americans have adapted some Japanese traditions to suit their own tastes and situations. One of the most striking of these adaptations is Spam *musubi*, which is an *onigiri* made with a slice of grilled Spam, the canned meat product made by the Hormel Company of Austin, Minnesota, sandwiched by rice and wrapped with a strip of *nori*. This dish is actually a Hawaiian mutation, not a mainland JA thing. Although Spam in general is relentlessly denigrated in mainstream U.S. culture, Hawaii has the highest per-capita consumption rate for the product in the world. Spam was introduced to Hawaii

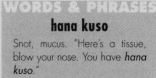

WORDS & PHRASES

hana kuso

Snot, mucus. "Here's a tissue, blow your nose. You have *hana kuso.*"

Benkyo-Do, a popular San Francisco diner and shop for mochi manju, or sweet rice cakes filled with various beans, invented a Japanese American hybrid: mochi filled with peanut butter.

Chopsticks

I was taught how to use ohashis when I was little . . . don't remember at what age, I must have been born with them in my hand. One has to use ohashis when eating Asian food . . . because it just wouldn't taste as good. Hahaha!

Loryce Hashimoto, Sansei

dakko

A child's hug, but more commonly used to mean pick up and carry a child. "Come here, baby, you want me to *dakko* you?"

via the U.S. military, which made it a culinary staple during World War II because it didn't need refrigeration and could be eaten hot or cold right out of the can. The impact of the military on Hawaii has been so strong that Spam has become a mainstay of the state's diet.

For JAs from Hawaii, Spam remains part of the family menu, as does Portuguese sausage, another Hawaiian import brought to the islands by the first Europeans. In most JA grocery stores, you're sure to find Spam and Portuguese sausage, and in many JA diners a breakfast of eggs and Portuguese sausage or Spam is a common sight. In San Francisco's Japantown, a Denny's restaurant that is no longer there served a Hawaiian menu that included fried rice and eggs with Portuguese sausage.

Other JA variations on Japanese dishes include JA potato salad, which is made with carrots and green peas plus a dash of soy sauce to the mayonnaise base. One snack I've come to love is *kakimochi*, a Japanese-style variation of the Mexican tortilla chip made from a family recipe.

Although gelatin desserts are popular in Japan, the JA community has taken Jell-O to unheard-of heights of culinary art. There are multi-colored, multi-layered slabs of Jell-O at family feasts and quivering combinations of Jell-O and whipped cream (or Cool Whip, the preferred JA substitute because the containers can be reused).

Mochi and the special foods of New Year

The high point of the JA food calendar happens at the New Year. That's when extended families come together and pull out all the stops, whipping up favorite contemporary recipes as well as the most traditional recipes, the ones handed down from their grandparents and great-grandparents (that is, except for the Jell-O desserts and the potato salad).

The Japanese tradition of New Year's isn't like America's, where the big party happens on New Year's Eve and you spend New Year's Day watching football games and nursing a hangover. In Japan, New Year's Eve isn't the main event; New Year's Day is. That's when Japanese start the new year with a sparklingly clean house and a feast. In fact, it may be the most important holiday of the year in Japan.

New Year's Eve, which is called *omisoka*, isn't an excuse for partying but a day of staying home and cleaning. Just before midnight families settle down to eat special *toshi koshi soba*, or end-of-the-year noodles. Temple bells start ringing in the New Year at 11:45 P.M. with 108 rings to banish the traditional 108 evil passions. At midnight, everyone toasts *akemashite omedeto gozaimasu* to welcome the New Year, which is called *oshogatsu*.

After midnight and into New Year's Day, people visit Shinto shrines to pay their respects to their ancestors, burn the previous year's good luck charms, and buy new ones. The first visit to the shrine every year is so special it has its own name: *hatsu mode*.

On New Year's morning, instead of tuning in the parades and football games, Japanese start feasting on a variety of traditional cold foods that are only made for this time of year, called *osechi ryori*. These foods include *kuromame*, black beans for good luck, and *ozoni*, a clear broth with vegetables and sticky *mochi* rice cakes, or (my favorite) *oshiruko*, a thick soup of sweet *azuki* bean paste with sticky *mochi* floating in it. Most of these foods are prepared in advance so mothers won't have to cook for several days. Traditional decorations for the home include pine branches and bamboo for doorways, displays of *kagamimochi*, stacks of Japanese oranges and flat round *mochi* cakes at home altars, and origami cranes, a symbol of longevity and happiness.

Beginning the next day and for three or four more days, Japanese make a point of visiting relatives and friends, settling old scores, and catching up with everyone's lives. It's all part of an effort to begin the New Year with a clean slate, a fresh start. Children are given *otoshidama* envelopes filled with money.

Sadly, I don't remember getting any loot for New Year's. Nor do I remember a lot of New Year's Day feasts and a lot of visiting going on. I was too young. Or maybe it's because we were a U.S. military family living off base in suburban Tokyo and didn't have a lot of family close by. I do remember eating a lot of *mochi*, though, both grilled and dunked into sugar and soy sauce and all gooey in the special New Year's soup.

New Year's feasts in JA households are a cross-cultural blend. Here's one year's menu: raw and fried oysters, shrimp cocktail, tempura shrimp and vegetables, eel sushi rolls, king crab, plum-flavored rice, *onigiri*, *nishime* (a sort of vegetable stew), macaroni salad, sashimi, *gyoza* (fried chicken dumplings), *shirae* (strained tofu and spinach mixed with ground sesame seeds and sweet miso paste), *kanten* (a gelatin dessert), cake, brownies, cheesecake, and lots more.

Growing up with food values

On New Year's we always had the most bizarre food of all of our friends. My father enjoyed all the real strange stuff like whale blubber, *namako*, *kazanoku*, *kombu*, and other stuff that I can only remember tasting very bad. Food is a celebration with family, though. You relish the quality, not the quantity (my mother's belief). My father grew up during the Depression and in internment camp and felt it was important not to waste food. We could not leave until we ate everything on our plate. Also if we had leftovers, we ate it until it was gone.

Scot Kamimae, Nisei-han

Japanese dorm food

In college I found there were a lot of easy dishes that made for great dorm food. *Ochazuke* was something I ate a lot during this time. It's a lot tastier than instant Mac and Cheese.

Ian Ferguson, Japanese Irish mixed-race Canadian Sansei

WORDS & PHRASES

mu-mu
Humid. "It sure is *mu-mu* today, I can hardly wait for fall to arrive."

Mochi madness

For me, the most vivid memories of the New Year are of the sticky rice dumplings called *omochi*.

Omochi, or just *mochi*, is made by pounding the hell out of sticky rice until it becomes glue-like, and then forming it into small balls that can be heated over a fire or in a pan until crispy on the outside and hot and gooey on the inside. The traditional way to make *mochi* for the New Year is to smash with a large wooden mallet at the glutinous mound of rice that has been placed in a huge mortar carved out of a stump of a tree. It takes at least two people—one to swing the mallet and one to reach in after each smash to turn the *mochi* over and make it smooth. The handler has to be quick and do his work before the next swing of the mallet or he'll get his fingers smashed, something I've seen happen and still wince at!

Prepared *mochi* is sold hardened and often frozen, either round or squared off like little bricks. The bricks are softened by grilling, and are hard on the outside but gooey and hot on the inside.

Mochi is also made year-round as a special soft pastry snack, sometimes with sweet *azuki* beans inside (*mochi manju*), and comes in white, pink, and tea green colors. There are endless variations of *mochi* available year-round in JA community grocery stores. In Little Tokyo in Los Angeles, for example, two of the oldest Japanese pastry stores in the United States, Fugetsudo and Mikawaya, have been making *mochi* for generations. When I was growing up, my mom used to make trays of *mochi manju* every week and sell it to the Japanese groceries where we lived, both in Washington, D.C., and in Denver.

JA-style *mochi* is a specialty of its own, and a surprise for Japanese when they taste it: fruity *mochi*, made with *mochiko* (the packaged sweet rice flour that's used to make *mochi* if you're not using fresh rice and pounding it) and Jell-O and fruit nectar for flavor. The *mochi* is baked in a casserole dish instead of being steamed, which is how *mochi manju* is made. The colorful pieces of *mochi* are a true JA delicacy and a delight for your Japanese friends and family.

There's even *mochi* ice cream, an unlikely melding of Japanese and American taste sensations and a truly Japanese American invention. The snack was actually created by Joel Friedman, a Caucasian who's married to Frances Hashimoto, the president of Mikawaya in LA's Little Tokyo. Friedman, the company's CFO and controller, found a way to wrap the family's trademark *mochi* around balls of ice cream, and now they've become a nationally distributed favorite, with other companies also getting in the act.

Recipes you can try

Gil's teriyaki sauce

1 cup soy sauce (use the low-sodium stuff, it's
    better for you)
½ cup water
½ cup sake
½ cup sugar

Heat water, soy sauce, and sake almost to a boil in saucepan, then add sugar and stir until dissolved. Cool and use as a marinade.

Note: You can vary this basic recipe a number of ways, beginning with the addition of green onions, fresh ground pepper, garlic (*lots* of garlic), ginger, lemon or lime juice, crushed red pepper, a dash of chili oil, sesame seeds, and/or a dash of sesame oil. You can also use beer instead of sake, a trick I discovered during my low-budget college days. The correct *Japanese* way is to use *mirin* (sweet rice cooking wine) instead of sake and sugar, and add a tablespoon or two of extra sugar depending on your preference. The mirin adds the lustrous glaze, the *teri* that goes with the *yaki* (which means to grill or cook).

Photo by Wataru Ebihara.

Fugetsu-do in Los Angeles's Little Tokyo is a landmark, family-owned business that has made sweet bean-filled mochi manju since 1903. After internment, the Kito family struggled to re-establish the shop (the landlord demanded four years of back rent and then kept the Kitos' equipment); the current location opened in 1957. As a side note, the fortune cookie, so closely associated with Chinese restaurants, was first invented at Fugetsu-do early in the twentieth century.

Apricot Mochi (24–32 pieces)

1 16-oz. box *mochiko* (sweet rice flour)
2 3-oz. boxes apricot-flavored gelatin
1¾ cups sugar
1 12-oz. can Kerns apricot nectar
12 oz. of water
katakuriko (potato starch) for coating the cooked *mochi*

Preheat oven to 350°. Grease 9x13" glass baking pan. In a large mixing bowl, combine *mochiko*, gelatin, and sugar. Mix well. Add nectar and water and mix on medium low with hand mixer until well blended. Pour into a baking pan and cover tightly with foil. Bake for 55 minutes. Remove from oven and cool with foil on for another 15 minutes.

Remove foil and cool for several hours before cutting. Gently take out the whole slab (use a spatula and try not to stretch it much) of *mochi* from the baking pan and place it on a large cutting board that's floured with potato starch. Use a large, sharp knife to cut away the

WORDS & PHRASES

osoi

Slow, late. "Gee, the service here is *osoi*," or "The bus is *osoi* today."

Japanese food

My memories of Japanese food are always associated with special occasions and in particular my grandmother. My most vivid memories of Japanese food always involve New Year's Day at Grandma's house and the colorful and abundant display of Japanese food laid out on my grandparents' table just waiting to be eaten after hours of preparation . . . and, of course, a photograph of the table always had to be taken before everyone got to eat. Grandma also produced various yummy dishes when we went to her house to eat dinner. But she always made sure to have something American on hand in case we didn't like what everyone else was eating.

Lisa Sasaki, Yonsei

edges first. Then cut strips lengthwise and into individual pieces. Roll the pieces in potato starch to keep them from sticking together. Brush away excess starch from pieces with a pastry brush before serving.

Note: You can use other combinations of gelatin and nectar such as strawberry gelatin with strawberry kiwi nectar, peach gelatin with peach nectar, and grape or raspberry gelatin with apple nectar (kids really like this flavor).

Erin's JA Fried Rice

> 3–5 cups cold leftover rice
> 4–8 pieces bacon
> 4 eggs, beaten in a bowl
> green onions (or regular onions, or both)
> misc. vegetables: diced celery, bell pepper, fresh snow peas, fresh bean sprouts, or frozen mixed vegetables
> fresh cilantro
> fresh ground pepper
> soy sauce

Cut bacon into ¼-inch strips and cook in a large frying pan or wok and drain the grease, leaving some in the pan. Add vegetables according to how long they need to cook (celery, then green peppers, snow peas, frozen vegetables, etc.). Then stir in eggs and scramble into small bits using a spatula. Add rice. Drizzle soy sauce and add pepper to taste. Add bean sprouts, cilantro, and green onions last.

Note: You can easily make this a one-pan meal, not just a side dish. There's no right or wrong way to make fried rice. Use different meats such as turkey bacon, pepper bacon, hamburger, chicken, or *charshu* (roast pork). If you use lean meats, add some canola or olive oil. Use any diced vegetable—broccoli, onions, carrots, green beans, sliced tomatoes, or shredded cabbage instead of bean sprouts. It's a great way to get rid of your *nokori*, or leftovers.

CHAPTER 5

Language

OK, OK. I'll admit it. My mom was right.

When I was a kid and we moved to the United States, she tried to make my older brother and me study Japanese using elementary school primers. She told us that it was important to learn to read and write *Nihongo*.

But my brother and I were more interested in learning American cuss words and the contents of the TV Guide than in buckling down and memorizing *hiragana* and *katakana* (never mind *kanji!*).

Now, I regret my slothfulness. I know that if I could read and write Japanese—especially that icky *kanji*—I'd have a good chance at working in a job where I could travel to Japan. But I never learned to read and write. I'm functionally illiterate in Japan.

The worst part is that even my conversational Japanese is lousy because I was too young when we moved to the States to have a well-developed vocabulary, and simply because I haven't used my feeble speaking skills much at all. Like many Nikkei I know, I've grown up with my parents (or mom, at least) speaking mostly Japanese to me, and replying in English all my life. When I'm in a situation where I'm expected to reply in Japanese, the little bit of conversational *Nihongo* I have locked up in my brain goes on a jailbreak, and even the most common words and phrases seem to escape me.

One time during college I was invited to be part of an exhibit of Japanese artists in New York City. Though I was flattered and even sold my painting at the show, I didn't remain a part of the group because I felt uncomfortable. The other artists were all very warm and eager to include me in their organization, but I was embarrassed at not being able to converse with them in their language. There were English-

Old-fashioned Japanese

Both my sister and I are pretty much anachronisms in a lot of ways. Until I was in high school, our spoken Japanese was pretty much Meiji- and Taisho-era Japanese. We are both married to men born in Japan, although my husband was raised in Spokane, Washington. Both my sister and I speak a lot of Japanese.

Masaye Okano Nakagawa, Sansei

Speaking Japanese

I wish I knew more Japanese. It is very important to me as I see it as part of my culture. My grandma speaks only a little English, and I wish I could talk to her more.

Jill Nakawatase, postwar Nisei

Courtesy Erin Yoshimura.

JA cool in LA in the mid-1960s.

Future generations and language

At this point, being able to use proper English is more important to me, but I do want my children (if I have any) to know Japanese.

Miku Maeda Rager, Shin Issei

Speaking Japanese

We were not allowed to speak English at home when living with my father. My stepmother's English was pretty much nonexistent. We did not go to Japanese school, but were allowed to see two Japanese movies every week and sometimes three in one weekend.

Masaye Okano Nakagawa, Sansei

WORDS & PHRASES

nani?

What? Huh? Short form of *nan desu ka?*

speaking members, and one sculptor was a white Columbia University professor who was the longtime companion of a Japanese artist. Maybe it was also because I was intimidated artistically, but I felt like too much an outsider because of my poor language skills.

Typically Japanese—and therefore JA

One common feature of Japanese American language is that the version we speak is, for the most part, an older, often arcane version of Japanese. For instance, that common and ever-so-useful phrase "Pardon me, but where is the bathroom?" might come out as "*Sumimasen, o-benjo wa doko desu ka?*" The parts would be correct, but the language has evolved in Japan. Even up until a few decades ago, the word for bathroom was *benjo*, or *o-benjo* to be polite. But in recent years Japanese have begun to use the even more indirect word *otearai*, which means "place to wash your hands," or *toire*, the Japanese pronunciation of "toilet." So if you use the older word *o-benjo* people in Japan might look at you as if you were mentally disadvantaged, or had perhaps been asleep for decades like an Asian Rip Van Winkle.

Yet, in the United States, at a typical Japanese American get-together, you might hear the word *o-benjo* spoken regularly, as guests ask the host where the bathroom is, or as family members pack their leftovers and get ready to go home. Often, the word is used as a verb meaning "to go to the bathroom" instead of just as a noun. Uncle Harry might yell from the door to leave, and Auntie Mary would reply from the kitchen where she's still saying her goodbyes, "Wait a minute, I have to go *benjo*." Or JA parents might ask their children before leaving on a car trip, "Do you have to go *benjo*?"

I mentioned *enryo* before—the rule that good JAs are supposed to have enough self-control to leave the last bit of food on a platter out of respect, and allow someone else to grab it. If a JA is a guest at someone else's home, he or she would never gorge on the food and would always allow others to get theirs first. Of course, this means that when all the people around a table are Japanese or Japanese American, there's a good chance that last bit of food will be . . . *wasted*.

And that's *mottainai*, another one of those words that JAs grow up hearing. It means "wasteful." But more than that, the word also carries an element of guilt, like "how shameful to be so wasteful."

This value, like *gaman* and *shikataganai*, the two words that helped JAs survive the internment, looms large in the JA community. It's the reason JAs seem obsessed with saving and reusing containers and bags of all sorts, from margarine tubs and whipped cream containers to boxes and even bread bags. I've never been in a JA home that didn't have a huge stash of twist ties in a kitchen drawer saved from bread and other packaging.

It's a very Japanese concept to have a word mean so much more than its simple definition. But then, that's what the Japanese language is like: imprecise, subject to contextual weight and emphasis. For most JAs, however, the language is more direct. That's because unlike English, most of us only know a few Japanese words, if any at all.

Growing up in a bilingual household

Many of us have childhood memories of Japanese being spoken, if not by our parents (if they're Sansei or even Yonsei), then certainly by our grandparents or great-grandparents, other relatives, or family friends. What we heard may have been a curious JA mixture of Japanese and English—sentences in English with a few Japanese words thrown in— or English spoken with a strong accent. I've grown up with Japanese accents so I find it easy to understand Japanese people when they speak English. I find it amusing that Americans sometimes assume that if you speak with an accent, they can just shout their words and you'll understand better. Especially with Japanese, if you don't raise your voice but instead just speak more slowly, usually they'll understand. Or better yet, write down what you need to say; most Japanese can read English better than they can speak or understand it.

Accents are an unavoidable part of merging cultures. Language is the front line of global diversity, where people from one country are faced with learning another country's language to communicate. Most Americans don't have the opportunity—or need—to move to another country and adapt to life there. In some cases, Americans who go overseas simply keep acting American and assume that their foreign hosts can speak English and others will adapt to them as if they were still in the United States. Other Americans won't get the chance to live or do business abroad, and even if they studied French, German, or Japanese in school their vocabulary will slowly fade away.

Those of us who grew up with parents for whom English is a second language have varying degrees of ability to juggle both languages and process the words in our brains as if they weren't different. It's hard to explain, but when I hear Japanese I can't translate each sentence

Baka

Food words and the odd cross-over word like *baka* (stupid) were the only Japanese words spoken in our household when I was growing up. There weren't that many Japanese traditions we observed that I can think of: taking your shoes off, New Year's Day celebrations, food, and that's about it.

Lisa Sasaki, Yonsei

Turning Japanese

My parents always told me that I'm Japanese. However as a child, I would occasionally be surprised to wake up in the morning, walk into the bathroom to look into the mirror, and see a Japanese boy (me) in the reflection.

Scott Takeda, Yonsei

Speaking Japanese

Growing up, I wanted to go to J-school, but my mom didn't have time to take us. Later in life when I was frequently asked if I spoke Japanese once people found out that I was JA, I felt ashamed that I couldn't—which later became a weird sort of pride that I couldn't. These days, it's mostly lamenting that I can't.

Kristin Fukushima, Japanese Caucasian mixed-race Yonsei

WORDS & PHRASES
beta beta

Sticky. "Who spilled Coke on the floor? It's all *beta beta* over here."

Courtesy Yayoi Winfrey.

A hapa celebrates her Japanese side.

Language

At home we spoke only Japanese, so my sister didn't know any English. She didn't pass her first grade.

Jack Kunio Miyasaki, Nisei

shikataganai

It can't be helped. Another value that helped JAs endure internment. "When a tornado destroys your house, *shikataganai*." See also *shoganai*, p. 60.

word-for-word. Nevertheless, I can get the gist of what's being said. When I watch a Japanese TV news show, for instance, I can understand what's happening without being able to tell you the specifics of what's going on. It helps, of course, that there're so many English words now being used in Japanese; I recognize more of the new words than my mom. Growing up, I could interpret for my mother if someone was speaking English too fast for her. I also got used to explaining what she told me in Japanese to others in English.

But I have to admit, there were times when I got somewhat embarrassed being around people who didn't speak English very well. It's a reminder that Americans think we're different, that we're outsiders. I suppose this happens to any immigrant culture, when second-, third-, and fourth-generation descendants of anyone from another country become more and more Americanized. Unlike some more recent Asian immigrant communities such as the Vietnamese or Cambodians, JAs seem to become less Japanese—that is, able to speak the language of their heritage—as they become more Americanized.

It's my name; please don't mangle it

It's easy to make fun of how Japanese pronounce or mangle English, but let's face it, many Americans—including Japanese Americans—have a hard time with Japanese words. The fact is, a lot of JAs can't even pronounce their own names correctly.

Asakawa. Ah-sa-ka-wa. Pretty simple, right? Very phonetic. At least, I think so. Yet, all my life I've heard my name mangled by people who don't take the time to read it. They see seven letters and the fact that it's not, well, *American,* and assume that it's hard to pronounce.

I've gotten so used to it from clerks and phone solicitors that I let even their more creative mispronunciations—"ASK-a-wah-wah," "Ask-a-COW-a"—roll off my back. I seldom try to correct people when they get my name wrong. But it's different when Japanese Americans can't handle Japanese names. Don't get me wrong—my partner Erin reminds me that I don't say "Asakawa" in a strictly Japanese way; I tend to use a broad, Americanized pronunciation even if the individual syllables are correct. I have an American accent, which I guess I can live with. But some JAs act like Japanese names are *foreign*.

At a Japanese American community dinner, one of the speakers, a

Sansei whose grandfather had been interned, was acknowledging people who were in attendance. He stumbled over several of the longer Japanese names then came upon one with two syllables. "Thank you for having an easy name to pronounce," he quipped from the podium.

I winced.

It irked me because JAs should have enough of a connection with our heritage to be able to pronounce names in Japanese. Was it unfair of me to think this way? I suppose this problem may be inevitable when a community of people concentrate so hard on assimilation that certain language skills fade.

I remembered how disappointed I was when I attended the national convention of the Japanese American Citizens League in Philadelphia and heard California representative Bob Matsui pronounce his name "MATT-suey" and, like the speaker above, stumble over a list of names of people—*heroes*—involved in the JACL's efforts to help attain redress for internment.

I asked for thoughts on the name game from other JAs and, not surprisingly, found a diversity of opinions. For starters, one Sansei living in Japan noted that correct pronunciation is relative, and no matter how perfectly we Nikkei might think we speak *Nihongo*, a Japanese might think our accents are awful—a good, and humbling, point.

If you've heard your name mispronounced all your life, eventually you begin to think that *you're* the one who's wrong. In my case, I just pronounce it the best I can. You should do the same (or as best you can, for an American), and correct others when they mangle your name. From non-Japanese, I'll accept "Ah-sa-WOKKA" or "O-SACK-a-wah." I'll correct JAs if they say my name incorrectly because I feel they should make the effort.

Learning Japanese

Especially for younger JAs, it's becoming more and more important to hold onto Japanese-language skills. Without the ability to communicate with Japanese people, we'll lose our ability to learn from our ancestors.

Besides the tried-and-true method of taking lessons in a classroom setting, there are a number of other ways to learn the Japanese language on your own. You can use classroom-proven visual techniques, such as *hiragana* and *katakana* jigsaw puzzles and Japanese vocabulary flashcards. This may make you feel like a child in grade school, but remember, that's what you are when you're learning a new language. There are magazines such as *Nihongo Journal*, the *Hiragana Times*,

Courtesy Erin Yoshimura.

Nisei children with their Caucasian schoolmates, circa 1920s.

Racism from WWII

My first boyfriend in high school was a third-generation American Greek. He told me that his father didn't want him to date me anymore because he had fought in WW2. This really pissed me off since my mother survived bombings in Tokyo by Americans in WW2 and ended up marrying one.

Harusami Pickrell, Japanese/Welsh/
Scottish/Irish/Native American
mixed-race Sansei

hapa

A term for a person who is part-Japanese, meaning "half" (also *haafu,* and the derogatory word *ainoko* in Japan), increasingly used by other ethnicities. "Keanu Reeves is *hapa,* part Chinese and Hawaiian." The term is actually of Hawaiian origin but has been widely adopted by JA and other Asian American communities.

---

and the dearly departed *Mangajin* (you can find copies on eBay) that feature articles in both English and Japanese. Hundreds of books crowd the shelves at bookstores and libraries everywhere with such enticing titles as *Japanese Made Easy, Read Japanese Today, Kanji Power, Japanese for Busy People, 13 Secrets for Speaking Fluent Japanese, Basic Business Japanese, Let's Learn Katakana, Let's Learn Hiragana, Japanese in 10 Minutes a Day,* and *Conversational Japanese in 7 Days.* Yeah, right. Sure. Whatever.

Not surprisingly, I also happen to be a junkie for high-tech ways to learn Japanese. I own a Berlitz CD-ROM for business Japanese that is pretty helpful. It features a fun vocabulary quiz with a Tokyo subway motif. If you answer correctly you get to move to the next station on an actual subway map of Tokyo. I also tried another CD-ROM, *Exotic Japan,* which includes primers on both Japanese language and culture using nineteenth-century woodblock prints of the Tokaido road as stopping points on the educational journey. CD-ROMs are attractive because of the extra features they can provide, such as the ability to change the animated speaker from male to female so students can identify more easily with the lesson.

Unfortunately, none of these low- and high-tech tools have helped me become fluent in Japanese. Eventually, I get bored, or frustrated, or both, and put them all aside. Both the Berlitz and *Exotic Japan* CDs are filed away in a box somewhere in the basement, and it's been several years since I've clicked around in them. I know, I know—it's a waste of money: *mottainai.* How's that for a quick Japanese lesson? It's a word I grew up hearing every time I left food on the table, broke a brand new toy, or ruined or outgrew a new piece of clothing. I know that word well.

Anyway, I feel guilty about buying all these gadgets, and I promise to find the discs and try them out again sometime soon.

Recently I bought *Instant Immersion Japanese,* a four-CD-ROM set that includes vocabulary and pronunciation lessons on two discs, "Talk Now!" and "World Talk Japanese," a dictionary, translation, and *kanji* reference tool on the "JquickTrans" disc, and an interactive tour of Japan called "Voyage in Japan." The price was irresistible—under $20—so I thought I would try it. It's been interesting and helpful so far.

At about the same time, Erin purchased a package called *Ultimate Japanese* that includes a 512-page textbook and eight audio cassettes. The cassettes come in two versions. The first is all in Japanese, to be used with the book at home. The second set is bilingual and is handy for learning on the go. The tapes are full of Japanese conversations that are translated line by line with long pauses so that you can repeat them for pronunciation practice. I was pleasantly surprised at how much of the Japanese conversations I could understand before the English-speaking announcer translated the sentences for us.

The Internet is an incredible resource for Japanese language information and education. There are Web sites out there that pronounce the words you click on, and sites that teach *katakana* and *hiragana* using animated brush strokes for the user to follow. There are software add-ons for your Web browser that allow easy (and free) translation of *kanji* and other Japanese characters so you can visit Japanese Web sites and practice by seeing the Internet from a Japanese Web surfer's eyes.

Technology has helped bust the language barrier in amazing ways in just the past decade. CD-ROMs are as antiquated as cassettes. Those language classes are now saved as MP3 files that you can listen to using iPods, smartphones, or other digital audio players. And an entire generation of "apps"—software programs that didn't even exist a few years ago—are available via download today, many for free. Just about the most useful is Google Translate, one of the many digital tools that Google makes available for no cost. It can translate words or phrases between many languages, including English to Japanese and vice versa. Most amazingly, it can translate text that you type in (on computer, tablet, or smartphone), or do the same with audio that you speak into the microphone on your phone, tablet, or PC, or even text that you submit by photograph.

This last feature is a terrific help if you're looking at a sign in Japanese and can't read it. The Google Translate app will read it for you—just take a photo of it. Once it's entered, you can click to see the translation with its definition, or hear the translation. The app doesn't replace learning a language and being able to hold conversations, but it certainly helps you get by if you're traveling to Tokyo or meeting someone from Japan. You can also click on the Japanese word or phrase to hear the correct pronunciation spoken.

I've used Google Translate by saying something in English and playing it back for a Japanese person in their language. I've also asked a Japanese person to speak into the app so I can hear it in English. The app is also handy for emails or letters to Japanese family or friends. I'll *write* a note in English, copy and paste it into Google Translate, and

Expats and JAs

As we grew older, by sixth grade, you could tell there was a division between the expat kids and the *eijyu-gumi*, the Japanese American groupies. It's mostly because friendships start to be based on talking, especially if you are a girl. The guys played basketball and that was their main basis for choosing friends. But it's harder for girls. Also, a lot of the Japanese kids went to the same schools. I went to a private school that none of the Japanese students attended. It was harder for me to make friends. Plus, I didn't know or care about the music they listened to and didn't know the stuff they were talking about because I didn't know Japanese pop culture! When the fourth Japanese exchange student came to live with my family, I was influenced a lot by her tastes and hobbies because she was around my age. She was the one that got me interested in Japanese television and music. Because of that, I got seriously connected to Japan.

Alisa Sanada, postwar Nisei

WORDS & PHRASES

ojiichan

Grandfather or elderly man. "*Ojiichan* sure gets grumpy when the Broncos lose." *Ojiisan* is more formal, *jiichan* more casual.

Benefits of being able to read and speak Japanese
I speak, read, and write Japanese. This has been one of my most important assets as I navigate my identity in the U.S., because I have found that these skills often set me apart from other mixed-race Asians and Japanese Americans. I find that I am better able to communicate with immigrant and first-generation Japanese despite my cultural differences.

Emily Chapman, mixed-race Nisei

WORDS & PHRASES
wakatta
Understood, understand. "Yes, *wakatta*. I know what I need to do before I can go out."

then copy and paste the Japanese version into my email or document. Be warned, though: Google Translate isn't perfect, so warn the person you're speaking with that some of what's translated might not make much sense. I preface emails to Japan by saying, "I'm using Google Translate so please excuse me if what I write is not correct."

Just searching the iTunes App Store or Google Play Store will turn up a number of Japanese apps. One handy app pair is IMI (which means "meaning" in Japanese) for Android phones or tablets and IMI WA (which means "the meaning is") for iOS. I have IMI installed on my Android phone and IMI WA on my iPad; the content is a bit more advanced and geared toward teaching yourself vocabulary and grammar by giving you definitions and examples of the word used in the context of sentences. As its ultimate nerd feature, IMI/IMI WA can animate the Kanji strokes so you can properly learn to write the words you've translated.

These digital education tools are an incredible way to help you communicate with Japanese speakers and go far beyond the basics of rote memorization of recordings to help you learn Japanese.

All of this effort is worth it if I can expand my career options and achieve personal goals such as eventually finding a job that will take me to Japan on regular trips. Japan's economy is still huge and hugely important. My interest isn't out of mere greed, though. I love my culture and have family members in Japan. I want to visit again as soon as my budget allows, and the next time I'm there I don't want to have only halting conversations in broken Japanese with taxi drivers. I'll always be more American than Japanese, but I want to be a little more balanced and try to be less obviously a foreigner.

For young people, there is a growing array of avenues for exposure to the sound, rhythm, and vocabulary of Japanese. *Okasan and Me* is an interactive project with a music CD and a booklet. It was created and sung by Hawaii-born Sansei Cynthia Konda, now living in California. The songs whimsically mix Japanese and English together with an ear toward making *Nihongo* familiar for kids age two and up. The titles include "Alphabet Go Sei Style," "Touch My Toe, Arigato," and "Taiko Drum Jan Ken Pon." The instrumentation includes traditional sounds from the *taiko* drum, shakuhachi flute, and shamisen lute. The package is available at various JA stores around the country and via Konda's Web site, www.okasanandme.com.

JAs
Today

CHAPTER 6

It's Hip to Be Japanese!

If cultural trends ebb and flow like the ocean being pulled by the magnetic mysteries of the moon, the tide is definitely running high for all things Japanese these days. Ever since the 1997 publication of Arthur Golden's enjoyable novel *Memoirs of a Geisha*, there's been a slow buildup of interest in Japanese culture, which seems to be culminating in a veritable tsunami of influences from the west shores of the Pacific lapping on the beaches of the United States.

This commoditization of Asian culture is nothing new. Americans have flirted with various forms of Asian style at various times over the decades, whether because of the sheer exoticism of the Far East or because our military spent time in Asia (there's an obvious cycle of Asian "war brides" from post–World War II Japanese women to brides from Korea and Vietnam and Southeast Asia marrying GIs during military engagements). Maybe it's a combination of both. Certainly, Asian women have long been objectified in Western sexual fantasies.

Food, as always, is an early harbinger of cultural change. As each new Asian community establishes a foothold in America, a wave of new restaurants emerges. Food fans have tasted a culinary shift over the past twenty years. The long-established Americanized Chinese and Japanese restaurants have been joined by many restaurants serving Vietnamese, Korean, and Thai food as young non-Asians have increasingly explored more distant culinary shores.

In the past couple of years, I've noticed a resurgence of Japanese restaurants, albeit often the Americanized type of "fast food" Japanese that serves up not-too-traditional bowls of gloppy teriyaki beef or chicken served atop over- or undercooked rice. Now that sushi's become an American staple, there are sushi bars galore, of varying

Connecting with Japan via social media
Ironically, Facebook is how I now primarily connect with Japan. I found some Japanese activists and now I wish I could read their latest posts on, say, Fukushima or environmental issues. The combination of scientific and political terminology is just way beyond my ability to parse.

Eri Izawa, Nisei

Dating
Hot white chicks don't gravitate toward JAs. Just like in my occupation (sales), I have to work harder than the white guys to accomplish the same results.

Scot Kamimae, Nisei-han

Courtesy Erin Yoshimura.

JAs had their own beauty queens, like this one in Denver—and they still do at LA's annual Nisei Week.

gaman

A very basic Japanese value that encompasses endurance, perseverance, self-control, and self-denial. "You have to go *benjo*? *Gaman*, we have a long way to drive still." On a more serious note, *gaman* was the concept that helped JAs endure internment: "We better *gaman* and bite the bullet. They'll figure out sooner or later that we're patriotic Americans."

quality. There's even the combination of sushi bar with the new American tradition, the all-you-can-eat buffet. These buffets may offer good value, but the sushi often isn't very good, and it just doesn't feel right to snarf down sushi by the handful with no regard to the delicate presentation of a true Japanese meal.

But it's not just sushi that's in with Americans. Thanks to *Memoirs*, there's been a surge of interest in geisha—an often misunderstood symbol of artful talents—and traditional fashion, including Japanese style elements such as kimono sleeves and Westernized versions of the traditional dress, topped off with chopsticks used as hairpins. Even pop star Madonna got into the act, donning a kimonoesque robe for a music video. A stack of new books about geisha have appeared on bookstore shelves in the last few years.

Articles in respected publications such as the *New York Times* have officially announced the Japan-fad, opening the way for Americans to feel hip and cutting-edge by mimicking and co-opting styles and artistic expressions that are sometimes hundreds of years old.

You can even have the Japanese experience in your own kitchen. A recent mail-order catalog from the haute kitchen retailer Williams-Sonoma, a bastion of tasteful, upper-crust American consumerism, featured four pages of "Asian style" with such "classic" (I'm being sarcastic here!) Japanese products as stainless steel chopsticks that look like something a surgeon might use to remove a kidney, "Square Asian Plates" (I didn't know that it took European ingenuity to invent the round plate!), and bamboo placemats and runners.

The text next to one inviting photo of a table setting crowed, "Even a few simple strokes can create a visually exciting table and set the stage for Asian-style dinner parties, exotic potlucks, and other gatherings." The photograph shows a careful arrangement of bamboo place mats (they look like misplaced sushi *maki* rollers), square plates, bowls, wine glasses (not very Japanese), candles (surrounded by moss no doubt yanked out of the backyard), and a bunch of silly river rocks laid out just so to capture the essence of a Zen garden.

My mother immediately saw through the well-intentioned but phony style, and worried that anyone who didn't know better might think this is really how Japanese eat their food. "*Inchiki* Japanese style," she huffed, and walked away.

She's right. It's weird to see Japanese culture being shaped into something that's not a true reflection of Japan but more of a mix and-match hybrid that depends on shallow style as a hook to reel in consumers, like catching carp in a pond.

On the other hand, at a time when prejudice and bigotry against Asian Americans continues, I'd rather have the spirit of Japan introduced even in diluted form as something that's hip and desirable. Even phony style can help bridge the cultural gap between the United States and Japan, and I'd rather have a conversation with someone who has an earnest, if misguided, appreciation for my roots than someone who looks at me and sees only a yellow face and feels only hate.

When these "Japanese lite" products hit the shelves of Kmart, Target, and Wal-Mart stores nationwide, I'll know that geisha chic has so saturated the fabric of American life that it's about to fade. Then we can concentrate on what may prove to be the ultimate power in U.S.-Japan relations: *Pokémon!*

The power of anime

Pokémon has become a staple of Saturday morning cartoons for American kids. For you few who haven't seen it, *Pokémon* is an animated series about a trio of kids who go around searching for creatures called Pocket Monsters (shortened to "Pokémon" in the typical Japanese way because it's cooler). The show is exciting, funny, and, in its own way, wise. The episodes I've seen have all had underlying themes of being accepting of others. It's become incredibly popular in the United States even though it's so obviously a quintessentially Japanese creation.

What is it about Japanese animation, or anime, that's so distinctive? There's a graphic sensibility that's more dynamic than most U.S. cartoons. In fact, it's hard to hang the "cartoon" label on Japanese animation; it's too sophisticated for that term. But beyond the sophistication in style, Japanese animators have created a distinctive look for their creations: large round eyes, tiny button noses, and expressive mouths that can cover the entire face when a character yells, to great comic effect. With their roots in manga, or comics, the artists have taken the look of Japanese comics and added the magic of the classic early Disney movies *Bambi, Snow White and the Seven Dwarfs*, and *Sleeping Beauty.*

Osamu Tezuka, the undisputed "God of Comics" and the creator of many of Japan's best-loved characters including *Astro Boy* (*Tetsuwan Atomu* in Japan) and *Kimba, the White Lion*, reportedly watched *Bambi* eighty times and memorized every frame. He grafted cinematic

Inferiority complex

I'm unhappy about the stereotypes of Japanese males being nerdy and unmasculine. When I was younger, it gave me an inferiority complex, though now I think it's more cool to be of Asian descent with the infiltration of Japanese mass culture, ie: *Pokémon*, Miyazaki, and other anime.

Glenn Asakawa, Sansei

Mixed-race upbringing was a blessing

For me, being born of a Japanese national was the greatest blessing. I grew up leaving a Japanese home, entering an American school, and returning home. It granted me an adaptability most of my American friends do not have, and a knowledge of my ancestors I could not have gotten any other way.

Marty Davies, mixed-race Nisei

WORDS & PHRASES

inchiki

False, phony, imitation, cheating. "No, you can't copy someone else's homework—that's *inchiki.*"

Astro Boy, Ultraman, Pokémon, Hello Kitty … it's hip to be Japanese!

Spirituality in anime

I am a great fan of *anime* spirituality—the lessons of perseverance, caring for others, and the message that compassion is more powerful than selfishness.

Eri Izawa, postwar Nisei

gomen nasai

Sorry, or excuse me. Also used casually as just *gomen*. "*Gomen nasai*, I didn't mean to hit your car," or "*Gomen*, can you move over and make room for me?"

techniques to the cartoon form, such as extreme angles and lighting, and found new ways to show slow motion and other special effects from the motion picture world.

In Japan, the audience is different, too. Anime (sometimes called "Japanimation") is a huge industry and has devoted fans among every age group, from kids to adults, men and women. Anime is considered a mainstream art form, with the films of Hayao Miyazaki such as *Princess Mononoke* and *Spirited Away* setting box office records. Most U.S. anime fans are Caucasian, but a growing number of Asian Americans (including me) see anime as a reflection of our heritage.

From my childhood in Japan, I have fond memories of many imported American television cartoons like *Bugs Bunny*, *Woody Woodpecker*, *Superman*, and *Spiderman*. But I also clearly remember the black-and-white image of *Testuwan Atomu* and *Tetsujin 28-Go* (*Gigantor* in the United States). The animation was crude, but the distinctive features were there. I remember my infatuation with the robot superhero in *Eighth Man*, the cool-driving Speed Racer, and the noble Kimba. (By the way, Disney spokespeople deny that Tezuka's *Kimba, The White Lion* had any influence on the company's later megahit *The Lion King*.)

In the past few years, anime has become increasingly popular—not just the stuff for children, like *Pokémon*, but also anime for older viewers. The cable television station Sci-Fi Channel regularly broadcasts anime. And in every video rental shop there's an entire section dedicated to anime. Some of the shows are intended for adults. But many of the mainstream releases, including titles such as *Project A-Ko*, *Sailor Moon*, *Doraemon*, *Akira*, and *My Neighbor Totoro* (a cute anime that my nieces are crazy about), are available dubbed into English (I prefer subtitles) and (except for *Akira*) are family-safe.

One anime I'm proud to own, *Hotaru no Haka* (*Grave of the Fireflies*), avoids every cliché of cartoons, from its beautifully detailed, almost photographic drawings to its heartbreaking story of two children orphaned at the end of World War II. It is almost documentary-like in its unflinching bleakness, and you won't be able to watch it without a box of tissues nearby. It's certainly not a "cartoon" in the American sense of the word.

Anime continues to grow in popularity and influence. The Web site AnimeCons.com lists over two hundred conventions for fans of anime and cosplay in 2015 alone, mostly in the United States and with a few in Canada, the UK, Brazil, Australia, and elsewhere (but not Japan). *Pokémon* is well known, but it's been joined by a plethora of other series from the mainstream and familiar, such as *Dragon Ball Z* and *Sailor Moon*, to newer, cutting-edge titles like *Full Metal Alchemist* and *Mushi-shi*.

Increasingly, fans of anime who are into cosplay (from "costume play") will dress in character at Japanese festivals like Denver's annual Cherry Blossom Festival and even at pan-Asian events like the Colorado Dragon Boat Festival. The passion for anime is much appreciated, of course, but there is an element of cultural appropriation when the "costumes" are merely bathrobes or nightgowns with flowery "Oriental" prints being worn as kimono, or when the makeup and costumes are over the top. But there are many fans who are so into the world of anime that when they do cosplay, they take it seriously and create detailed and accurate costumes from scratch. They're not all teenagers or people in their early twenties, either. I once met a Caucasian anime fanatic in his mid-thirties who has spent hundreds of dollars putting together a very realistic aluminum-and-plastic recreation of a sci-fi robot warrior character. Fans like him, and the ones who are so turned on by anime that they go on to study Japanese in school, or even head to Japan for college, are a reflection of how powerful the influence of Japanese pop culture can be.

Over the years, anime has made the leap onto the big screen, and results have been mixed. *Astro Boy* was a 2009 computer-animated version of the early television series that did OK, though its digital modernization was off-putting to some older fans (like me). The 2008 Hollywood blockbuster version of *Speed Racer* was a crazy mix of live-action acting against computer-graphics backdrops, and the film bombed despite featuring some big stars and direction from the Wachowski siblings, who gave the world the *Matrix* trilogy. A 1988 anime series, *Akira*, is being considered for live-action Hollywood treatment, but its development has been stalled (in part because of protests from Asian Americans at the original plan to shoot the film with Caucasian actors).

Hayao Miyazaki, the talented storyteller and creator of beloved anime including *Princess Mononoke* and *Spirited Away* as well as earlier

Devotees of Japanese animation love to engage in cosplay, dressing up (or down) as their favorite characters and showing their style at conventions attended by thousands of like-minded fans and cosplayers.

Japanese at heart?

Many people assume that I am very Japanese because of my fluency in the Japanese language, but I don't think I'm very "Japanese." Of course, this depends on your definition of "Japanese." Comparable to who and what is an "American?" I know how to act like a Japanese and "pretend" like a Japanese, but am not truly Japanese at heart.

Kathy Ajisaka, Sansei

WORDS & PHRASES
gacha-gacha
Cluttered or messy. "Clean up your room, it's so *gacha-gacha* you can't find anything in there."

A publicity still from Speed Racer, *an early animation that made the leap from its Japanese roots to the big screen.*

Challenges of growing up mixed race in the 1960s

I'm an older *hapa*, born in 1960. Growing up, there were not a lot of us around, and very few Asian role models. People couldn't guess that I was half Japanese, they would assume I was white, or if I was tanned, they would mistake me for Mexican or Native American. Once the other kids found out I was half Japanese, I would be teased and called names. I remember once coming home from school and asking my dad what a "slope head" was. I remember how angry he got when I told him some kid called me one. . . . I was really concerned there was something wrong with my head!

Harusami Pickrell, Japanese/Welsh/ Scottish/Irish/Native American mixed-race Sansei

hits like *My Neighbor Totoro*, retired from anime in 2013 after completing his final film, *The Wind Rises*, an overtly antiwar biography loosely based on the man who designed the Mitsubishi Zero fighter during World War II. Even though the film caused controversy with its message (and Miyazaki's public statements criticizing Japan's role in WWII and lack of apology for it), *The Wind Rises* earned the biggest opening of any film in Japan and was released in the U.S. in 2014. Although the animator says he's retired from animation, he's continuing to draw manga and helping to write scripts for his son, who has taken up the family business. Miyazaki also continues to oversee the Studio Ghibli Museum in western Tokyo.

Even if Miyazaki has really retired (he's quit before, but come back for more), anime remains one of Japan's most potent exports.

There are lots of books that will help you get acquainted with anime (check the resources list at the back of this book). One publication in particular, *The Anime Companion*, volumes 1 and 2 (Stone Bridge Press, 1999, 2005) clarifies the uniquely Japanese features of anime. It's an engaging and enlightening encyclopedia of sometimes obvious, and often trivial, references in anime. The author, Gilles Poitras, an anime fanatic with eagle eyes, catches every reference, explains it, and tells you where to watch for it in various shows. For example, an everyday bit of Japanese life like the sweet dish *anmitsu* can be seen being eaten in *Urusei Yatsura* and *Electric Household Guard*. Other cultural touchstones include entries for *geta* (wooden sandals) and *sotoba* (Buddhist graveyard tablets).

The point of the books isn't to analyze anime obsessively but to show how much of true Japanese culture appears—and is absorbed by Western viewers—through the innocent entertainment of anime. They are a great resource for fans of anime as well as people interested in Japanese culture. The hard-copy editions are no longer in print, but much of the text lives on and the author's mission continues on his Web site at http://www.koyagi.com.

Animation has come full circle, and Americans are set to learn from the style and stories from across the Pacific. I'm sure Osamu Tezuka, who died in 1989, is smiling in heaven at the thought of countless American anime fans watching and absorbing every nuance of Japanese culture.

The man in the lizard suit

I can't help but wonder at some of the unexplainable mysteries of life. For instance, why is it that a country that is one of the world's leaders in technology, automation, and robotics still produces movies featuring a man in an ugly rubber lizard suit thrashing scale models of cities?

That's the question that flashed through my mind while I watched Godzilla destroy the Hokkaido city of Nemuro—my mother's home town—in *Godzilla 2000*, the latest in a long line of Godzilla movies made in Japan and distributed in the United States (not all have made it to American theatrical release, and two more have been completed in Japan since this film).

The quality of the rubber suit and the model city has improved since *Gojira* (the Japanese pronunciation of the monstrous dinosaur-like creature) first stomped through Tokyo in 1956. But with the rise of computer animation and digital special effects, the film seems a throwback to an earlier age of clunky, old-fashioned fright features. That's exactly the point, I've decided.

Godzilla 2000, like most of the other Godzilla movies—this was the twenty-fourth starring the 300-foot lizard—is meant to be just a little bit tongue-in-cheek. It's not supposed to be all big-budget blockbuster production values with seamless special effects and modern technology. Go rent *Jurassic Park* if that's what you want.

Or, you could rent the 1998 American-made *Godzilla*, which was a big-budget blockbuster with flashy effects, and a failure at the box office. Sure, the '98-model Godzilla looked more realistic. It was a lot scarier and more violent, too. But, it turns out that people don't want a scary, violent Godzilla ripping through New York City the way the aliens in *Independence Day* did. They want Godzilla to be an actor sweating it out in a heavy suit, destroying a toy version of Tokyo, which everyone knows will be rebuilt for the next go-round.

Hollywood misjudged Godzilla. But Toho, the Japanese studio that created Godzilla, understands that corniness and camp are two of the ingredients that Japanese film audience's love about the monster. Toho made a lot of money off the 1998 failure because Hollywood licensed the character and licensed it again for everything from lunch boxes and toys to a series of Taco Bell commercials co-starring a Chihuahua. But Toho was smart and retained the rights. Even if the

Ultraman, a '60s Japanese sci-fi TV hero, is a cult figure in Japantown.

Identity crisis

Sometimes I used to say I felt too white for Asian Americans, too Japanese for Japanese Americans, too mainstream for indie people, and too indie for mainstream people.

Alisa Sanada, postwar Nisei

WORDS & PHRASES
okaasan

Mother. "*Okaasan* always told me to sit up straight or I'd be bent over when I'm old."

Courtesy Lisa Sasaki.

JAs are a rarity in professional football, but plenty of JAs grow up playing sports throughout high school and college.

American version flopped—and it did—the studio knew that Japanese audiences would come back for more of the same formula that had been used for decades.

I guess the lesson here is, "If it ain't broke, don't fix it."

Gojira Ni-sen Mireniamu (literally, *Godzilla Millennium 2000*) actually picks up where the first film left off, as if the years of cataclysmic battles with such outlandish other creatures as Mothra and Ghidorah had never occurred, never mind the invasion of New York City. In the first film, nuclear testing in the Pacific awakens the long-dormant Gojira (a combination of the Japanese words for whale and gorilla), and the monster threatens Japan with indiscriminate carnage. The message was clear and poignantly relevant to the Japanese in the 1950s: Mess around with mother nature in the form of atomic bomb tests in the Pacific Ocean and a mutant monster will rise to punish humankind.

The *Godzilla* movies may be something of a joke in the United States, but the monster has made an impact. In one celebrated poll, the three Japanese best known to Americans were Emperor Hirohito, Bruce Lee (who was from Hong Kong), and Godzilla.

I must have watched a lot of the *Gojira* films when I was a kid in Tokyo. I believed that some of these monsters could really exist deep in the sea or out in outer space, and that Japan's capital could someday be destroyed by a giant moth, or even a tidal wave. That era's special effects were crude and seem silly now, but they were state of the art back then. The latest incarnation of the monster, *Godzilla*, was released in 2014, and though it was a computer-generated lizard, it captured the spirit of the Japanese original much better than the 1998 flop.

The movie industry has come a long way since 1954, and so have the limits of what we consider to be science fiction. A lot more things seem possible today. When the first *Godzilla* movie was made, the moon landing wasn't even a possibility. Now, as the *Matrix* movies have shown, filmmakers can depict anything realistically on screen. But I bet in Japan the *Gojira* movies will continue to feature a man in a lizard suit. And that's the way it should be.

unchi

Poop, defecation. The casual form of *unko*. One of those early words children learn. "Mom, my stomach hurts. I need to *unchi*."

Ameri-kana

One of the more interesting things a Western traveler will notice in Japan is how often English is used—in signs and slogans (often slogans that don't make much sense) on everything from packaging and tee-shirts to advertising copy and even the mass media.

The English alphabet is scattered everywhere, and it's not used for the purposes of helping American tourists get around. English is almost a second language in a way; in fact there's a debate going on in Japan over whether to acknowledge English as an official second language. One of my favorite anecdotes about this cross-cultural phenomenon is about the Japanese gas station chain, Cosmo, which spells out its name proudly in the Roman alphabet for its logo. I once asked an older taxi driver if he could read the signs. He replied that unlike a lot of younger Japanese, he couldn't read English, but "Cosmo" meant "gas station" to him by association, so he wasn't offended that the company chose to use a name that many Japanese presumably couldn't even read.

At the time, I found it far-fetched that Americans would accept signs and symbols in a language other than English along our roads. The thought of a U.S. gas station chain with its signs written in Japanese was quite a fantasy.

Recently I've been noticing how, as Asian culture begins another of its periodic resurgences in the West, Japanese is showing up stateside. And I don't mean English spellings of Japanese words, but words and phrases written in Japanese characters.

For the uninitiated (which includes me, since I can't read or write it despite my mom's efforts when I was a kid), a quick introduction to how the Japanese language is written out: Unlike English, which is written with twenty-six letters, Japanese have to stuff their heads with a minimum of three completely different systems of symbols to read their morning newspaper. The largest group is the *kanji*, or Chinese pictographs. Most characters, and there are thousands, many of them very complex, represent a separate word. They can also be used in combination with other characters to make even more words. The other two alphabets are *hiragana* and *katakana*, each of which includes forty-six different characters.

These *kana* letters don't have meaning on their own like the *kanji*, but are used to represent syllables. For instance, the first five characters represent the sounds for "ah," "ee," "oo," "eh," and "oh." The next five represent "kah" "kee," "koo," "keh," "koh," followed by "sah," "shee," "soo," "seh," "soh," and so on.

Why have two separate *kana* alphabets? *Hiragana*, the more

Parents and grandparents

My parents met on a blind date set up by their friends. It turned out that they were both the only Japanese people that they knew so it seemed logical to their friends that they would like each other. My grandparents had an arranged marriage even though they were Nisei. This was especially hard on my grandmother, who saw her American friends marrying by choice rather than tradition. I always thought it was rather ironic. Although on the surface a blind date and an arranged marriage seem like opposite ends of a spectrum, when you think about it they share some interesting similarities. Trusted family and/or friends find someone whom they think will afford you a "good" marriage or relationship and then arrange for the two of you to meet. Of course, the main difference is the element of choice that was available to my parents but not to my grandparents.

Lisa Sasaki, Yonsei

shi-shi

Pee. A common version of *oshikko*, a fancier word. Some witty JAs say "five-four-four" to mean "Go pee," because *go* is five in Japanese, and *shi* is four.

rounded of the two, is used to phonetically spell out words of Japanese origin; the angular *katakana* is used to denote foreign words. Somewhere along the line the Japanese decided that foreign words should be written in a different alphabet, so they'd know at a glance that the words they represent weren't originally Japanese. For all the words written out in English throughout Japan, there are many more written out in *katakana*. (The prevalence of foreign words in Japanese isn't just in writing. Listen to Japanese newscasts via satellite or the Internet. You'll hear many English words sprinkled throughout, although they're often abbreviated or their pronunciation is mangled. These days, though, language seems to be a two-way conversation.)

Images derived from the "Orient" seem to be appearing more often in American pop culture. Dragons are commonplace (the Asian variety, not the European dungeons-and-dragons type), and local department stores invariably stock clothing with Asian motifs. Those motifs increasingly include Japanese and Chinese alphabets. I now own several baseball hats with the *kanji* characters for "love" and "heart," and I've even seen a line of baseball caps with the *kanji* characters for various American universities' mascots on them (I wonder how North Carolina's "Tarheels" translates).

Because *katakana* is meant for use in Japan with foreign loan words, it is ideal for slogans on clothing in America. You can buy a long-sleeve tee-shirt from Abercrombie & Fitch, a store popular with teenagers, that has the name of the chain spelled out in *katakana* down the sleeve: "Ah-bah-ku-rom-bii an-doh Fi-chi." Guess Jeans offers tee-shirts with "Ges-su Jiin-zu" in *katakana* across the chest. And another popular brand of clothing for young people, Union Bay, features a line of *katakana* underneath its logos that spells out "hip-pu hop-pu," or hip-hop, as its stamp of contemporary authenticity.

Does this mean that America is on the verge of accepting Japanese in everyday life and commerce? Of course not. As with every cultural trend that's embraced and then inevitably dropped, such use of Japanese on American products will probably disappear along with whatever the "in" color is this summer.

I'm trying to memorize *katakana* before the fad fades, though, so I can walk through a store and read some of the Japanese. It'll make me feel pretty darned smart, knowing that most Americans won't have a clue what they're wearing on their chest, or across their butts.

For now, I like the idea that my old cab driver could come to the U.S. and see Japanese strewn across the American cultural landscape. The only problem is, he could read it, but would he know what the heck "Ah-bah-ku-rom-bii an-doh Fi-chi" is?

Hai! Karate

By the late 1960s, Asian martial arts had caught on enough for Bruce Lee to co-star in *The Green Hornet* TV series and for Hai! Karate, a popular aftershave, to run a series of amusing TV commercials. But it was in the 1970s, thanks in large part to Lee's subsequent film career, especially the 1973 release of *Enter the Dragon* and the Fall 1972 launch of *Kung Fu,* a TV show starring David Carradine with his eyes taped back playing a *hapa* Asian, that martial arts became pop culture.

Courtesy Randy Kirihara.

Along with that interest came the explosion in Japanese martial arts disciplines including karate, judo, aikido, and others. American kids by the droves signed up to get thrown around practice mats and learn to count to ten in Japanese as they performed their *kata*, or basic forms. In the late 1970s, *Saturday Night Live*'s superstar comedian John Belushi started a recurring skit that paid tribute to Toshiro Mifune's samurai characters, and though he walked a fine line between stereotyping and satirizing, he managed to capture the essence of the rough swordsmen Mifune often played in his films. The image of the ninja, the silent, black-clad assassins of the samurai era, also became popular with a series of low-budget American movies that paled in comparison with the classic Japanese ninja movies of the 1960s.

The stage was set for *Shogun,* James Clavell's epic novel, and more importantly, for the 1980 TV miniseries starring Richard Chamberlain as a Westerner in medieval Japan (with Mifune co-starring as the shogun, Lord Toranaga). The TV movie sparked another wave of interest in things Japanese in the West, as did Arthur Golden's 1997 novel *Memoirs of a Geisha* and its 2005 film version.

Hollywood's infatuation with Japan—both with the country's history as well as its pop culture—continues. The 2003 movie *The Last Samurai* was a blockbuster starring Tom Cruise as an American soldier who finds himself in Meiji-period Japan during the late 19th century. He naturally falls in love with Japan and a Japanese woman, somewhat incredibly becomes a samurai warrior after just a few months of training, and helps lead Japan to its modern era. The story might be mostly fantasy, but the producers of the film were actually

Baseball was establshed in Japan in the late 1800s and has long been popular among JAs. This JA team photo dates from 1910.

Which side?

I'm not very Japanese . . . more American. Or more Japanese-American. Whatever the hell that means. Maybe the best of both worlds (or maybe the worst of both). I can tell you when I feel the least Japanese: when I'm in Japan or with my Japanese-national friends.

Stann Nakazono, Sansei

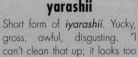
yarashii

Short form of *iyarashii.* Yucky, gross, awful, disgusting. "I can't clean that up; it looks too *yarashii.*"

Courtesy Lisa Sasaki.

Playing baseball in JA-only leagues was a rite of passage for many Nisei and Sansei, even into the 1960s, because Japanese weren't accepted on many Little League teams.

Sticks and stones

I have been called Jap a few times when I was young. My son plays baseball and the opposing team players will call him "chink." Yes, this is even in 2014.

Lisa Imamura, mixed-race Sansei adopted by Nisei parents

ohayo gozaimasu

Good morning. Also simply *ohayo* in casual conversation. "*Ohayo gozaimasu.* Would you like some eggs for breakfast?"

pretty respectful about accurately capturing the look of Japan during that era. Other films have stretched reality with fantasy portrayals of Japan, like *Ninja Assassin*, an extra-violent American film starring Korean matinee idol Rain that glamorized ninja as a mercenary clan of killers who conduct assassinations even today, and the 2013 *kaiju* or monster movie *Pacific Rim*, written and directed by Guillermo del Toro, an affectionate tribute to the Japanese monster films he grew up watching.

The 2014 film version of Godzilla was much better than the 1998 take on the monster precisely because it stuck closer to its Japanese roots. The giant lizard was initially criticized by Japanese fans as being too fat, but the movie was well received when it opened in Japan. Moviegoers there gave it the stamp of approval—Japanese culture is now completing the pop-culture cycle and heading home after being ingested and remade in American fashion.

The sporting life

If you asked most Americans twenty years ago what they knew about Japanese sports, they'd probably only come up with "sumo." Yet another aspect of the current Japan fad, sumo has reached the West—with amateur sumo matches between Caucasian wrestlers and with those obnoxious blow-up plastic costumes that allow wearers to slam against each other in bars and at parties.

But Japan's national sport for many decades—even during the prewar and immediate postwar years—has been the American game of baseball. Baseball was introduced in the late 1800s during the Meiji Restoration when Japan was absorbing all things Western like a sponge. The quality of athletes is as high as anywhere in the world, and in the past decade, Japanese professional players have been increasingly imported into the Major Leagues. The first was pitcher Hideo Nomo in the mid-1990s. Nomo was treated as almost a novelty, but in the seasons since, players such as Ichiro Suzuki of the Seattle Mariners have become marquee players who are an increasing draw for fans.

Some notable Asians and Asian Americans have made their mark on professional sports—among them NBA superstars Yao Ming from Shanghai and Jeremy Lin, who was born in Torrance, California, and golf superstar Tiger Woods, who is African American and Thai. A handful of NFL players are Pacific Islanders, including Rey Maualuga of the Cincinnati Bengals. Increasingly, Asian athletes have reached the heights of sports such as golf (Michelle Wie) and tennis (Michael Chang). There has been a stream of players from Japan recruited to Major League Baseball since Hideo Nomo was imported by the Los Angeles Dodgers in 1995 and Ichiro Suzuki was drafted by the Seattle Mariners in 2001. But few Japanese Americans have been in the sports spotlight, outside of skating (Apolo Ohno, Kristy Yamaguchi) or hockey (Paul Kariya, a Japanese Canadian in the National Hockey League).

Wataru "Wat" Misaka broke the "color" barrier in professional American basketball in 1946. (From the documentary Transcending: The Wat Misaka Story.*)*

Travis Ishikawa, a mixed-race Japanese American whose father is a Sansei, is a Major League Baseball player for the San Francisco Giants, and hit the three-run home run that won the National League pennant for his team in 2014. You can't get much more high profile than that for a JA in sports.

The first notable Japanese American in professional sports was a record-setter named Wataru Misaka. A Nisei who grew up in Ogden, Utah, "Wat" Misaka was a basketball star who led the University of Utah to an NCAA championship in 1944 in spite of the racism he faced, and then, after serving two years in the U.S. Army during WWII, led the University of Utah to another national title in 1947. That year, Misaka was drafted by the New York Knicks—he was the first athlete of color to play in professional basketball (in the same year Jackie Robinson broke the color barrier in baseball).

Ironically, Misaka's career in pro basketball was brief (the Knicks let him go during his rookie season, and Misaka turned down an offer to play with the Harlem Globetrotters show team), but he went on to much greater professional glory as a champion in the Japanese American National Bowling Association (JANBA). Now in his 80s, Wataru Misaka still plays in JANBA tournaments around the country.

JAs online

AAPIs have embraced the Internet as a primary way to communicate—we've been early adopters of all things digital and, now, of social media on the Internet. According to a 2013 Nielsen study of Asian American consumers, "Asian Americans are digital pioneers, adopting

Prejudice

Prejudice hurt me the most through its effect on my self-image and confidence. I was subjected to occasional verbal assaults from strangers and jokes from friends. Also growing up, the media really shaped the way I judged beauty, power, and success. The complete lack of representation of Asians in media led me to believe that Asians could not attain any of those attributes. The community I grew up in was also very white, which didn't help me in my quest for an Asian role model. These things combined to give me a very negative self-image and low confidence that I am only now starting to reverse.

Jill Nakawatase, postwar Nisei

Courtesy Ron Mori.

Very cool to be tooling about in 1978 on a Yamaha Enduro bike.

Identity

I consider myself both Japanese and American. Japanese American is an identity that defines my cultural and ethnic background. I identify with Japanese American history, culture, and community. Asian American is an identity that defines my political beliefs and passions. Though a demographic category defined by Caucasian America, I strongly believe an Asian American identity is crucial to cultivating positive change for people of color.

Kota Mizutani, Shin Nisei (child of recent immigrants)

WORDS & PHRASES

binbo

Poor. "We can't afford to go on vacation this year; we're too *binbo*."

technology faster than any other segment. With higher rates of smartphone usage, online video consumption, and internet connectivity, they are redefining the way they watch, listen, and interact."

When *Being Japanese American* was published in 2004, I was posting columns online on my Web site, which I had started as a weekly article for Denver's Japanese community newspaper, a weekly called the *Rocky Mountain Jiho* that has since been shuttered. In 2006 my online column was converted into a blog, just one indication that blogging programs like Wordpress, which I use, have made it so easy for people to "publish" themselves online that I hardly have to worry about HTML and complicated programming code. Writing a blog isn't so different these days from, say, writing a report using Microsoft Word.

I still blog at www.nikkeiview.com, although I admit I'm not as regular about writing weekly as I was when the *Jiho* was around with deadlines for me to meet. But I am a frequent user of Instagram, the popular image-sharing social media platform. I have my Instagram set so when I post a photo from my mobile phone, it will also be posted on Twitter and Facebook. . . . And as an Asian American, one of the things I photograph most is food, glorious food. There is an actual genre using the hashtag "#foodporn" on social media so people can search for images of food. My research is anecdotal, but Asian Americans seem more inclined to post #foodporn than other people. And I'm seriously guilty of shooting #foodporn. It started innocently as a fun way of sharing the wonderful meals we ate at restaurants. But now my social media followers expect me to chronicle every meal!

There are many sources online for news and commentary about Asian Americans, such as Angry Asian Man (a daily must-read for me) and 8 Asians—I've added a section for AAPI blogs in my list of Resources at the end of this book. This network of online AAPI media is essential to our sense of identity because newspaper and TV stations generally don't cover our news unless it's about a horrible crime or some pre-teen Asian American genius who's about to go to Harvard. We are, after all, still defined by the "model minority" myth. When AAPIs are stereotyped or suffer some racist attack, it's the Asian American blogosphere that spreads the word first. In some cases, AAPI bloggers can lead to coverage by mainstream media.

When Phil Yu, creator of the Angry Asian Man blog (no, he's

not a particularly angry dude), shared the local news coverage in Philadelphia of racist attacks against Asian high school students, the resulting national outrage led to national mainstream news coverage. Such examples are rare, but it's nice to know we now have the clout to move the media needle even a little bit, from time to time. Before the Internet, blogs, and now social media, where news can go viral in an instant, local news about Asians stayed pretty much local, if it got covered at all.

The other big change that came along the year the first edition of this book was published was the founding of Facebook, a Web site that originally only accepted college students as members, enabling them to share with their peers updates about their lives in text and photos. It was the dawning of today's social media industry.

The next year, in 2005, YouTube was launched, and in 2006, the same year Facebook opened its service to everyone, not just college students, Twitter was launched. Dozens of new social media sites debut every year, but these three, along with Instagram, a site that lets users share photographs, have been the major avenues for most sharing of content. Facebook alone hosts 1.5 billion users, and YouTube's 1 billion users upload 100 hours of video every *minute*.

Of the pantheon of new media stars made possible by the popularity of YouTube, one of the top stars is a Japanese American, Ryan Higa, who goes by the YouTube username "NigaHiga." He has over 13 million subscribers for his YouTube channel and also posts on a second YouTube channel, HigaTV, that has over 2 million subscribers. Higa, who's just twenty-four years old, posts a mix of funny commentary and parody skits in rapid-fire monologue intercut with loosely directed scenes acted out with an ensemble of friends. He doesn't necessarily cover JA topics, or rarely even wider Asian American topics, though he does criticize racist jokes about Asians.

Ryan Higa isn't the only AAPI celeb on YouTube. He leads a pack of Asian American video stars who produce everything from makeup tips to more comedic commentary. At one point, most of the top ten YouTube celebrities were Asian American. That's an amazing feat, considering that Asians historically have been invisible in the mainstream media.

Courtesy Phil Yu

Angry Asian Man is a must-read blog for news about Asian Americans.

Stereotypes

The stuff like Mickey Rooney in *Breakfast at Tiffany's* really offends me. Also white people playing Asian parts in movies, TV, stage, etc. The ignorance people sometimes express in terms of the internment. The lack of Asian actors in any situation. In science fiction movies there should be more of us, since we comprise a majority of the world's population.

June Inuzuka, Sansei

WORDS & PHRASES

kokujin

African-American, or black person (unfortunately sometimes used in a derogatory manner). "Michael Jordan is *kokujin*."

Nikkei and their love of nicknames

Hideo's mother used to affectionately call him Hidebon, so this eventually evolved into "Bonehead." Suematsu was Sue even before Johnny Cash wrote "A Boy Named Sue." Noburo, for I don't know what reason, answered cheerfully to "Chink." Kiyoshi actually saw nothing wrong with being called "Cowshit."

Iwao became Wahoo, and during a period when my friend Katch had a crush on Wahoo, we teased her by calling her "Minni Ha Cha." Hey, I'm not kidding about any of this! I don't know whether this was typical of JCs everywhere, but we lived in a mainly immigrant community called Queensborough, a part of New Westminster City, and people like my husband, who is from Vancouver, considered us to be "hicks" and looked down on us. Among the Vancouverites there were many colorful nicknames: YY, Doc, Hippo, Sparrow, Chipmunk, Freak and Swede (they were brothers), Shine, Bowey. My father's military captain did call him Frank because he found "Katsuji" a bit of a mouthful. By the way, I think most of these nicknames were shed once we were shipped off to the camps, and I don't think they were ever used by *hakujin* friends.

Lois Hashimoto, Canadian Nisei

yasashii

Easy or simple. "That recipe was *yasashii*, but it's such a fancy meal."

J-pop and the sound of young Japan

Mainstream American pop fans have long ignored Japanese music. For all most rock fans know, Japanese music is still rooted in the traditional sounds of the koto, shamisen, and shakuhachi, and is best listened to as accompaniment to Zen meditation or a ritualistic tea ceremony.

Mostly, that's because American pop music fans have very little patience or interest in music that is sung in a foreign language. The odd exception will garner attention in the United States—Kyu Sakamoto's "Ue o Muite Aruko" (better known in the West as "Sukiyaki") is the best-known example of a Japanese song that became a hit in America. With a name change it overcame the language barrier and became a number-one hit in 1963 on the strength of its mournful, hummable melody.

These exceptions have been cultural flukes at best—blips on the radar screen, not planned or expected. Japan's music industry has the same full range of styles and artists as we do here—from older pop crooners and jazz musicians to folkies, big-haired rockers, and leather-clad punks. But we'd never know it from the few musicians who've managed to cross the Pacific.

Japan's first attempted invasion of the U.S. pop charts after Sakamoto was in the late 1970s, in the form of Pink Lady, the duo of Mie Nemoto and Kei Masuda who had a huge hit in Japan with a remake of the American disco tune "In the Navy." The two were cute enough to be noticed by an American TV executive who made the ill-fated decision to create a variety show around the women as a summer filler series. Although the show had an American co-host who tossed ethnic humor around in an attempt to keep viewers interested, the women couldn't speak English very well (they sang phonetically), and the series didn't even last a month. Pink Lady barely cracked the U.S. charts in 1979 with "Kiss in the Dark," but never made a lasting impression. They broke up in 1981 after returning to Japan and trying to respark their careers. Japanese musicians haven't made it on the U.S. hit charts since then.

Outside the mainstream, however, Japanese music has thrived in America. As young Japanese discovered punk rock and turned their amps up to eleven, their noisy thrashing caught the attention of some cutting-edge American rock fans. In the early 1990s, a Seattle label tried to import and make popular a Tokyo punk band called Blue Hearts that made music as energetic and catchy as the Clash. They failed, but another Japanese punk group, a much smoother sounding female trio (now duo) called Shonen Knife, became underground sensations when U.S. avant-garde groups such as Sonic Youth and

Nirvana proclaimed them the best thing since . . . sushi. Their songs had a twist—the tunes dwelt on whimsical topics like buffalo and tomato heads and were sung with absolutely no irony. The approach was somewhat one-dimensional, though, and despite the best efforts of their U.S. label, Shonen Knife never built a fan base beyond the thin cutting-edge and a handful of rock critics.

A more recent attempt by an American company to import a Japanese group was Pizzicato Five, the duo of Yasuharu Konishi and Maki Nomiya. Konishi, a musician and record producer with an obsessive knowledge of American disco and R&B of the 1970s, created catchy sonic soundscapes for singer Nomiya to dance across. The duo was popular on the dance club circuit, but never made it big. Other groups from Japan that played dance-club music based on 1970s R&B have made some inroads, like Fantastic Plastic Machine, but they've been cult favorites at best, and mostly unknown to the general public.

The group Dreams Come True has made a strong attempt at breaking through with their slick, soulful pop. Their toe-tapping brassy sound and mellow ballads would appeal to fans of Earth, Wind and Fire or Luther Vandross, but they remain virtually unknown despite wider distribution in the West than most Japanese artists.

Finally, though, Japanese rock seems poised to make a bigger impact on the U.S. scene, without the help of record companies and their marketing schemes, without TV exposure, and even without radio airplay. Thanks in large part to the Internet, with its ability to let fans build spontaneous Web sites and share music files with each other, "J-pop," as the genre is now called, is catching on.

J-pop artists actually cover a lot of stylistic ground. The love for '70s R&B is still there, but so are hard-rock guitars, and the hip underground dance sounds of techno and trance. Fans of anime, or Japanese animation, seem also to be interested in J-pop because of the movie soundtracks.

I'm just a novice, but my favorite J-pop artists include the eclectic duo Puffy (Yumi Yoshimura and Ami Onuki, who have toured the States), the more traditional pop star Ayumi Hamasaki, and the edgier Utada Hikaru (who was born in New York and educated in the United States).

Courtesy Erin Yoshimura.

Nisei soldiers on leave play a baseball game with their interned friends.

No checkbox for mixed race

When I was younger, taking standardized tests, they used to only give the options "Asian, White, Black, Hispanic, Pacific Islander" and you could only pick one. When I was very small I looked very Japanese and I was proud of that, but as I got older I started looking more and more white like my dad. Most people now can't tell I'm *hapa* except for other Asians. It's kind of weird since I always identified as being more Japanese and being proud that I was *hapa*.

Emily Porter, Japanese Caucasian mixed-race Yonsei

WORDS & PHRASES
otosan

Father. "My *otosan* took me out to the baseball game."

For now, listening to J-pop is like tuning in to early rock and roll. There's that feeling of cultish appreciation shared by a small but growing group of fans. I doubt it'll stay this way much longer. Some of these artists deserve worldwide attention. Thanks to the Internet, they're getting it.

JA musicians have made even less of a mark than Japanese artists in the music industry. I can name only a handful of well-known JA musicians, including the new-age artist Kitaro (who's Japanese but has lived in Colorado for years); the fusion jazz band Hiroshima, which was formed during the "Yellow Power" era of the 1970s in California; Jeff Kashiwa, a former member of the contemporary jazz band Rippingtons and now working solo; and New York jazz singer Lionelle Hamanaka. Of these contemporary jazz stars, Hiroshima's known for mixing traditional Japanese sounds—koto and *taiko* drums—with the propulsive instrumentation of fusion.

Although some Japanese classical musicians are well known (conductor Seiji Ozawa and violinist Midori, both now living in the United States, come to mind), JAs are making inroads into classical music, too. Maestro Kent Nagano, a Sansei born in California in the early 1950s, served as the Music Director and Conductor of the Berkeley Symphony since 1978, and since 2000 as the Music Director of the Deutsches Symphonie-Orchester Berlin. The busy Nagano is also Music Director of the Los Angeles Opera, as well as principal guest conductor for a number of other symphonies. He's been named as a candidate for the top job at several high-profile symphonies, including the Chicago Symphony Orchestra and the New York Philharmonic, but in early 2004 he was named Music Director of the Montreal Symphony Orchestra (being fluent in French helped), and he'll take over as conductor in 2006. He's made a splash on the music scene because he's a baby-boomer with the shaggy hair of a Beatles fan. His handsome looks and vivaciousness have helped to attract younger fans to the classical canon.

Over in the rock field, James Iha is one of the few visible JAs at the national level. The former Smashing Pumpkins guitarist these days plays with A Perfect Circle.

Mike Shinoda, founder of the hip hop rock band Linkin Park and a side project, Fort Minor, is a mixed-race Los Angeleno whose JA heritage is most clearly outlined in a moving Fort Minor song, "Kenji," about an uncle's experience in a wartime internment camp. Shinoda's father is Japanese American. Shinoda is also an artist, and his work has been on exhibit at the Japanese American National Museum.

Judith Hill is half African American and half Japanese, and although she's a gifted songwriter and composer, her voice is what has brought her into the spotlight. A background singer for Michael Jackson, she was rehearsing a duet she was to sing with him on his "This Is It" tour when Jackson died from an overdose before the show could debut. Hill was the most notable performer among a star-studded stage at the memorial concert to Jackson that was televised around the world. But instead of capitalizing on her acclaim she chose not to take advantage of her relationship with the late King of Pop. Instead, she toured as a backup singer and wrote original songs. When she felt ready for the spotlight, Hill earned it on her own merits, as a contestant on the reality television contest "The Voice." She didn't win, but she was one of the finalists, and the attention has boosted her career.

Some JA musicians are local heroes, playing clubs in their hometown scenes, like Curt Yagi and his band The People Standing Behind Me, a popular group in the San Francisco Bay area.

Mia Doi Todd is not a household name, but she has been a Japanese American pioneer as a singer-songwriter, releasing her first album in 1997 and, most recently, her ninth album in 2014. A Los Angeles–born musician, she has a low throaty voice and an artistic musical palette that at times evokes middle-era Joni Mitchell.

Another artistic JA singer-songwriter who deserves more fame for her well-crafted, alternative folk-rock is New York-based Rachael Yamagata. Her first record was released in 2002, and to date she's recorded three full albums and five EPs.

Other JAs are finding success as singer-songwriters in the YouTube age, recording sparely produced independent pop records. San Francisco–based Goh Nakamura has released three full-length albums and also acted in a couple of indie films. Kina Grannis, a mixed-race JA from Mission Viejo, California, first came to prominence when she won a Doritos contest and had her song played for a Super Bowl audience in 2008. She has released five albums and has gained a following through her YouTube videos. Meiko is a young singer-songwriter from Georgia who is one-quarter Japanese. She's released three albums of her quiet, introspective songs. All the tracks on her 2008 debut album received exposure on various television series.

These musicians may not all be superstars (yet), but they have the potential to gain national acclaim—all it might take is for every reader to buy their music!

It's not that JAs aren't out there making music. Whether it's because so many of us were forced to take music lessons as kids and it turned us off to playing, or because of our cultural training not to stand out and bring attention to ourselves, there just aren't many JAs

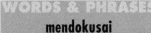

WORDS & PHRASES

mendokusai

Not worth the trouble, or more casually, pain in the butt. "I'm not going to volunteer to make that dish, it's too *mendokusai*, and takes too long."

Goh Nakamura is a San Francisco–based musician.

Being JA in Seattle

As twentysomethings, sis and I ended up hanging out in Seattle's International District watching old samurai flicks at the Kokusai. Sometimes, we'd go to the Toyo on Rainier—then, a very Black area. The Toyo owners would always put out little cups of green tea for us customers.

Yayoi Lena Winfrey, *hapa* Issei

WORDS & PHRASES
tomodachi

Friend. *"I've never seen a group of tomodachi like the ones in the TV show Friends."*

in the spotlight. Let's hope that changes with coming generations.

On the silver screen

When it comes to recent Japanese imports, anime may be making the biggest cinematic impression on the U.S. market, but there are plenty of devotees of non-animated Japanese films in America. Japanese film first made an impression in the 1950s with the classic early work of director Akira Kurosawa and actor Toshiro Mifune, such as *Seven Samurai* and *Rashomon.*

Yasujiro Ozu's steadfastly slow films were almost entirely shot from one angle (low, as if from the perspective of someone kneeling Japanese-style on a tatami mat) without fancy tricks like dissolves, fades, or pans. The simplicity of the directing forces you to absorb the characters and the dialogue and immerses you in the story, not in the artifice of cinema. His 1953 *Tokyo Story* is a classic about how postwar Japanese values changed and families drifted apart. His 1959 *Hello* updated the theme with a healthy dose of humor.

More recently I've come to enjoy the work of "Beat" Takeshi Kitano. His deadpan expression—made more so by a 1994 motorcycle accident that nearly killed him—has redefined the cold fury of modern Japanese gangster films. At the same time, he brings a bemused humor to his roles. A former comedian who is best known in America for his yakuza films, Kitano's 2000 U.S.-funded movie *Brother* is typical of his incredibly violent stories, while the 1999 *Kikujiro*, in which he portrays a tough guy with a soft spot for a kid he's accompanying on a trip, shows his more human side.

Other enjoyable recent imports include *Tampopo,* a wonderful story about a ramen shop; *Shall We Dance,* about the search for individuality through dance lessons; and *Afterlife*, a funny and smart film about life and death. I seek out Japanese movies at film festivals.

Despite the audience for Japanese films in the West, however, there isn't a genre that could be classified as "Japanese American cinema." Partly, that's because there are so few JAs who are recognizable faces in Hollywood productions. In fact, few Asian faces of any heritage are visible on the boxes that line the shelves at your neighborhood Blockbuster. George Takei, who played Sulu in the original

Courtesy Myleen Hollero.

Star Trek TV show and movies, is probably the most famous JA of all. Pat Morita, first as Arnold on *Happy Days* and then as Mr. Miyagi in the *Karate Kid* series, is also a familiar star. Okinawa-born JA actress Tamlyn Tomita has acted in a number of notable films, including *Karate Kid II*, *Picture Bride*, and *The Joy Luck Club*. But mostly we're relegated to supporting roles, such as the Japanese American characters in films like *Go for Broke!* (1951, about the 442nd JA regimental combat team in World War II that ironically starred a white guy, Van Johnson), and *Snow Falling on Cedars* (1999), or to playing the bad guys in numerous World War II movies.

Sure, there have been Asian actors who've won awards. Miyoshi Umeki won a supporting actress award in 1957 for her role as a Japanese woman who falls in love with an American GI during the Korean War in *Sayonara* (she played a submissive GI bride). Mako (Makoto Iwamatsu) was nominated for best supporting actor for the 1966 film *The Sand Pebbles* (he played a Chinese coolie). A Cambodian who had never acted before, Haing S. Ngor, won the best supporting actor award in 1984 for his role in the gripping film *The Killing Fields*. But those are the exceptions, not the rule.

On the positive side, Asians are showing up more in Hollywood movies these days, even if most are martial arts stars like Jackie Chan and Jet Li. It's progress. When *Kung Fu* premiered in 1972, the producers wouldn't allow Bruce Lee to play the lead role and instead hired David Carradine, taping back his eyes to make him "half Chinese."

There's a long history of "yellowface" in Hollywood movies. Warner Oland, a Swede, starred as Charlie Chan in the 1930s and 1940s. Actors including Christopher Lee and Boris Karloff have played the evil Fu Manchu, an icon of early twentieth century anti-Asian paranoia. Luise Rainer won an Academy Award for *The Good Earth* in 1938, playing the lead role of O-lan. Katherine Hepburn played a Chinese woman in 1944's *Dragon Seed*. Marlon Brando and Ricardo Montalban with their eyes taped back have both played Japanese characters.

Mickey Rooney played a racist stereotype of a Japanese—complete with squinty eyes, thick glasses, godawful buck teeth, and a tellible lacist ac-cu-cento in the 1961 film *Breakfast at Tiffany's*, which unfortunately is considered a "classic." So I'm happy to note that at least now we can have real Asians playing Asians.

There is an emerging generation of Asian American actors bubbling under Hollywood's mainstream. People such as writer/director/actor Lane Nishikawa (who's working on a feature film about the 442nd's famous rescue of the Texas "Lost Battalion") and playwright

Facing subtle racism

Like most Asians, I've encountered many people who make veiled racist comments disguised as compliments ("You speak such good English!," "I knew a Japanese person once . . . ," "You're Japanese? I love sushi!"). When I was in high school, I attended a television show taping with my classmates. There was a comedian that was supposed to entertain the audience between scenes and he started interviewing some of the audience members to help facilitate his jokes. He asked me, "Where are you from?" Not realizing that he was trying to find out my racial background, I answered truthfully: "The Valley." Comedian: "But where were you born?" Me: "The Valley." Comedian: "Well, where are your parents from?" Me: "My dad's from the Valley, and my mom's from L.A." Comedian, getting frustrated: "How about your grandparents?" Me: "They're from Idaho, Utah, and California." Comedian: "Come on, help me out here. Where are your ancestors from then?" Me: "Japan." Comedian then proceeds to make some stupid racist joke about Japan. In retrospect, I wish I'd made it harder for him and said something.

Mariko Yamashiro, Yonsei

WORDS & PHRASES

dozo

"Here you go." Polite word when serving someone, as in "Dozo, please have a seat," or "Dozo, I hope you like these pastries."

On feeling Japanese

I feel very "Japanese" but the Japanese side of my family is not what I think of when I think of "typical" Japanese Americans. On the whole, most of my Japanese family members are not quiet, passive, well-mannered, and afraid to make waves. (Gosh, talk about stereotypes!) My great-grandma left her husband in Japan and came to the U.S. with another man because her husband wasn't treating her well. My grandparents divorced in the early 1950s, which was not a common thing. My grandpa rode his Harley-Davidson in leather from his head to his toes and ended up marrying three very beautiful Japanese American women in total.

I feel "Japanese" but I think I act more "Chinese" (whatever that means)

I'm not as concerned with being polite and considerate as most other JAs I know. I know about *koden* [monetary gift at a funeral] but my mom never did this to my knowledge. This is really making me question why I feel so "JA" and tied to my community though I do feel a bit like an outsider.

Tamiko Wong, mixed-race
Japanese Chinese

Philip Kan Gotanda may not be household names, but they're already respected artists. A growing number of theater groups such as the East West Players in Los Angeles, Asian American Theater Company in San Francisco, and Northwest Asian American Theater in Seattle are training young Asian Pacific Americans and giving them the tools to move onto the national scene. As with music, hopefully, we'll be able to taste the fruits of this new generation's talents in a few years.

One JA who has made an impact is Oscar-winning filmmaker Steven Okazaki, who has directed both documentaries and independent feature films, many of which have been broadcast on public television. His films span a range of topics from JA and Japanese issues to AIDS and punk culture. A Sansei born in 1952, Okazaki directed his first film in 1982. *Survivors* is a short documentary about survivors of the Hiroshima atomic bomb blast. His second film, 1985's *Unfinished Business*, examines the 1980s court case that finally overturned the convictions of the three JAs who fought internment during the 1940s. His first feature film, *Living on Tokyo Time*, is a sweet comedy about a JA man who marries—and then falls in love with—a Japanese woman so she can stay in the United States. Okazaki won the 1990 Oscar for Best Documentary Short Subject for *Days of Waiting*, a film about Estelle Ishigo, a Caucasian artist who was interned along with her husband at Heart Mountain, Wyoming.

With the rise of the Gosei and Rokusei generations, there seems to be a more pan-Asian mentality developing in the film community. The 2003 release of critically acclaimed films such as *Better Luck Tomorrow* and *Charlotte Sometimes* were collaborations between young AAPIs, not just JAs, or Chinese Americans, or Vietnamese Americans. The momentum's building for such projects, as young people disregard the boundaries between the various Asian communities and work together to fashion a reflection of their own AAPI culture.

On the small screen

For many baby boomers, the most memorable Asians on TV may have been the young couple on the Calgon laundry detergent commercial from the late 1960s, in which the husband tells the (white) customer at his laundry that there's an "ancient Chinese secret" that makes their clothes so clean. His wife at the end of the commercial reveals the secret is Calgon detergent.

Except for outliers like the Calgon commercial, for decades prime-time TV hasn't focused on Asians at all. The few Asians of note on the small screen were mostly sidekicks or lesser characters, from Hop

WORDS & PHRASES

sukoshi

A little bit. Turned into "skosh" by GIs returning from Japan. "I can only speak Japanese *sukoshi*."

Sing (played by Victor Sen Yung), the cook in the long-running western *Bonanza,* and Fuji (Yoshio Yoda), the upbeat POW in *McHale's Navy,* who was treated like the PT boat crew's houseboy, to Sam Fujiyama (Robert Ito), the lab assistant to Jack Klugman's starring role in *Quincy, M.E.,* and the beloved Arnold Takahashi, the owner of the diner where the characters on *Happy Days* hung out. These were subservient or supporting roles, not starring ones. The closest AAPIs got to starring was with Bruce Lee's scene-stealing charisma as Kato, the Green Hornet's driver and sidekick.

That changed in 1994 when up-and-coming standup comic Margaret Cho was cast as a young Korean American woman in an Asian American family sitcom, *All-American Girl.* The show started promisingly as a showcase for Asian American family dynamics and cultural traditions (Cho was a hip twenty-three-year-old who fought with her more traditional "tiger mom"), but it lasted only a season as it struggled for ratings, with the producers tweaking the ethnic concept out of the series before its demise. The producers at one point told Cho she wasn't "Asian" enough, and hired a coach to help her act the part.

Asian Americans have begun taking their place among Hollywood stars. Some have starred in both movies and television series, like John Cho (*Star Trek*, the *Harold and Kumar* movies, and on TV most recently, *Selfie*, a sitcom, which was unfortunately canceled). Mindy Kaling has become an industry power, starring in her own eponymous comedy series, *Mindy.*

For years until her departure last season, Sandra Oh played a brilliant surgeon on the hit hospital series *Gray's Anatomy.* Lucy Liu is co-star of a hit TV show *Elementary,* Maggie Q is cast in movies as well as major network series (the latest is CBS's *Stalker*), and Kristin Kreuk is the fairer half of the action series *Beauty and the Beast.*

The hit series *Bones* has featured a mixed-race actor, Michaela Conlin, as a member of the crime-solving team of scientists helping the FBI. Mixed-race actor Chloe Bennet and veteran AAPI actor Ming-Na Wen both star as team members in *Marvel's Agents of S.H.I.E.L.D.* One new program, *Scorpion*, includes Jadyn Wong as one of its group of brilliant but antisocial nerds who fight crime, but she's a quirky character who's a mechanical genius with a strong New York accent. No "ancient Chinese secret" for her!

And the new version of *Hawaii Five-0* is chock-full of Asian Americans and Pacific Islanders in leading roles—Daniel Dae Kim, Grace

Publicity still from All-American Girl, *the first TV show featuring an almost all-Asian cast.*

On growing up in a non-Asian community

I grew up in an area that was primarily Latino and white, with less than 1 percent of the population being Asian. So while I attended a JA church and played JA bball, as a child I didn't connect those things to my identity or sense of JA-ness. Thus, growing up in La Habra, I felt often pulled between being hypervisible as Asian and therefore different from everyone else, but also invisibilized as my mixed-ness often would be read as Latina/ambiguous/white to others (to the point where when I was a senior in high school, someone I had gone to school with since elementary school was shocked that I was JA, and not Latina as assumed).

Kristin Fukushima, Japanese Caucasian mixed-race Yonsei

Park, and Masi Oka—unlike the original *Five-0* series that aired from the late 1960s to the early 1980s. Even *Walking Dead*, a series about a zombie apocalypse that takes place in the Deep South, has included an Asian American, Steven Yeun, as one of the group of survivors.

One heartening feature of all these characters is that the actors who play them don't have to speak with Asian accents. They're not playing *Asian* roles, they're playing roles that happen to be played by Asians. They're not immigrants, they're not martial artists or any of the typical stereotypes. Sometimes their Asian heritage might be mentioned (the Sandra Oh character's back story as a Korean American was referred to a couple of times on *Gray's Anatomy*), but it's not a big part of who the characters are.

In early 2015, ABC launched another attempt at the concept, *Fresh Off the Boat*, based on the memoir of celebrity Chinese American chef Eddie Huang, whose family emigrated from Taiwan to the U.S. in the 1990s. Many AAPI bloggers have been eagerly following its development, and there's confidence that this is the show that can accurately reflect our lives, because the network executives and producers are much more diverse than during Margaret Cho's ill-fated show and because Huang has had a strong influence in how the show is produced.

The title is an insult that's even used by Asian Americans aimed at other Asians, to make fun of recent immigrants. To be fair the phrase should be Fresh Off the Plane these days, but FOB has stuck

In the show, the mother does have an accent, but that's because she is the recent-immigrant counterpoint to the Americanized young Eddie Huang character (played by Hudson Yang), who listens to rap music and straddles American culture at school and Chinese culture at home. It's a cultural juggling act that many Asian Americans—including me with my Japanese American dual lifestyle: Japanese at home, American with my friends—grew up balancing. In one early scene young Eddie tells his mother he wants "American food" for lunch because when he brought Chinese food to the cafeteria his friends teased him for eating worms.

These days, thanks to the emergence of Asians in mass and social media, we don't have to be ashamed of bringing "exotic" food to school, like Eddie.

JA lit

Ironically, one of the best-known books about Japanese Americans was not written by a JA. *Snow Falling on Cedars,* David Guterson's evocative bestselling novel, which was made into an atmospheric but confusing 1999 movie, tells the story of lingering prejudice toward Japanese Americans who returned after internment to a Puget Sound island community.

Asian American literature as a genre is growing steadily, with JAs contributing. Especially in nonfiction, JAs have cranked out histories and sociological tracts by the dozen. But there's a rich catalog of JA fiction too. John Okada's *No-No Boy* broke ground in 1957 with its pioneering fictional exploration of the internment but, more importantly, of the conflict within the JA community over those who said "No" to two important questions in the government's Loyalty Questionnaire about fighting in the U.S. military against Japan. The book's main character refuses the draft late in the war and is sent to prison for two years as a traitor (a fate that actually befell some JAs). Because the novel touched a raw nerve within the community, Okada was shunned and his book derided until long after its publication, when the Yellow Power movement praised its unflinching perspective. Sadly, Okada died in 1971, never having published another novel.

That same year, Yoshiko Uchida, a Nisei, published a book, *Journey to Topaz*, for teen readers that tells a fictional account of her family's experience. Uchida died in 1992, but she was a prolific author, writing books for both young readers and adults. Among her books are *The Bracelet*, a children's book that takes place in an internment camp, *Picture Bride*, and an autobiography, *Invisible Thread: A Memoir*.

The most widely known book about Japanese Americans, thanks to a 1976 TV movie, was *Farewell to Manzanar*, by James Houston and his wife Jeanne Wakatsuki Houston, a Nisei who was seven years old when her family was incarcerated in the California internment camp. The book, which was written for young readers, is still widely read in schools throughout the United States, and is often the first—and just about the only—introduction that American students get to internment, an era that's hardly mentioned in high school history texts.

Most of the notable books by JAs are about internment. E. T. Miyakawa's *Tule Lake* was first published in 1980 and reissued in 2002. It's a novel about the internment camp that was the repository

Publicity still from Fresh Off the Boat, *popular among Asian viewers for its honest depiction of the lives of an Asian immigrant family, based on the memoir by Eddie Huang.*

On being mixed race
To me, being mixed just sort of throws a whole second level of barriers and anxieties. Whether it's not being seen/recognized by folks/the community as someone who "belongs" to the community, or being told that *hapa* are "the Problem" or as it was once put—killing the community, there are always incidents that give me mini identity crises and make me question my JA-ness for a second.

Kristin Fukushima, Japanese Caucasian mixed-race Yonsei

WORDS & PHRASES
chiisai (chichai)
Small. "Gee, their new house is so *chiisai* for how much it cost. . ."

for the "No-No boys" and anyone else the government thought was anti-American and pro-Japan during the war. Hence, Tule Lake was the most violent camp, housing the most bitter and angry JAs.

In 1999, Rahna Reiko Rizzuto's powerful *Why She Left Us* tells the story of internment through the eyes of various members of a JA family, including the Yonsei generation that still feels the aftereffects of a mother's abandonment of an illegitimate daughter.

Rahna Reiko Rizzuto's 2010 book, *Hiroshima in the Morning*, was a memoir of her 2001 trip to Hiroshima on a fellowship to interview survivors of the atomic bombing. It evolves into a commentary on marriage and motherhood, but the narrative arc gets upended when the September 11 attacks happen while she's in Japan and her husband and two sons are in New York City. The book is an emotionally brave exploration of Rizzuto's past and present.

Internment is the setting in *The Red Kimono*, a novel published by mixed-race Arkansas author Jan Morrill in 2013. The book follows a family from the San Francisco area who are sent to Rowher Relocation Center in Arkansas and the tragedy of losing a father to a hate crime after the attack on Pearl Harbor. Told from the perspective of three young protagonists, it is written in an engaging style and obviously informed with a lot of careful historical research as it tracks the family's forced journey to Tanforan, a racetrack south of San Francisco that was converted into a temporary camp, and then on to Rowher. The book is an intriguing study of racial enmity and the need for forgiveness. By the time they reach the unexpected conclusion, readers will feel as if the characters are part of their own family.

The camp experience is only tangentially a part of Los Angeles author Naomi Hirahara's fine series of mystery novels starring Mas Arai, a crusty older Japanese American gardener who is mostly retired but has a knack for stumbling into—and then solving—murderous crimes. Hirahara, a journalist, began channeling her familiarity with the LA JA community into plots involving Mas Arai over five novels that earned her an Edgar Award and a loyal following. She has now retired Arai and launched a new series of books featuring a young Los Angeles bicycle cop, Ellie Rush. Hirahara has also written nonfiction books, including profiles of Japanese American leaders and histories of both JA gardeners and Southern California's Japanese American floral industry.

Another journalist, Roxana Saberi, who is half Japanese and half Iranian (and a former Miss North Dakota!), covered a more contemporary lockup in her compelling account of a nightmarish imprisonment in Iran's notorious Evin prison in the 2010 book, *Between Two*

Worlds: My Life and Captivity in Iran. She was accused of espionage against the government of Iran and gave a false confession under duress. Her sentence was suspended and she was given her freedom after 101 days thanks in part to efforts from Amnesty International Human Rights Watch, Asian American Journalists Association, Committee to Protect Journalists, and other international organizations. Saberi returned to journalism after her release and now works for Al Jazeera.

Julie Otsuka's 2002 first novel, *When the Emperor Was Divine*, is a slim, impressionistic look back at internment, primarily through the eyes of a girl whose family is uprooted from San Francisco.

Ken Mochizuki takes a different approach to internment with his popular children's book *Baseball Saved Us* (illustrated by Dom Lee) about how the most American of games brought together the children in the internment camps and focused their energies and spirit. In another children's book illustrated by Lee, *Heroes*, set in the 1960s, Mochizuki tells the story of a Japanese American boy during the Vietnam War era who's tired of always having to be the enemy when he and his friends play war. Mochizuki has also written a book for teen readers, *Beacon Hill Boys,* about a group of JA friends growing up in Seattle during the 1970s amidst the unspoken family stories of internment. These last two are semiautobiographical; Mochizuki was raised in Seattle, and was a teenager during the seventies.

Cynthia Kadohata, another baby-boomer JA, has avoided writing directly about internment, although the aftereffects of internment are woven throughout her stories. She made a splash with her first novel in 1989, *The Floating World*, about a struggling JA family in the 1950s. She has since published *Kira Kira*, a book for young readers about the relationship of two Japanese American sisters whose family moves from Iowa to the South—a rarely-touched-upon topic of JAs who don't live on the West Coast. She has also written non-JA themed books, including a science fiction novel, *In the Heart of the Valley of Love.*

Dale Furutani is one JA author who writes in a completely different genre. He's the first Asian American to win major mystery writing awards, including the Anthony Award and the Macavity award, and he's been nominated for the prestigious Agatha Award. His books include *Death in Little Tokyo* and *The Toyotomi Blades*, featuring JA amateur

Blood Hana *is one of several novels by Naomi Hirahara featuring Mas Arai, a Japanese American gardener turned sleuth in southern California.*

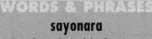

Overt racism

When I was young people would ask me if I could see out of my eyes. At my first job in New York City, they would say "Remember Pearl Harbor!" jokingly. I worked as a salesgirl at a clothing store, and one of the girls said, "Here comes a Jap," and I said I am standing right next to you. Also when I started in real estate, one of the agents called me a gook.

Carol Nichols, Sansei

Tak Toyoshima's "Secret Asian Man" comic chronicles the JA—and AAPI—experience.

private investigator Ken Tanaka. He's also written a samurai-era trilogy set in Japan that combines swordplay with sleuthing.

Well-known JA poets include Lawson Fusao Inada, Garrett Kaoru Hongo, David Mura, and Mitsuye Yamada. The best-known JA playwright is Philip Kan Gotanda, whose work includes *Fish Head Soup* and *Sisters Matsumoto*. Gotanda is also a filmmaker. But Lane Nishikawa, better known now as a filmmaker and actor, began his career as a playwright with his one-man show, *I'm on a Mission from Buddha*, and other plays including *Mifune and Me.*

North of the border, notable Japanese Canadians in literature include poets such as Sansei Roy Miki, who was born in a Canadian internment camp. Poet and novelist Joy Kogawa's 1981 *Obasan*, about her childhood experience in internment, and its 1992 sequel, *Itsuka*, set during the Japanese Canadian redress movement, are among the best known of Japanese Canadian books. *Obasan* made enough of an impact that Joy Kogawa's childhood home was purchased by The Land Conservancy in 2006 to be maintained as a historic landmark and "symbol of hope, healing and reconciliation."

The ever-increasing number of JA writers being published is proof that a Japanese American voice in literature is finally evolving.

On the cutting edge

There's a wave of JA culture that's part of the AAPI mentality taking hold. It's edgy and hip, and combines an interest in Japanese contemporary culture such as anime and manga, but gives it a distinctly American, culturally omnivorous spin that includes hip-hop, other Asian cultures (especially an appreciation for all types of Asian food jumbled together), poetry, fine art, traditional culture, rock and roll, and the Internet.

A hapa looks proud of her roots.

Musicians such as Cibo Matto, the New York-based group of avant-pop musicians that includes Yuka Honda, Miho Hatori, and Sean Lennon; the collective of pop intellectuals who create the cutting-edge Web site and retail stores under the umbrella of Giant Robot; trendy urban areas such as Sawtelle in West Los Angeles, miles from the established JA centers of Little Tokyo and Gardena—all of these are part of the new wave. Sawtelle is particularly striking because in a four- or five-block stretch of Sawtelle Boulevard you can find older JA businesses such as nurseries and shops selling ceramics next to dozens of hip new restaurants that span the gamut, from cheap ramen shops and Korean barbecues to upscale sushi bars and unique eateries like Furaibo, a Japanese chain that's one of my favorites because they serve unusual traditional dishes such as *natto*, fermented soy beans, in a raucous, à la carte "dim sum" atmosphere.

Also part of the rising AAPI culture is "Secret Asian Man," a weekly comic strip drawn by Boston-based artist Tak Toyoshima, a Sansei. Toyoshima serves as both activist and critic for the AAPI consciousness, by railing against racism and the tribulations faced by Asians in America. He also skewers political righteousness when things get too overwrought and pompous. He's a refreshing voice to be welcomed by every generation.

Pan-Asian bridges are also being built with events such as Dragon Boat races and festivals across the country. As young Asians discover that they can raise their voice higher by banding together instead of keeping to separate communities, it'll be fascinating to see how the JA culture continues to evolve, and how culture from Japan continues to be absorbed into the West.

The look of SAM, Secret Asian Man

The look is definitely a mix of Japanese and American styles. A lot of the best Japanese comics illustrators and animators tend to draw little caricatures of themselves with big expressive heads. Akira Toriyama's *Dr. Slump* series was a big inspiration, as was Tezuka Osamu's *Astro Boy*. SAM isn't a literal caricature of me, he's a semi-stereotypical representation of Asian males in general. Bowl cut hair, eyes that are tiny compared to his eyebrows, tiny mouth, no nose. I love iconographic looks so I wanted to simplify him as much as possible.

Tak Toyoshima, Sansei, creator of "Secret Asian Man" comic strip

CHAPTER 7

JA Communities

Sometimes I wish I lived on the West Coast, where Asians are everywhere and there are long-established pockets of Japanese Americans who've lived, worked, and shopped for generations.

Because the West Coast was the destination of the original wave of Asian immigrants, there are long-established Pacific-rim communities there, especially for Chinese and Japanese. For the Japanese and Japanese American population, these central areas have names like "Little Tokyo" and "Japantown."

Denver doesn't have the kind of Japanese presence you can find along the West Coast. Instead of Little Tokyo we have "Tiny Tokyo," a one-block downtown development called Sakura Square. In spite of its size, it's a fine focus for the Japanese community, with a high-rise apartment building for seniors, a grocery store, the Denver Buddhist Temple, a couple of Japanese restaurants, and a few shops. I love Sakura Square, but it's just a tantalizing taste of Japan, with a Japanese American flavor (because of the area's JA population, much of which settled in Colorado after internment).

Japantowns

In contrast to Sakura Square, when I visit Little Tokyo in Los Angeles, it's astounding how, well, Japanese, it is. Instead of just a taste of Japan, it's a feast.

It's a similar experience when I travel to San Francisco and visit the city's J-town, or Nihonmachi. I feel as if I'm visiting Japan without leaving the United States. Many of the signs are in Japanese, and everywhere you can hear Japanese being spoken. Even the Denny's

The Japanese-Chinese mix
I grew up with a Chinese last name but I look more Japanese. Japanese thought I was Chinese and Chinese thought I was Japanese.

Caroline Tu Farley, Japanese Taiwanese mixed-race Sansei

Facing racism

We lived in the "colored" section of town (Pasadena) and our school had more minorities than the primarily white school across town. But I didn't experience real racism until I moved to the East Coast, where I was constantly asked what I was. A black guy called me "mamasan" once, as if he were speaking to a prostitute. I've had non-Asian men ask me when I was going to give them a "massage." I've had kids call me "ching, chang, chinaman."

June Inuzuka, Sansei

restaurant that used to be in J-town, a typical American diner everyplace else, fit with the local culture. Beneath the sign is "Deh-nee-zu" spelled out in *katakana* characters, and the restaurant served a special Hawaiian-style breakfast menu with fried rice and Portuguese sausage (which was delicious), *kimchi*, and *saimin* noodle soup.

From the view of a visiting tourist interested in Japanese culture, J-town is a dream. It's close to all of San Francisco's tourist hotspots—Fisherman's Wharf, the Muir Woods redwood forest, Golden Gate Park with its beautiful Japanese Tea Garden, and the city's new, beautiful Asian Art Museum. But for an infusion of heritage, there's nothing like hanging out in J-town and its Japanese shops and, of course, its many restaurants. There are four—four!—Japanese grocery stores within a several-block area and CD stores that exclusively sell Japanese recordings.

Highlights include the comfortable Benkyo-Do, a small diner and pastry shop that sells wonderful *manju*, traditional pastries made with sweet bean paste enclosed in sweet, sticky rice dough or other wrapping; and Kinokuniya, the Japanese bookstore chain (there's also one in LA's Little Tokyo, as well as outlets in other California cities, Seattle, Portland, Chicago, New York City, and Edgewater, New Jersey), with a wealth of books and magazines in Japanese, plus an impressive section of English-language publications about Japanese culture, arts, and history.

San Francisco's J-town also had a terrific store called Nikkei Traditions that sold a variety of artsy items, gifts, and clothing that combine Japanese and Japanese American traditions. It was the first Sansei-owned business in J-town and had a distinctive JA flavor that was different from that of the purely Japanese stores. Nikkei Traditions also sold a series of CDs of popular pre– and post–World War II Japanese songs recorded by Japanese-American bands and artists in Hawaii from the 1930s to the 1950s. A second Nikkei Traditions shop in San Jose's smaller but old-fashioned Nihonmachi is still open.

There are stores featuring antiques, handicrafts, toys, Japanese office supplies, and pop culture collectibles such as Hello Kitty and Ultraman. Soko Hardware is a treasure trove of cool stuff. A family-owned hardware store in the grand tradition with goods stacked to the ceiling, the shop carries not only ordinary hardware items such as brooms and tools, but it stocks Japanese appliances and kitchen gadgets, *washi* (hand-made paper), calligraphy and ink-brush painting supplies, lots and lots of ceramics and lacquerware, and crafts including dolls. The Japanese Cultural and Community Center of Northern

California (JCCCNC) may have an unwieldy name, but the center is a vital resource for the community, and it's also located right there in J-town.

Scattered throughout are *puri-kura* photo booths (a Japanized version of the phrase "print club"), a Japanese invention that allows you to take pictures of yourself that are printed on sheets of tiny stickers, an improvement on the familiar passport photo booths.

The restaurants are terrific, though on our latest trip there, instead of sushi places, Erin and I sought out ramen restaurants.

We loved the food so much that on one evening we had dinner twice. We ate early at Mifune, ordering tempura and *soba* and sukiyaki *udon* (sukiyaki ingredients served in a sweet-flavored broth with fat *udon* noodles). A few hours later, after seeing a movie, we were curious enough about Sapporo-Ya that we had a second dinner, this time ramen. It was fine, though the noodles, which the restaurant makes every morning using an old machine by the entrance, had a different flavor and texture from what we were used to.

We even discovered a Japanese dessert creation at Sophie's Crepes, which in typical Japanese fashion takes a Western concept—the French crepe—and turns it into a new product, rolling crepes into a cone for ingredients including green tea gelato topped with *matcha* syrup, sweet *azuki* red beans, and whipped cream. We liked Sophie's Crepes so much we returned for another dessert after lunch our final day, a last stop before heading to the airport. I think I had enough of a Japanese culture fix to last me a while, but I can hardly wait to go back to Japan—via J-town.

Community organizations

During one trip to San Francisco, I had the pleasure of meeting Paul Osaki, part-owner of the original Nikkei Traditions store. More importantly, he's the executive director of the JCCCNC, an organization with a hard-to-remember name but an unforgettable impact on the community it serves. The entire time during our stay at the Best Western Miyako Inn in Japantown, I kept seeing vans drive by with the name "Kimochi" ("feeling") painted on the side. I didn't realize until we visited the JCCCNC, which turned out to be just down the

Courtesy Erin Yoshimura.

TRI-STATE BUDDHIST CHURCH 1966

JA Boy Scouts. The Buddhist church in Denver had its own scout troop.

Cultural regrets

I believe that some of the values that my very traditional Nisei mother instilled in me such as *haji* and *shikata ga nai* sometimes hold me back from going "outside of the box." My mother always encouraged me to blend in and not stand out. Probably my biggest regret was to not try to communicate more with my paternal grandmother to learn more about her life. Thankfully, older cousins and aunties did and can share that through recipes and stories.

Pam Yoshida, Sansei

WORDS & PHRASES

mottainai

Wasteful with a hint of regret or guilt. "You're throwing away that tube of toothpaste already? *Mottainai.* I bet you can get another week's worth out of it."

Courtesy JANM.

The Japanese American National Museum anchors one corner of Little Tokyo in Los Angeles.

Taunted by other children

I have experienced "nuances of racism"—usually it is not overt but things people say, looks, the way they treat you. When I was younger, I was often taunted on the playground. When I was in grade school, I had to do a demonstration speech. My mom suggested making sukiyaki. Well, the kids started called me that. I was mad at my mom for suggesting the idea, but I was really mad at the kids that called me the name.

Caroline Tu Farley, Japanese Taiwanese mixed-race Sansei

baka (bakatare, bakayaro)

Fool, idiot, dummy, trivial matter. "You thought you could ask her out? What are you, *baka?*" or "Hey *baka*, what're you doing?"

street from the hotel, that Kimochi is part of the JCCCNC's stable of community services.

The JCCCNC puts a premium on its role within the community. Osaki, dressed casually in jeans and a fine Hawaiian shirt, stepped out of his office, which was busy with staffers working on a myriad of programs and initiatives, and gave us a short but very impressive tour. In one climate-controlled room, community members, including senior citizens, were using state-of-the-art computer equipment to learn about technology and the Internet. Paul showed us a beautiful gym where JA and non-JA teams play basketball, a library of JA historical archives (someone was doing research just then so I didn't have a chance to dig around), a studio for pottery classes, and facilities or facilities under construction for other art studios, including a complete photography darkroom.

The building that the JCCCNC purchased for its operations is deceptively small—it occupies most of a block. Much of the space is taken up by smaller nonprofits for which the JCCCNC serves as an umbrella.

The tour ended with Osaki leading us through a bustling kitchen into a cafeteria full of a couple hundred older Japanese eating lunch and socializing. The scene was profoundly moving because it proved how food and culture can bring a community together to achieve common goals. Osaki explained that the food program is run by Kimochi, one of the many groups based at the JCCCNC, and the vans we saw all weekend were driven by volunteers to deliver food to house-bound clients.

The incredible work of the JCCCNC is managed mostly with the energy and commitment of volunteers and reminds me of the Little Tokyo Service Center (LTSC) in Los Angeles, where longtime executive director Bill Watanabe accomplished similar heroic feats of community building. The LTSC also owns a building, as well as a low-income apartment building called Casa Heiwa, which serves not only Japanese people but all the diverse communities of downtown LA. The LTSC also provides healthcare and classes and offers its constituents access to computers, technology, and the Internet. Watanabe has also overseen the purchase and renovation of a theater nearby. The LTSC is obviously a powerful force in Little Tokyo.

These organizations are essential to the larger Japanese

communities of the major West Coast cities. They're the heart and soul of the population, providing a spirit of cultural renewal and preserving the heritage of the community.

Other organizations are crucial to preserving Japanese-American heritage (for contact information, see the resource list at the back of the book). For example:

The National Japanese American Historical Society (NJAHS), based in San Francisco's J-town but with a new partnership and facility at the Presidio, is a nonprofit organization that preserves, promotes, and disseminates materials relating to JA history and culture. The organization distributes a quarterly publication, *Nikkei Heritage*, that's full of thoughtful articles and essays on a single theme each issue. The NJAHS also creates videos, traveling exhibits, workshops, and other materials to chronicle the JA population.

The Japanese American National Museum (JANM) in Los Angeles, anchoring one corner of Little Tokyo, is a wonderful resource. A permanent exhibit tells the story of the JA community's immigrant roots, the tragedy of the internment years, and the community's rebirth in the decades since the war. The museum also features revolving exhibits of deserving but little-known Japanese American artists, as well as valuable displays that preserve the history of not just the JA community but the entire area's multicultural heritage. In 2002, JANM also organized the first-ever All-Camp Summit of survivors from all the wartime internment camps and held a series of panels about those experiences (for some, it was the first time they had ever spoken about it because of their humiliation and shame), the long road to redress, and the current state of civil rights and prejudice in the country.

The Japanese American Museum of San Jose celebrates the history and culture of JAs in California's Santa Clara Valley. It began as an outreach program, part of a project to research farmers in the area, and grew into a workshop to develop family histories. Part of the small but dedicated Japantown culture that still exists in San Jose, the museum crystallizes the JA community's efforts to preserve the past and hand down cultural traditions to future generations.

Community without J-towns

It's becoming more difficult to identify JA communities because they are increasingly decentralized and nebulous. Whereas the first generation of immigrants were often forced to create Nihonmachi to live and work together in because of racial prejudice and language

Being JA in Texas

There wasn't much of a Nikkei culture there, I think, and even if there was, I guess I never knew about it. All the Nisei were around my age, went to Japanese school, and could at least speak Japanese, regardless of their level of reading and writing skills. Some of my friends had better writing/reading skills, especially because they went through all the grades and actually studied during their years in Japanese school. I think Dallas, when it comes to Japanese people, is mostly dominated by an expat community. There are lots of families that come for business reasons. The Japanese school is probably the center of the Japanese community. Japanese Americans were way in the minority, and I never thought much about Japanese Americanism.

Alisa Sanada, postwar Nisei

WORDS & PHRASES
samui
Cold, used for weather, or personally feeling chilled. "The wind got *samui*. I need a jacket."

Midwestern JA life

I grew up in Kansas City, Missouri, where there were about seven other Japanese families in the area. There was no Japantown or Little Tokyo or other Japanese community, and it pretty much meant we were on our own. In the early years, my friends were Italian-American. In an Italian neighborhood, with black hair and brown eyes, I looked like everyone else. But later in the suburbs, it did not seem to matter very much.

Peggy Seo Oba, Sansei

A community of farmers

Back in the 1930s there were many Japanese families vegetable farming in our area (Ft. Lupton, Colorado), so they purchased a piece of property and built a gathering place and it was called Showa Hall—I assume because it was built during the Showa period. During summer months they taught Japanese to the children.

Jack Kunio Miyasaki, Nisei

and cultural barriers, the history of post–World War II JAs is more about assimilating into the American mainstream. It's common now for JAs to live far apart from each other, in the suburbs of any given city.

Of the forty or more Nihonmachi that were scattered across the country early in the twentieth century, there are only three districts (larger, that is, than ones such as Denver's one-block Sakura Square) left—in Los Angeles, San Francisco, and San Jose. Even along the West Coast, Japantowns aren't as clearly delineated as they used to be, and many of these self-contained districts are slowly fading away as population patterns shift and urban renewal makes way for newer developments. It's a constant struggle. San Francisco's Japantown, for instance, battled urban renewal in the 1960s and 1970s and is now working to find ways to keep its businesses Japanese-owned.

Some Nihonmachi, as in the case of Seattle's Japantown, were the victim of wartime internment when the neighborhood was gutted as businesses and homes were sold off, or deserted and families were shipped off to camps. Even after the war, the former residents and businesses were unable to reclaim the original Nihonmachi. The Japanese supermarket Uwajimaya is one of the few remaining landmarks of that earlier era still standing in what's now part of Seattle's International District.

Seattle's Nihonmachi once flourished. Like similar areas in other cities up and down the West Coast, the district was established by Japanese laborers who immigrated in the late nineteenth and early twentieth centuries. As the city's Japanese community grew with the arrival of picture brides and the birth of the Nisei, these JA families established their own segregated social and economic neighborhood in the south end of Seattle's downtown.

Seattle's Japantown at its peak included homes as well as churches, grocery stores, theaters, language schools, hotels, restaurants, bathhouses, and other businesses serving the Japanese community. The JA population in Seattle reached its high point of about 8,500 in the 1930s, but decreased during the Depression. In 1940, a large part of Japantown was torn down to build a public housing project. The war and evacuation of everyone of Japanese ancestry shut down the district once and for all. Many of the original buildings are still there, at least, and the JA community is now rallying with plans to restore and preserve the heritage of their Japantown roots.

In the postwar years, among the factors that led to the demise of the Nihonmachi in many communities was the pressure to assimilate as Americans, and the need for many JAs to distance themselves from being identified as foreigners. Anti-Japanese feeling still ran strong, especially in California, where decades of tirades against the "Yellow Peril" of Asian immigration had been instilled in the Caucasian majority population. So, moving back to a concentrated Japanese community where their foreign-ness would be emphasized all over again looked less inviting than spreading out into the suburbs and attempting to integrate with the larger culture. Many Japanese simply didn't want to move back to California, where they'd lost everything they had and still weren't welcome. Some had already settled during the war in the Midwest and along the East Coast. There are significant JA populations even today in Chicago and Philadelphia, even without a well-defined Japantown.

A tiny start for a Japanese garden in suburban America.

Because Colorado's governor had invited Japanese to move to the state before internment, a lot of JAs settled in and around Denver and in rural areas where Japanese had already settled in the first decades of the twentieth century. The area around Denver's current Sakura Square development, which was built in 1972, must have looked like Seattle or San Francisco's Nihonmachi in the years immediately following the war. Within a few years, though, many families had moved back to the West Coast to rebuild their lives.

Even then, in many cases, Japanese culture was snuffed out within the home. Only English was spoken among family members, and children were no longer encouraged to take Japanese language or dance classes. Thus, many in the later Nisei and the Sansei generations were cheated out of their heritage. "I never learned our language because of my parents' fear of what might happen to us. I regret to this day not learning at my mother's knee," explained Marge Taniwaki, a Nisei who had been interned at Manzanar as an infant. This was a common experience for young JAs in the years after the war.

For decades, until the "Yellow Power" movement of the 1970s sparked an interest in their heritage, for the sons and daughters of immigrants being American was more important than being Japanese—even if it meant denying the community that had once supplied and supported their values.

Now, the three remaining J-towns are working together to preserve their heritage. San Francisco's Japantown and Los Angeles's Little Tokyo have both been substantially redeveloped since the 1960s

Fifth generation JA still connected

I connect with my Japanese heritage through the traditions that my family participates in, such as *obon odori* or *mochitsuki*. I enjoy eating savory Japanese dishes as much as I enjoy eating Japanese sweets. In order to better understand my Japanese heritage, I studied the Japanese language in college and studied abroad in Japan for a semester. Additionally, there are the small things that I do to relate to my Japanese heritage, such as taking my shoes off at the door, folding plastic bags for storage, or observing Japanese food etiquette.

Craig Hirokawa, Gosei

WORDS & PHRASES

toki-doki

Sometimes, from time to time. "I come here *toki-doki* to try the squid."

Small community

There weren't too many Japanese families in Lodi, California, where I grew up, and we probably knew all of them. I'd say roughly fifteen families or so. Lodi is a very white community, although it is starting to diversify. Asians were like 0.5 percent of the population. There is a substantial Latino population. The Japanese families gathered at the local Buddhist church. I would see Japanese children at Sunday school when I was young and at events like *bon odori*.

Jill Nakawatase, postwar Nisei

Being JA in the South

After World War II, the Yenari family moved to New Orleans where they rented a large house in the suburbs. As the Yenari sons grew up, the Issei often rented extra rooms out to other Nikkei who came to New Orleans to attend school. Many of these Nikkei remembered the wonderful Japanese dishes my grandmother Kaoru would prepare for everyone. This informal boarding house seemed integral to fostering a sense of community among Nikkei in a city with very few Japanese.

Midori Yenari, Sansei

WORDS & PHRASES

gasa-gasa or goso-goso

The act of talking a lot and saying nothing. "Geez, the boss is just *gasa-gasa* all the time. Why do we even have to go to the meetings?"

and 1970s. There are far fewer JAs living in those areas and they've become concentrated hubs of Japanese and JA businesses. San Jose's small Japantown is quaintly intact—its few blocks are marked with historic designation signs, and its small shops and Buddhist church remain in their original buildings, all nestled in a quiet residential neighborhood.

In 2002, the California Japanese American Community Leadership Council, a coalition of JA groups interested in the historic preservation of the remaining J-towns, managed to pass in the California Legislature Senate Bill 307, which provided $150,000 to study what it would take to protect the J-towns' cultural flavor. The law broke new ground in preservation efforts. Instead of designating a specific building or property, the bill targeted the preservation of arts and culture, allowing an entire neighborhood to be designated as a historic ethnic enclave. The bill could ultimately aide in the preservation efforts of any ethnic community in the state.

Also in 2002, California Governor Gray Davis awarded the three J-towns a $1 million grant from funds that had been set aside by the just-passed Proposition 40, which earmarked monies for historic preservation. The communities in Los Angeles, San Jose, and San Francisco are working together to develop preservation plans, and the funds from the two laws are being divided equally among them.

LA's Little Tokyo planned to use its funds to upgrade a garden in the Japanese American Cultural and Community Center, put up historic markers and informational kiosks throughout the district, and paint a mural. All three J-towns will erect an obelisk to mark their shared historic designation.

These communities are looking to the future by preserving—and celebrating—their past. They're an example the JA community throughout the country can follow.

Church life, newspapers, and the Wonder Years

Even without the Nihonmachi, the one place where the Japanese American community continued to evolve was within the churches, where bake sales and Japanese food festivals, Sakura Matsuri, *mochitsuki*, Hina Matsuri, *obon* dances, and JA sports leagues including basketball, baseball, and even bowling served as avenues to pass down the traditions and culture of the Issei to young JAs. The churches were often the only resource available for JA families who wanted their children to attend *Nihongo* classes on weekends.

Another avenue for sharing within the JA community is the

vernacular newspapers that publish news in both Japanese and English. They may have low circulation numbers and only serve small communities, but they maintain the flow of information with news about the local community and Japan, and also provide a vital pipeline for announcements about community events. Japanese community newspapers have included the *Northwest Nikkei* in Seattle, *Nichi Bei Times* and *Hokubei Mainichi* in San Francisco, the *Rafu Shimpo* in Los Angeles (which was founded in 1903), the *Rocky Mountain Jiho* in Denver, and the *Pacific Citizen*, the national newspaper of the Japanese American Citizens League, which is mailed to JACL members for free but is also available to nonmembers via subscription. Of these newspapers, the *Hokubei* and the *Jiho* closed in the 2000s, and the *Nichi Bei* is now published by a non-pofit foundation.

Courtesy Erin Yoshimura.

A family portrait at a Buddhist temple, circa mid-1960s.

The *Rafu Shimpo*'s story is typical of the JA press. The *Rafu Shimpo* (*Ra* comes from the Chinese name for Los Angeles, "Rashogiri," which in common Japanese practice was shortened, and *fu* is Japanese for "prefecture"; *Shimpo* is Japanese for "newspaper") was started as a news bulletin in Japanese for the immigrant community, but the newspaper eventually added an English-language section to serve the burgeoning—and increasingly English-speaking—Japanese-American population. The paper ceased publication when war broke out and JAs were interned. Its publisher, H. T. Komai, was imprisoned in a Justice Department Camp as a leader in the Japanese community and therefore a possible spy. After the war, his son relaunched the *Rafu Shimpo* with a circulation of only 500 in 1946.

Although many magazines aimed at a national Asian Pacific American readership have struggled, there are a couple of publications directed at a Nikkei audience that have found a niche. San Francisco–based *Nikkei Family Magazine*, a publication of the Japanese Community Youth Council (an organization formed to keep JAs in touch with their roots in Japantown), focuses exclusively on the lifestyle and culture of Japanese Americans, with feature stories and profiles. *Nikkei Heritage*, a quarterly magazine of the National Japanese American Historical Society in San Francisco, also spotlights JA culture, but from a historical perspective. Each issue has a theme—in the past the magazine has looked at the history of Japantowns, the effect urban

Pride in Japanese heritage

The more immersed I become in the non-Japanese environment, the more aware I am of being Japanese and am proud of my heritage. I still observe New Year's with the *kadomatsu*, *soba*, and *mochi* soup. But more than external practices, it's that deeply developed sense of being Japanese that reminds me often of who I am.

Frances Kakugawa, Sansei

WORDS & PHRASES
guru-guru
Spinning around. "You're so confused your eyes are going *guru-guru* in your head."

renewal has had on Nikkei communities, and the story of the Military Intelligence Service during World War II.

When my family moved to the Washington, D.C., area from Japan, it didn't occur to my eight-year-old mind that I was suddenly in a non-Japanese environment after having been raised in an almost completely Japanese society. We had moved to a suburb in northern Virginia that was the 1990s TV series *Wonder Years* come to life: homogeneous houses on wide, quiet streets, nicely trimmed lawns, the trees young and small (or nonexistent), and the population mostly middle-class and Caucasian. The Japanese elements of my family were confined to the inside the house: my mom's cooking, some décor, my parents' use of Japanese, and our habit of taking off our shoes at the door. My mom had Japanese friends in the area whom she would visit. Most important was our regular trip to the Japanese grocery store in D.C., where we'd stock up for the following week.

By the time we moved to Denver, I was so Americanized I only thought of myself as Japanese when I was at home. It's different now, of course, and I'm glad I'm connected to my culture—half the fun lies in discovering how Japanese I've been all along, and in nurturing that side of myself so that I can be more aware of and in touch with my roots.

Nikkei, not just JA

I identify myself as a Japanese American, but I use the term Nikkei or Nikkeijin freely. Yes, Nikkei refers to the Japanese stock market index, but that's not what I mean. Nikkei means "of Japanese descent," and Nikkeijin means someone of Japanese descent who is non-Japanese, a citizen of another country. The term includes a significant number of Japanese Canadians and Japanese Latin Americans.

According to a 2012 post on the Web site Japan Talk (http://www.japantalk.com), there are 1,204,205 Nikkei living in the United States. But there were even more in Brazil, over 1,500,000, with significant numbers as well in the Philippines (120,000), the United Kingdom (100,000), and Canada (81,300). There is a large population of Nikkei in China (over 30,000) but fewer numbers in places like northern Europe, India, and Africa (in 1992, Egypt had a Nikkei population of a mere 120!).

The first Japanese-government–sponsored group of laborers was sent to Hawaii in 1885 to work on the sugar and pineapple plantations, but it didn't take long for entrepreneurs to send laborers from Japan elsewhere. In 1886, forty workers were sent by an Englishman to Thursday Island in the Pacific, and a hundred Japanese were sent to a sugar plantation in Australia. The first Japanese immigrants to Mexico were twenty-eight laborers sent to start a farm colony in Chiapas. Japanese didn't arrive in Brazil until 1908, but the Portuguese-speaking country became the largest stronghold of Nikkeijin in Latin America, second only in the Americas to the United States.

The first 790 Japanese landed in Peru in 1899, with a portion of those moving on to Bolivia to work in the rubber forests there. Japanese Peruvians are commonplace enough (there were 55,472 in 1993) that a Japanese Peruvian, Alberto Fujimori (he was nicknamed "Chino" in his country), became Peru's president in 1990. In 2000, he fled the country after a series of scandals. The final scandal was that although he was a Nisei born in Peru, his birth was registered with the Japanese consulate, making him a dual citizen. He never renounced his Japanese citizenship, making him legally ineligible to run for president in Peru, but allowing him to apply for political asylum in Japan, where he stayed until being extradited in 2007 to face several trials. He is currently in prison, though his family has asked for a pardon on medical grounds.

Peruvian Japanese are still embroiled in a controversy over the same internment that JAs were subjected to during World War II. In 1996, almost a decade after the U.S. government's official apology to Japanese Americans for the internment, a class action suit, *Mochizuki v. the United States*, was filed to gain redress for the wartime incarceration of 2,000 Japanese Latin Americans, most of whom were from Peru. When the war began the United States pressured Latin American countries into signing a unity pact to protect the Western hemisphere, which included the forced repatriation of Axis officials through the United States. Peru sent to the United States not only Japanese officials to be repatriated to Japan, but also people who had nothing to do with the Japanese government, including women and children. Many were simply kidnapped by the Peruvian police and handed over to the U.S. authorities. These Latin Americans of Japanese descent, whether citizens of Japan or of Latin American countries, were imprisoned in a U.S. Justice Department camp in Crystal City, Texas, during the war.

Courtesy Lois Hashimoto.

Japanese Canadian girls celebrate the fifteenth anniversary of the Queensborough Japanese School in 1940.

Cherished traditions

I am very American, but still stay close to my Japanese-American heritage. *Oshogatsu, obon,* and some other Japanese traditions are important to me and my family. I also love Japanese food items including *manju/mochi* and certain Japanese dishes.

Bill Imada, Sansei

WORDS & PHRASES

mecha-kucha

All messed up. "How can you figure out what part goes where? It looks all *mecha-kucha* to me."

Growing up Japanese Canadian

My life until the evacuation (when I was almost fourteen) was lived almost entirely within the JC community, except for public school. Of course we went to see American movies (Gene Autry was my idol), but especially when I was younger, I accompanied my parents to see Japanese movies at the Buddhist church in town. These were silent movies, and the Issei man who showed the films did all the vocals, both male and female. I liked the modern romances. There was no kissing in these "picture shows"—the lovers gazed soulfully into each other's eyes. And the heroine would address her loved one as *"anata"* and it seemed to be the equivalent of "dearest."

Fast forward to 1945, I was almost seventeen. I was still in the internment camp of Slocan, which was emptying out quickly as more and more families headed out east to Toronto, to Montreal. A nice young man two or three years older than me walked me home from a dance—probably one of the many "farewell" dances—and before leaving me kissed me lightly on the cheek. I was startled: I think my eyes popped wide open, my mouth gaped like a goldfish. I think I must have frightened poor George with my reaction, because he hurried away, but what I was thinking was: "Wow! Japanese boys kiss! What do you know! Oh wow!" I went to bed really excited and happy.

Lois Hashimoto, Canadian Nisei

Japanese Canadians, eh

The first Japanese Canadian was a sailor and laborer from Yokohama named Manzo Nagano. He arrived in 1877 in Vancouver and worked for seven years before briefly returning to Japan, opening a restaurant in Seattle, and finally settling in Victoria to become a successful businessman and major figure in the local Nikkei community. In 1977, the centennial of Nagano's arrival in Canada was marked by a ceremony naming a mountain after him—an honor yet to be bestowed on any Japanese American.

The first group of contract laborers from Japan arrived in Canada as mineworkers in Vancouver in 1891. The Japanese immigrant experience in Canada was similar to the Nikkei experience in the United States. They fought prejudice and racist legislation, established ethnically segregated communities, brought wives from Japan and began families (the first Canadian Nisei, Katsuji Oya, was born in 1889), formed churches for worship (the first Christian church for Japanese parishioners opened in Vancouver in 1894, and the first Buddhist temple in 1905), started up Japanese newspapers, and found ways to maintain their heritage in the new world.

In 1919, because half of the fishing licenses in British Columbia were given to Nikkei fishermen, the government began reducing the number of licenses made available to anyone "other than white." Japanese immigration was limited several times in the years leading up to World War II. Even though over 75 percent of the 23,303 Nikkei living in Canada at the start of 1941 were Canadian citizens, they were all required to register when war broke out against Japan. Parallel with the JA internment experience, over 12,000 people of Japanese ancestry were evacuated from "protected areas" declared along the coast of British Columbia and sent to internment camps inland. Though not as restrictive as the camps to the south, the Canadian government passed a law that allowed it to sell off the property of the Nikkei that it had held in custody.

Toward the end of the war, Japanese Canadians were allowed to enlist in the military, and many were allowed to resettle throughout the country, so long as they were east of the Rocky Mountains.

Today, the heritage of the Japanese Canadian community is preserved by organizations such as the Japanese Canadian National Museum and the National Association of Japanese Canadians.

CHAPTER 8
Scrapbooking Your History

For many of us, the most tangible record of our family's Japanese roots is the old, dusty photo album. If we dig back far enough, we're all likely to find the same wedding photo of the groom in a Western suit and the bride in a kimono and traditional coiffure, both looking so grim as to belie the notion of a happy occasion that Americans typically associate with weddings. It may be a picture of our grandparents, great-grandparents, or great-great grandparents, but they sure weren't having fun that day. In the case of the bride, it's possible it wasn't a happy day at all, because the marriage was either arranged by the family in Japan, or she undertook a rigorous trip from Japan to the United States as a picture bride only to discover that the photos she'd been sent of her husband-to-be were either taken years before, or that the wonderful life promised in his flowery letters (quite likely written for him by someone else) was purely fiction.

If you don't find rigid wedding photos, you're sure to come across stiff family photos with children looking as uncomfortable as their parents.

My immediate family's photo albums from the 1950s and 1960s aren't so different from those of any other American family—shots of us at tourist attractions, on trips, and during holidays. The albums that include my father's and mother's earlier lives—pre–my brothers and me—show two young people caught up in romance, my dad skinny and handsome in his GI uniform, my mom beautiful as a former "Miss Nemuro" (she was a beauty queen in her hometown of Nemuro) should be.

Holding on to heritage

I consider myself pretty Japanese. But maybe it's more that I'm pretty Japanese American. I still use some Japanese phrases and random vocab. Like *kore kore*, *oisho*, *shoyu*, and things like that just out of reflex. I know how to make Japanese rice well and some other dishes. And I have some frugal/hoarding tendencies with cardboard and things. Japanese snacks are always in stock at my house, as is rice and *ocha*.

Emily Porter, Japanese Caucasian mixed-race Yonsei

Mitsuko and Masao Yoshida settled in Hawaii.

Courtesy George Yoshida.

Photos, postcards, and other memorabilia

During a 1994 trip to Japan to find out more about my father's family history, I was given some photos from his childhood. My grandfather, a carpenter, had come to Hawaii in the early twentieth century and become a successful building contractor in Honolulu. My father was born in Hawaii in 1933. In one photo (see page 129), taken in the late 1930s, my father's family are all staring glumly into the camera. But the little details in the image convey a lot of information despite the stiff, posed portrait. In the sepia-toned picture taken in Hawaii, five boys and three girls flank my grandparents. (My grandfather had given all eight children American first names, so I have to think he had planned to stay in Hawaii.) Both adults are wearing traditional kimono, as are all three daughters. The boys stand straight-backed and wear ties, the two oldest in suits. My father—the youngest son—is the only one wearing shorts, and looks like he'd rather be outside playing.

The family is lined up in front of the kitchen counter, carefully arranged on the shiny wood floor. Curiously for a Japanese family, everyone's wearing *geta* or shoes inside the house except for one of the boys, who's barefoot. In the background is a vase of beautiful Hawaiian flowers, and glass-fronted shelves display china and drinking glasses. Along the top of the wall are several framed pieces—what looks like a maritime print of a ship, a large work of calligraphy, and a photo of the Showa Emperor and Empress—all hung in the typically Japanese style, very high and leaning out at a severe angle, all the easier for people sitting on the floor to look up at.

To the right of the family, frilly, American-style drapes and pull-down window shades partially cover a window that glows brightly with the Hawaiian daylight. Within a couple of years, this light would give way to the dark years of war.

The details are fleeting, but they've been captured forever in family albums. I've always been glad my family kept a lot of photos. I only wish we'd taken movies and, more recently, videos to chronicle our history. With the current popularity of scrapbooking, it's a perfect time to explore your own family history as a JA journey. Ask your relatives for not only photos, but old letters, documents (such as immigration papers, tickets for the ship your ancestors took across the Pacific, documentation from their time in the internment camps), and other bits of family flotsam that capture the essence of the past. Then assemble them into books or collages. Although many families destroyed or left behind memorabilia when they were interned, you may be surprised at what they have been able to save, storing them away in a trunk, an attic, or basement.

One of the great treasures I discovered after my father passed away was his collection of postcards. As a child, I remembered my dad was interested in stamps and went out of his way to buy the first edition of stamps released in Japan. (I got some of those when he died, too.) Because of his interest in stamps, I began collecting stamps when I was a kid. But I had never known that he had a box of fascinating Japanese postcards, some dating back to the early twentieth century, that he could only have collected when he was a kid himself. I was able to show them to my mother, who translated the dates and descriptions on the back for me and, more important, helped me date the postcards according to the Japanese system of naming years by the emperors' reign (for instance, 1939 to us was "Showa 14," the fourteenth year of the reign of Hirohito, the Showa Emperor).

One terrific way of creating a virtual scrapbook that everyone can share is to post all this material and documentation online and create a Web site.

Courtesy Lisa Sasaki.

By the time Nisei and Sansei got married, Western-style formal wear was chosen over traditional kimono. This is a wedding photo from 1941, of Harry and Helen Nitta.

Climbing the Japanese family tree

Possibly the most satisfying way to learn more about your Japanese ancestors is to get a copy of your official family registry, or *koseki*. Since 1872, the *koseki* has been the official record, required by law, of births, deaths, marriages, divorces, and adoptions in every Japanese household. It's a legal document that's filed with the local city government, with a copy at the Ministry of Justice. The *koseki tohon* is the current family registry; the *joseki tohon* is the "emptied" registry of deceased or married family members, with their names crossed out.

A *koseki* looks like a genealogy chart that shows every Japanese citizen's family tree and lists the family's town or village, which for many people has been the same for generations.

Because Japanese immigrants weren't allowed to become U.S. citizens, the Issei registered the birth of their Nisei children with Japa-

Family history

My paternal grandfather had been trained to be a suicide bomber, but the war was already winding up and he didn't become an actual pilot. My maternal grandfather was a college student working at a weapon factory in Hiroshima that was less than 1 kilometer from ground zero. Most of his classmates died instantly, but my grandfather miraculously survived. Both of them are well and active to this day.

Miku Maeda Rager, Shin Issei

Climbing the family tree

I have been working on my family tree. However, due to the small size of my family and my limited knowledge of the Japanese language, I am having a difficult time with the research. I currently have the family tree back to my paternal great-grandfather and back four generations on my mother's side.

Scot Kamimae, Nisei-han

WORDS & PHRASES

onara

Fart. "Gross, Dad—that *onara* is *kusai!*"

nese consulate officials in the nearest U.S. city, to be transferred to the family's hometown *koseki*. If the Nisei were registered on the *koseki*, it officially made them Japanese citizens.

The details of a family's lineage can be revealing. In 1994, with my mother as translator, I was able to get my father's family *koseki* from the city hall of Fukui, near where my father's family originated. We spent three dull but worthwhile hours getting the Asakawa family records and trying to sort out details. We found out my grandfather had already been married and divorced in 1910 before going to Hawaii, and had had a son by his first wife. Inexplicably, the records also showed my grandfather had legally divorced his second wife, my grandmother, after he took the family back to Fukui in 1940, even though she had died in Hawaii the previous year.

The most important piece of information any JA will need when researching a family *koseki* is the village (*mura*), town (*machi* or *cho*), or city (*shi*) where the family ancestors resided. Without that detail, or if you only have the prefecture (*ken*), it will be worse than searching for a needle in a haystack. Once you have the right locale, you must then contact the local authorities to request a copy of the *koseki*. Ideally, you should travel to Japan to ask for the information in person, or have a family member in Japan make the inquiry. The process can be complicated if the village or town of your ancestors has been incorporated into other municipalities.

Once you have the right place, you'll have to find the right government office. This is where it helps if you're there in person, or have someone you trust doing the research (although if you have someone doing the work for you there may be other complications—make sure the person has power of attorney and formal papers proving he or she is working on your behalf). You can contact the office by mail—you can get the proper forms, in English, from the Japanese American National Museum (JANM) in Los Angeles. But the most reliable way to get a *koseki* is to go there in person to ask for it. It doesn't hurt to have your mother there to serve as interpreter and speak with the clerks working in the Japanese bureaucracy.

Once you have your *koseki*, of course, you'll need someone—your mother again—to translate all the information it contains. If she hesitates or gives vague translations, stop and ask for explicit, word-for-word translations. Her reticence could mean there's something juicy in the record that nobody in the family knew before, like an illegitimate child, or a secret marriage.

Some people specialize in helping JAs discover their family history. Chester Hashizume of Los Angeles gives workshops at JANM about how to research this information. JANM has a wealth of information helpful in researching family histories, as do a handful of organizations across the country (see the resources at the back of this book).

Immigration records

As one JA put it regarding having a copy of the ship's manifest that lists your great-grandfather, "It's surprising how comforting it is to know he actually did come." It makes concrete the connection your family has to your ancestors in Japan. It makes tangible the journey your family members undertook to come to this country and start a new life.

Courtesy Glenn Asakawa.

For many JAs whose family settled in the United States in the late nineteenth or early twentieth century, immigration records may be found in the archives for Angel Island in San Francisco Bay where their ancestors almost certainly disembarked. EllisIsland.org includes information on immigrants who arrived on the West Coast. You can also contact the National Archives for passenger lists of immigrants who arrived on ships. The National Archives Web site has forms available for ordering ship passenger arrival records for 1820–1959. You'll need to know as much as possible about your ancestors' arrival, including full name, year of immigration, and if possible, the ship's name.

The Asakawa family pose for a portrait in Hawaii, circa late 1930s. The author's grandfather, Kyutaro Asakawa, was a successful contractor in Honolulu until 1940, when he suddenly decided to move the family back to Japan. The author's father, George Hisayuki Asakawa, is the youngest son, wearing shorts.

Researching internment history

For many JA families, the *koseki* and immigration records are documents of the distant past. A more recent, and perhaps more vivid, piece of family history is the information filed with the U.S. government about every person of Japanese ancestry who was incarcerated during World War II.

Much of the information might be mundane, but some of it could be dramatic and powerfully moving. In many cases, information about the internment years completes a family puzzle with pieces that have been missing—and unspoken of—for decades.

The Hirasaki National Resource Center at the Japanese American National Museum has access to the War Relocation Authority database for every internee. A former internee or family member can go to the museum and look up summaries of the 1942 Form 26, which

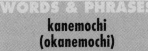

WORDS & PHRASES

kanemochi (okanemochi)

A rich man, as in "Don't make your uncle Joe mad. He's *kanemochi* and you want him to like you."

Yayoi Lena Winfrey, shown here with her mother's family, is the daughter of an African American GI.

Japanese pride

Be proud that you are Japanese—my father told us that constantly, and we were. It gave me the confidence to be myself and not wish that I was white like so many people I know. This confidence relieved me of the burden of having a "chip on my shoulder."

Toshiko Kikuta, Canadian Nisei

shiranai

Don't know. "Uh, what happened to the money you gave me? *Shiranai.*"

was completed by inmates entering the camps directly or through the assembly centers. JANM also has each camp's Final Accountability Roster, which lists individuals by family unit and records when they entered and left the camps.

For individual family records, JANM can provide information on how to order an internee's complete file from the records of the War Relocation Authority at the National Archives in Washington, D.C. You can initiate this process yourself by contacting the National Archives. You'll have to jump through a few hoops before they will release information to you, though.

To locate the right records, they will need as much of the following information as you can provide: your family number if you have it, the name of the evacuee, date of birth, head of family, name of War Relocation Center, and your name and address. You will receive a price quotation for copies in about ten working days. The cost depends on the number of pages in the case file.

If you're requesting information for someone other than yourself, and they were born less than seventy-five years ago, you will need to provide a signed authorization from the internee allowing the administration to release the records to you. It's to protect the internee's privacy. Call or write to the Old Military and Civil Records division at the National Archive and ask for a War Relocation Authority Evacuee Case File Request form. Or go to the Many Mountains Web site and download a copy of the form from http://manymountains.org/pdf/naraWraFileRequest.pdf. (The site administrator, Brian Minami, has put together a wonderful collection of documents, including poetry and oral histories.)

Recording your family history

There's plenty of research you can do on your own to learn more about your family's past. The most powerful connection to your roots will come when you record an oral history, whether it's of your parents, grandparents, great-grandparents, or other family members. The original Nisei generation is quickly passing on—many are already in their 80s—and many have been so deeply affected by the experience of internment that they've gone out of their way to avoid sharing their life stories. Like the traumatized veteran who refuses to tell war stories to his grandkids, an entire generation of JAs has kept mum about their lives.

Now is the time to capture their oral histories, on audio or video. These recordings don't have to be museum quality, but they'll be better resources for future generations if you keep a few simple rules in mind before you set up your camera or tape recorder.

Courtesy JANM.

A display about internment at the Japanese American National Museum in Los Angeles.

- **Do some research first:** Don't just start recording your Auntie Millie and let her roll with her memories. If you do some work upfront and know some of the milestones in her life, you'll be able to guide her memories more effectively and avoid wasting time, tape, or hard drive space.

- **Have materials on hand:** Photo albums or other family artifacts can jog memories or help you guide the interview toward the subjects you're interested in.

- **Be sensitive:** Remember, internment was a particularly traumatic time in many a JA's life. If Auntie Millie isn't going to open up about it on the first interview, don't force it. You're not trying to tape a Barbara Walters tell-all segment.

- **Be sure your subject is comfortable:** You may be at this for a couple of hours, so be sure both you and Auntie Millie are comfortable and relaxed, and that you're facing each other.

- **Check your equipment (and know how to use it):** The worst thing you can do is record an hour of Auntie Millie's precious memories and then discover that the recorder never turned on or the tape broke.

- **Set up properly:** Place the microphone as close as possible to Auntie Millie, and check sound and light levels in the room before you begin.

- **Have the subject ignore the recorder or camera:** Make

Going home to Japan—sort of

It felt like going home in a weird way, yet it was still foreign in that I wasn't fluent in the language. Surprisingly I still felt very much at home, especially when visiting distant cousins who still live in my grandfather's hometown of Tana.

Midori Yenari, Sansei

takai

Literally high, but if used in the context of prices, expensive. Handy word in American restaurants when you want to complain. "Gee everything here is so *takai*."

Making mochi *at New Year's in Sunnyvale, California, 1961.*

Courtesy Barbara Horiuchi.

A business that connects to Japan

I'm part-owner of Nikkei Traditions [a shop in Japantown in San Jose, California]. The store puts me in a very unique position to reach out more by requiring that I learn and research when reviewing products for the store. I am also involved with the *kime-komi* doll craft.

Pam Yoshida, Sansei

ganbatte

A variant of *gaman* that's an imperative statement: "Come on, don't be a wuss. You can run five more laps! *Ganbatte!*"

it a conversation with you, not the camera or microphone. It'll help Auntie Millie to stay relaxed and to think of more stories if she's in eye contact and facing you at all times.

- **Start broad and narrow it down:** Start the interview with general background questions and get more specific, digging for more detailed information as you go along.

- **Save difficult, controversial, or potentially disturbing questions for later:** They won't be as disruptive if Auntie Millie is already in the groove.

- **Make your questions short and direct, and ask only one at a time:** Save your follow-ups until after Auntie Millie has answered the first question.

- **Keep your questions open-ended:** Avoid questions that can be answered with a "Yes," "No," or other simple reply. Your questions should be a starting point from which the stories can flow; they're not just to extract specific information. Ask questions about how or why things happened, or ask about how she felt during a certain situation, or her opinion about something. Open-ended questions will prompt longer, deeper responses.

- **Pay attention but don't interject:** Maintain eye contact and use facial expressions and body language to show you're listening and paying attention. Don't jump in with extraneous comments that break Auntie Millie's train of thought. And avoid "filler" responses that don't mean anything, such as "sure," "yes," and "uh huh." You'll regret it later if you keep hearing yourself on the recording, and it's distracting.

- **Take notes:** You'll be glad to have notes as a way to ask follow-up questions, clarify information, and to compare against the recording later to know where you are in the interview.

- **Keep the recorder on:** Unless there's an interruption, such as a phone call or a visitor, don't turn off the recorder even if Auntie Millie wants to say something off the record. You can edit out comments later if you have to.

- **Keep the interview about the subject:** Remember, this is about *her*, not about you. Let Auntie Millie tell her story and don't jump in with your reactions or comparisons to your life.

- **Get permission:** If you're going to be using the interview or transcript for any purpose other than for your private family use—say you want to donate a transcript to a library, university, museum, or organization—remember to respect Auntie Millie's privacy. Get her permission and have her sign a legal release form.

Courtesy Midori Yenari.

The Yenari family on the steps of their Boyle Heights home in 1920s Los Angeles.

Preserving your family's legacy

The final thing you can do to hold on to your heritage is to care for the artifacts that contain that legacy. This means more than just the photo albums and home movies stacked in the closet, but also the clothing, artwork, documents, recordings, and other objects that have been passed down through the generations or simply stored away.

There are a multitude of rules for museum-quality preservation of collections. But even following some simple rules of thumb will help save your private collection for future learning and sharing.

- **Make an inventory:** You're working with antiques and historical records. Be careful with everything, but make an inventory so you'll know what you have. Treat everything as if you could make a fortune off it on *Antiques Roadshow*.

- **Control the environment:** The first rule of preservation is to minimize humidity and temperature extremes. Don't store artifacts near sources of heat (like stacked next to the water heater) or where it's damp (like near a washer/dryer). At

Blending in in Japan

I'm lost in Japan right now. Actually, I'm not really lost. I know where I am (on a bullet train to Kyoto). And I'm not hungry, or thirsty, or in need of shelter, or anything like that. And I'm not really searching for directions (though I did get lost in Tokyo's Narita Airport and subway system). However I think I've lost my identity. My individuality. In Colorado, I stuck out. I'm "That Asian Guy." Here in the Land of the Rising Sun, it's different. I'm just another guy on this bullet train. Just another Asian face in a sea of Asian faces. You could mistake me for that businessman with a cell phone glued to his ear, or that student reading a book. For the first time in my life I'm just a "Regular Joe."

Scott Takeda, Yonsei

Issei Kaoru Sato Yenari and her eldest son, Hajime, in the kitchen of their Tacoma, Washington, home (circa 1917).

Courtesy Midori Yenari.

Coming to America

In the early 1900s, my grandfather Seo gambled his passage money away and was given a loan by a man he met in Yokohama.

Peggy Seo Oba, Sanseii

yakamashii

Noisy, fussy, often used for children. *"Yakamashii!* Stop your complaining!"

the very minimum keep the environment stable—if it's cold, it should always be cold, not fluctuate up and down.

- **Protect the collection:** Keep artifacts out of harm's way and protect them as much as possible from flooding, fire, and pests such as rodents or insects.

- **Don't just handle with care—don't handle, period:** Once you've decided to add something to your family's archival collection, put it away. If you'll need it frequently, make a copy or take photos if it's an object. If you must handle an artifact, use cotton gloves to protect it from the oils on your fingers.

- **Keep out of direct light:** Especially for photographs, documents, and artwork, direct light can be harmful. When your artifacts are stored, they should be stored in the dark.

- **Keep them separate:** For documents, photos, artwork, or photo albums, place acid-free paper between pages or photos, and place negatives in individual sleeves. There are a number of archival elements you can purchase, such as acid-free mounting corners for photos, or polyethylene or polypropylene sleeves without "plasticizers" to protect loose photos and negatives. Never laminate photos or documents in an attempt to protect them.

- **Don't use tape:** Don't use tape to display photos or documents, and don't use tape on the backs of photos or documents that are torn.

- **Care for old home movies:** Movie film—usually cellulose nitrate or cellulose acetate—will deteriorate with time. Moisture, heat, and acids hasten the process. If your old movies smell like vinegar, your acetate film is breaking down and becoming brittle. Keep film reels in a cold, dry place (but don't refrigerate), and if possible, professionally transfer the images to video or digital formats.

- **Care for videotapes:** Keep videos out of sunlight and away from sources of magnetic fields (TVs, electrical appliances, and power tools). Snap out the tab on the spine of the tape so that it can't be accidentally recorded over.

- **Remove staples and paper clips:** When storing your collection, discard staples, paper clips, pins, and even Post-It notes. They can rust or damage important documents.

- **Roll textiles:** Flat textiles such as towels and tablecloths can be rolled up for storage.

- **Don't use dry cleaner bags:** If you're storing clothing on hangers, do not use dry cleaner bags to protect them. Such plastics contain chemicals that can alter colors.

If you follow these rules, you'll have artifacts that will last for generations, and in the event you donate your collection to a museum, they'll be well on their way to meeting the museum's standards for archival storage. Either way, you're preserving the past for the future.

The importance of family and community history

For me, understanding my history is what makes me feel most connected to my Japanese roots. Knowing the story of Japanese internment continues to remind me of the perseverance and strength the Issei and Nisei generations had and grounds me in the understanding of where Japanese Americans, and by extension Asian Americans, fit into the hierarchy in this country. Also, studying my family's genealogy has helped me feel more connected because I have been able to identify with specific towns, cities, and prefectures and have a better sense of where my family comes from.

Craig Hirokawa, Gosei

Homeward Bound

Traveling to any foreign country for the first time can be both thrilling and nerve-wracking. Everything is new and exciting, but you're truly a stranger in a strange land. For Japanese Americans traveling to Japan, the trepidation can be heightened because of the disconcerting feeling that everything is new but somehow familiar at the same time. Everywhere you look, everyone looks like us. That's what we think, anyway. The Japanese around us know in an instant, even before we open our mouths and speak in our halting, broken *Nihongo*, that we're not one of them. We're still outsiders, even in the land of our ancestors.

The feeling of being an outsider can be acute, but traveling anywhere outside your home environment is one of the surest ways to break down the barriers between people. Just seeing other cultures expands your world view and makes you appreciate where you came from and respect where others live. And if you're a Nikkei a trip to Japan can be an eye-opener for many reasons.

Even though I was born and raised in Japan as a kid—or perhaps because of it—I was reluctant to visit Japan when I got older. The main reason, I'll admit now, was my shame and embarrassment at not being able to speak Japanese anymore. Now that I'm older, I frankly don't care about my shortcomings and am happy to stumble along with my limited child's vocabulary combined with a fair-to-middling accent. Now I revel in standing out and I'm not afraid to let Japanese know that I'm Japanese American, and not quite one of them.

I've known many JAs who say they've never thought about visiting Japan. I sometimes wonder if deep down they feel that way for the same reason that I was initially reluctant to go visit the land of my ancestors.

Visiting Japan was like going home

I visited Japan when I was in high school on an exchange program for one month. It was a wonderful experience. When I looked around and was surrounded by Japanese people everywhere . . . I felt as if I had come home to my motherland! I remember feeling totally connected like I belonged there! I'd love to go back with my mom and kids!

Cindy Yoshida-Moromisato, Yonsei

When in Japan

I felt like a strange alien who looked like everyone else but thought and spoke completely differently.

Glenn Asakawa, Sansei

Disadvantages of being JA

Your parents tell you to be proud of your heritage because you are Japanese, but the Japanese don't think of you as Japanese and will flat out tell you, "You're not Japanese."

Masaye Okano Nakagawa, Sansei

Whiteness

I am SOOOOO white. I wish I knew more (about Japanese culture). I don't blame my parents since they were second and third generations themselves. And I hear lots of stories of how hard it was for them to be post–World War II kids, so their experience was far different from mine. However, I do wonder sometimes where I belong. When I went to Japan, it was very clear to me that I didn't belong there. I didn't look Japanese. I certainly didn't act Japanese, but I was.

Scott Takeda, Yonsei

Prefectural ties

My mother worked in the summer for a fellow Kumamoto-ken (Prefecture) family who owned a vegetable farm. There was a strong feeling of kinship among *Ken-jin* (prefecture people), I noticed. I often accompanied my mother to the farm when I was little, and to this day, my closest Japanese friend is the daughter of this farm family friend.

Lois Hashimoto, Nisei

WORDS & PHRASES

a-reh

"Hey" or "What?" "A-reh! What's going on here?"

That's the first thing that JAs must overcome if they are to enjoy traveling to Japan: accepting the fact that they aren't Japanese and not feeling as if they have to live up to an expectation of being Japanese. Caucasians don't feel any such pressure when they go to Japan. Because of their height/hair/skin color, they're already a novelty—the "other"—in Japan, so even the littlest attempt to be Japanese, such as learning a little bit of the language, elicits appreciative "oohs" and "aahs."

Not so for Nikkeijin who go to Japan.

It's easy to feel that because we look like the Japanese at first glance, we're expected to speak and act like them, too. If we don't measure up, we make ourselves feel as if we're deficient somehow. Looking Japanese and acting American isn't a novelty in Japan as it is for Caucasians who look American and act Japanese. If we act a little bit Japanese, the people there feel we're not Japanese enough, or at least that's what we say to ourselves. It's a lot of pressure to bear—self-inflicted perhaps, but it's there nonetheless. I've spoken with JAs who were treated rudely in Japan for this very reason. On the other hand, I've also known JAs who got along fine, just as I did when I first returned to Japan as an adult.

Strangers in a familiar land

When I entered a store while exploring Tokyo on my own, I was careful to announce right away, *"Sumimasen, watashi wa Amerika-jin desu. Watashi wa Nikkeijin no Sansei, to Nihongo ga totemo warui desu."* It's probably incorrect, but what I was trying to say was "Excuse me, but I'm an American, a Sansei Japanese American, so my Japanese is very poor."

That always elicited smiles of appreciation and exclamations of surprise. What's more, it broke the ice and everyone was friendly toward me. I found again and again that if I just acted natural and made an effort to communicate with the Japanese, I got along just fine.

Before one trip to Japan, my mother insisted that I go out and buy a nice-fitting plain suit and some "normal" clothes instead of the colorful, baggy, and generally extroverted clothes I was used to wearing. She didn't want me to stick out in Japan. It's certainly true that Japan is a stunningly conformist society—at least on the surface, and if you focus on the older generations. Most Japanese businessmen wear blue, black, or gray suits with quiet ties over a white shirt. Anything else would bring attention to oneself. Women, too, wear conservative, usually monotone outfits. Japanese children are taught such habits early, with their dark blue or black public school uniforms (with pleated skirts and blouses with sailor collars for girls) drumming conformity into their lives. Even the roads are monochromatic. If you see a brightly colored car zip by, you can bet it's either a foreigner or an uppity Japanese who imported a foreign car in a foreign color.

But don't let the pressure to be Japanese keep you from going to Japan. For a Japanese American, such a trip can be like going home.

There's an incredible rush for any JA—but especially for a JA who's not from the West Coast where Asians are common—who steps off the plane at Narita International Airport and sees so many Japanese faces, so many short people, so much black hair (and lots of black hair dyed brown, which is popular these days), everywhere you look.

And if you're open to and curious about Japanese culture and are not ashamed to let people know right away—and with pride—that you're a Japanese American (it seems to help if you tell them which generation you are), you'll find that the Japanese are as open and as nice to you as they are to other visiting foreigners. Sure, there may be some people who are rude because they expect you to speak and act more Japanese, but I bet you'll find many more people who are accommodating and welcoming.

Despite the language barrier, everything can seem oddly familiar to a Japanese American. In the cities this is true because *romaji*, the Roman alphabet, is so commonplace. Many products, brands, and even companies are familiar American icons: KFC, McDonald's, Dunkin' Donuts, Pizza Hut, and even Starbucks. They may have Japanese-oriented products (McD's has a Teriyaki McBurger, and you can get squid on your pizza), but you won't feel like a total stranger.

Photo by Glenn Asakawa.

Clockwise from rear left, Junko Asakawa, Mitsu Mori, Michelle Asakawa, Sage Asakawa, and McKenna Asakawa represent four generations of the Japan-America experience. This photo was taken during a family trip to Nemuro, Japan, during an annual festival.

Ways to go

There are any number of ways to go to Japan, starting with planning your own trip, whether it's a solo trek with overnight stays at hostels or *ryokan*, traditional inns, to elaborate package tours for a large group set up by an agency.

One way that's especially popular with young people is the Japan Exchange and Teaching Programme. You have to be young to

The burden of being JA

One thing that impacted how I see myself in relationship to my heritage is something my father once said to me when I was in high school. It was basically this: Every day when I am in public I represent my family and my community. While it is in no way fair or right, people see me first as Japanese. Whenever I do something wrong, people won't say, "Boy, that Lisa is a bad person." Instead they say something like "Boy, that Japanese girl was rude/mean/inconsiderate/etc." Over time, that comment could easily change into "Japanese are rude/mean/inconsiderate," especially if they happened to run into another Japanese (or Asian) person who confirmed that statement. My father's point was that, as a minority in America, I didn't have the luxury of anonymity, blending in with the white majority of brunettes and blondes. My behavior would not reflect solely upon me, but be painted onto unsuspecting Japanese everywhere. I was, therefore, an ambassador for my heritage. My father pointed out that Japanese Americans had gone from being hated and feared at the end of World War II to being respected members of the community today. He credited this transformation to the hard work of my grandparents and other Issei and Nisei who proved to their white neighbors through their actions that they were trustworthy, hardworking citizens of the United States.

Lisa Sasaki, Yonsei

be part of the JET Programme. The upper age limit serves to encourage young people right out of college to spend a year as paid English teachers in schools throughout Japan.

Exchange programs—whether they are operated through high schools, colleges, or friendship organizations such as People to People or Sister Cities International—also can arrange for Americans to go to Japan. JAs are likely to be well-served by latching onto one of these opportunities, because they often offer better prices than traveling as a tourist.

I managed a trip to Japan in the mid-1990s by attending the Japan-America Grassroots Summit. The Grassroots Summit is sponsored by the Manjiro Society for International Exchange, a nonprofit organization with offices in Tokyo and just outside Washington, D.C. The organization is named after Manjiro Nakahama, the shipwrecked fisherman who was the first Japanese to set foot on U.S. soil. His legacy inspired the Manjiro Society, which holds Grassroots Summits in Japan one year and the United States the next. People from each country converge for a week's worth of panels, homestays, and guided tours geared toward bringing people from both countries closer.

Before my 1995 trip, I half-expected the journey to be an elaborate package tour. Nobody could explain to me what happened at the summit. Would there be panel discussions? Lectures? Historical presentations? Sightseeing?

It turned out to be all of the above, and more. Attendance at the summit also included a two-night homestay with a Japanese family. The homestay is what makes the summit truly a grassroots experience. After attending the summit, the American participants—there were about two hundred, several dozen of whom were from Colorado—came home with a better understanding of how the Japanese live their day-to-day lives.

The one-on-one familiarity that comes from understanding seemed more crucial that year than at any time since the end of World War II. The fiftieth anniversary of the war added an emotional edge to already tense relations between the two countries, including controversies on both sides over the various commemorations of the war, difficult trade negotiations, and the massive public protests against the U.S. bases in Okinawa following the rape of an Okinawan teenager by three American servicemen. The homestay segment of the summit bridged the gap and reminded us that behind national differences lie plenty of individual similarities.

The summit took place in Kagoshima, a beautiful port city at the southern end of Kyushu that has as its centerpiece Sakurajima, a live and smoking volcano in its bay. I'd never visited anywhere south of Hiroshima, and it was a wonderful experience going to Kyushu.

Because of Sakurajima's majesty, I had decided on a homestay in Kagoshima to get to know the city and its volcano better. Attendees chose in advance from ten regional homestay locations, including remote villages such as Wadomari on Okinoerabu Island, a two-hour flight from Kagoshima, and Nishinoomote City on the island of Tanegashima, the headquarters of Japan's space program.

One reason it's hard to describe the summit is that much of its programming structure depends on where you spend your homestay. This particular summit opened with an afternoon of welcome speeches in Tokyo, but after a day of cultural performances (traditional music, dance, and a tea ceremony) and history lectures in Kagoshima, the attendees split into small groups according to their homestay locations. For the next two days, each locale planned its own agenda, from loosely structured sightseeing to quite serious panel discussions.

The Kagoshima homestay group spent the first day meeting with the city's mayor and lunching at City Hall, sitting through more history lessons, which are enlightening but a burden to endure during such an otherwise exciting experience, and a brief but beautiful traditional dance performance at a reception where we met our hosts for the next two nights. Then the eight of us in the Kagoshima group went off with our homestay families for our unique one-on-one experiences.

Not everyone got a real-life look at daily Japanese living, though. One Caucasian art teacher from Colorado who had his homestay in Wadomari had a wonderful time. But he was treated like a visiting dignitary, and villagers dressed their best to come visit him and take his picture. I doubt he got an accurate view of those villagers' lives. And some Americans got to see a somewhat privileged view of Japanese life, because they were assigned to wealthy homestay families and were showered with extravagant gifts.

Luckily, my homestay was with an unusually large (for Japan) family that doesn't live extravagantly and didn't treat me like a curiosity. Mr. and Mrs. Yamashita have eight kids who range in age from seven to twenty-three. Tsutomu Yamashita is a professor at the local technical college who works the long hours typical of Japanese employees; I didn't get to spend much time with him. Sayoko, my fifty-one-year-

A tranquil garden in Japan.

We're foreigners in Japan

I usually go every other year. I like Japan but often feel a bit odd when I am there. We look Japanese, but are not fully Japanese. Even the Japanese consider us foreigners. We have to write our names in katakana because we are foreigners in the eyes of many Japanese. Using our family kanji name is considered impolite and inappropriate.

Bill Imada, Sansei

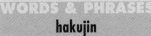

WORDS & PHRASES

hakujin

Caucasian (race is important—too important, I would say—to Japanese). "You're dating a *hakujin?* Do your parents know?"

Traveling to Japan

It felt so weird for everyone to be Japanese like me—blending in totally instead of standing out, being obviously different. Also, it felt claustrophobic in Japan. I also saw why my mom preferred the greater openness of America in terms of class differences and how they restrict people in Japan. Japanese society is very racist.

June Inuzuka, Sansei

Asking parents

My father was a traveling book salesman from Fukuoka, and met my mother on the job! They fell in love and had a son in 1908 (apparently before they were married, according to my eighty-seven-year-old American cousin), and my father caused great displeasure to my maternal grandparents. When my brother Kay (Katsuyuki) was two, my father came to Canada to seek a better life for his family. I don't know what kind of jobs he held in the first four or five years—I'd love to know, but when you're a kid, and growing up, you're so self-absorbed you don't think of asking these things, and then you're a grownup (supposedly, anyway) and you're absorbed with bringing up your own kids and providing for them, and so you still don't wonder about these things, 'til suddenly, it's too late! So many, many things I want to know, and yet, I wonder, would they have told me everything if I had thought to ask?

Lois Hashimoto, Nisei

old homestay "mother," was a housewife who volunteers with the local traditional dance troupe. She's a progressive woman who often invites foreigners to stay with her family to expose her children to people from other cultures. She speaks close to fluent English, as opposed to my stumbling Japanese. She used to run a restaurant in Kagoshima, and dreams of selling her local specialty, a deep-fried, meat-filled potato dumpling called *koroke*, in an American fast-food chain.

We spoke and shared ideas and knowledge for the next two days about the education system in Japan (she thinks it asks too much of her children); about racism; about the difference between Japanese and American work ethics; about things that affect our lives, not just our countries.

She took me to the 120-year-old local elementary school that her youngest children walk to every day; the local hospital, where her older son Shinya was having his sore throat investigated by a doctor (the prognosis: he didn't want to go to school); and Kagoshima's downtown entertainment district, where hundreds of bars with tiny, discreet square signs attract the working population after office hours. I slept on the floor on a futon, used their Japanese-style *ofuro* bath, and ate sukiyaki communally with the family.

Somewhere in between the talking and eating, we also squeezed in a lot of sightseeing, including a breathtaking ferry ride and a drive halfway up Sakurajima's smoking spout (the first night in Kagoshima it erupted in a fountain of ash that forced contact lens wearers to switch to their glasses). We also visited the mountainous area around Kirishima (a hot spring resort north of Kagoshima) and the local botanical gardens, where a Chrysanthemum Festival was being held.

I also did my best to have a cultural exchange at the most basic level: I ate as much Japanese food as I could, from *udon* noodles to a local rice-dumpling snack specialty called *janbo*. And of course I had the freshest sushi I had ever tasted in my life.

The climactic moment of the trip came at the end of the homestay, when all the American participants gathered back in downtown Kagoshima to join in an annual street festival parade. We were given short, festive *happi* coats to wear, and were instructed to watch the Japanese around us for cues to the dance movements.

The sweetest moment was later that same night when the Colorado delegation, including members of the Japan-America Society of Colorado, gathered at the dock after a ferry-boat farewell party and began singing "Moonlight Over Colorado" amid the tearful farewells, as an invitation to the 1996 Manjiro Summit in Colorado Springs.

The most lasting moment for me will be when I first stepped into

Sayoko Yamashita's home and in her family's doorway saw a crudely drawn sign with a Japanese and U.S. flag crossed and the words "Welcome Gilbert" written across it. The sentiment was sincere, and for the first time during my trip to Japan, I truly felt welcome.

Getting young people to Japan

It's one thing for older JAs—the Nisei or Sansei who are in their fifties, sixties, or older—to avoid traveling to Japan. At least the older JAs are likely to have had more exposure to their heritage just from their upbringing. It's the younger generations—the Yonsei, Gosei, and now the Rokusei—who are increasingly removed from their root culture, and for whom traveling to Japan can be a critical, life-changing opportunity.

Guess which one is the Japanese American visiting Japan on a business trip? The karaoke singer holding the microphone.

Many Japanese-language classes and JA churches regularly organize group trips to Japan. There are usually parents or teachers who come along as guides and chaperones, and the programs often include homestays with Japanese families and portions of the trip planned as packaged tours.

Several years ago, I watched enviously as a group of Japanese American kids from the Denver Buddhist Temple's Japanese language class left Denver International Airport on a ten-day trip with their teacher. The children ranged in age from ten to fifteen, and at departure they were more excited to be going on a long trip without their parents than they were to be seeing a foreign country.

At least the language barrier had already been scaled—or so I hoped—since the kids attended Japanese class together, and they'd received an introduction to common phrases and greetings. The problem, of course, was that some of the kids—especially the teenagers—may not have taken the class very seriously, as just a chance to socialize. They may have arrived in Japan just as green and unprepared as any other casual tourist.

Parents scrambled to make sure their little travelers had the essentials: passport, spending money in yen, and some knowledge about Japan garnered from introductory videos for the trip. For this the teenagers' response was "Why should I watch a video about Japan when I'm going to be there in person next week?"

Once in Japan, the trip was fantastic for the kids. They arrived

Advantages of being JA

How can one adequately express the gratitude and joy one feels for being allowed to have understanding and profound awareness of the strengths and weaknesses of two vastly different cultures? It is a terrible thing to be in the midst of the maelstrom, but when one is able to step back and see the big picture—to see more clearly the beauty of disparate cultures, and to bridge the gaps and sometimes even promote intercultural understanding and compassion—then one can inwardly rejoice and be thankful. Amen.

Eri Izawa, postwar Nisei

in Nagoya and moved on to Toyohashi, a small inland city, for their homestays. There, the kids met with the city's mayor and spent a day at a middle school to see how their peers in Japan spend their school days (the Americans were most shocked by the required school uniforms).

Such striking differences and the many surprising similarities are the things that should impress any young JA who visits Japan. Kids may find some of their trip to Japan a bore. But they'll come back with a profound appreciation for the country. Their connection to Japan won't be limited to just rice with dinner anymore. They'll have places and faces in their minds when they think of the country of their heritage.

Tips for your trip

Two common words of advice for any international travel are especially important in the case of Japan: Pack light. Not only will you find yourself dragging your luggage through huge international airport concourses and waiting in line at customs, you'll probably be carrying your bags onto buses and trains. Rooms in hotels and private homes can be severely small, like a one-person college dorm room. And, you'll want space for the souvenirs you'll be carting back from Japan.

Mix and match your clothes so you can wear them multiple times during your trip. Choose slip-on shoes if you're staying at someone's home because you'll have to take them off and put them on every time you come and go, and you won't always have room in the *genkan* portico to sit or kneel to tie your shoelaces.

If you're still hung up on the language barrier, there are high- and low-tech tools to help. See the chapter "Language" for high-tech solutions. The low-tech solution is of course a trustworthy English-Japanese dictionary or phrasebook. Memorize the most common helpful words, like *toire* (the Japanized version of "toilet") for "bathroom," *sumimasen* for "excuse me," *gomen nasai* for "I'm sorry."

For more advanced communications, technology has made possible the Wordtank, a calculator-sized way to read *kanji*. You enter the number of strokes that make up the character of interest and then scroll down until you see the one you're looking for. Once you have the pronunciation, it's handy if you have the dictionary—or someone with a larger Japanese vocabulary than you, but who can't read any Japanese. That describes Erin and me—she can read and write some Japanese but doesn't know many words. So when we travel in Japan, she can read the words out loud on signs and menus, and I'll translate them for her. We make a great team.

As part of your trip preparations, you'll have to stock up on the *omiyage* gifts that I mentioned in Chapter 3 for anyone you'll be meeting in Japan. Your long-lost family members or your generous homestay family will appreciate a nice gift. But not too nice, or it will put pressure on them to reciprocate. For travelers, the gift should ideally reflect your home. Be careful that it is not manufactured or printed in Asia, though. It's seen as rude to take anything made in Asia as a gift from the United States. Aside from hometown souvenirs, popular *omiyage* include packets of gourmet coffee for the adults, a Colorado Rockies baseball team magazine for boys, or a teen celebrity magazine for the girls. American pop culture is always a winner with young Japanese. You can take CDs, but avoid DVDs because they are likely to be coded to prevent them from working in DVD players in Japan.

Once you're in Japan, learn to spot the friendly neighborhood *koban* police stations where impeccably uniformed policemen can be incredibly helpful, even if they can speak little English. Besides, they don't have a whole lot to do. It's true that to a large degree Japan is relatively crime-free. Don't be shocked to find people who don't lock their doors, or leave their bicycles unchained at the crowded racks at train stations all day.

Typical guidebooks for travelers to Japan will have advice such as don't leave a tip for service workers and don't open your own taxi door (most taxi drivers will open the passenger door for you with an inside lever). But for JAs, the main advice I'd give is to be yourself and be proud you're an American, but at the same time stay curious and open to all things Japanese. Remember, you have one advantage over other Western tourists flocking to Japan: deep down, you're one of them, and the best thing about going there is that it'll awaken the Japanese in you.

Not visiting Japan

I have not visited Japan and until now, have not wanted to visit. I must confess that as time passes, I do fear that I may regret not going.

I have not wanted to visit because I do not speak Japanese. I have heard negative things from people who were obviously not well prepared for their visits.

Toshiko Kikuta, Canadian Nisei

Every visit to Japan brings discoveries

I have visited Japan several times, and I absolutely love it. From Tokyo to the Yanbaru of Okinawa, I feel very much at home and very much like a tourist at the same time. Each time I go is filled with amazing discoveries.

Susan Hamaker, mixed-race Nisei

JAs
Tomorrow

AAPI, Not Just JA

It's a fact: Japanese Americans are a shrinking community. While all other Asian Pacific American populations are growing, the JA population dwindled between 1990 and 2000, according to the U.S. Census, from 863,811 to 796,700 (Nikkei population numbers vary depending on the source). While the Asian Indian community in the United States grew by almost 110 percent, the Vietnamese community by 87 percent, Chinese by 48 percent, Korean by 35 percent, and Filipino by 31 percent, the number of Japanese dropped by almost 8 percent.

One of the main reasons is that JAs have the highest outmarriage rate of any Asian Pacific Islander population—close to 80 percent at its peak in the late 1980s.

This means that as a community, we face different challenges in maintaining our cultural traditions. It means we have an obligation to embrace diversity and accept mixed-race children as Japanese Americans. And, it means we have to work a little harder with both our *hapa,* or mixed-race members, as well as the full-blooded Yonsei, Gosei, and Rokusei to pass along our heritage and history. Because the JA community was established so long ago, the younger generations are naturally more assimilated into the larger American culture.

I know middle-aged JAs whose parents and grandparents encouraged them to be good Americans: get good grades, go to a good college, get a good job, work hard, avoid making waves—a byproduct of the internment experience. A consequence of the push for assimilation into the mainstream was the propensity of JAs to leave behind their Japanese culture, and also to date and marry non-Japanese.

In 2000, there were around 2.1 million Asian Pacific Americans of mixed heritage. For the first time ever, the 2000 Census allowed

The role of a mixed marriage

I've come to appreciate my culture and heritage more as I grow older and thankfully due to my wife, Michelle (who is Caucasian), who has taken an active role in helping me understand the significance of my culture and what it means to our two daughters.

Glenn Asakawa, Sansei

The future

JA culture will disappear. Most of the Nisei in the Seattle area have decided they know everything there is to know and don't need any Sansei to help with any of the organizations. They have a fatalistic attitude toward anything the Sansei try to do. I worked with a community group called Warashibe-kai that was attempting to organize all the JA organizations under one umbrella. We were trying to raise money to get the organization going. All the Nisei involved did everything they could to make the fundraising efforts fail.

A very visible organization is the Nisei Veterans organization in Seattle. They have never invited any of the Korean or Vietnam vets. There was a movement to get younger people involved so they created the Seattle Sansei organization. The Seattle Sansei became the worker bees for the Nisei Vets and had no part in the decision-making process. The Nisei Vets organization is shrinking as they die off. They have a ton of money and property but no one to use it due to their selfishness. In a few years the last World War II vet will be gone and so will the organization.

The JACL does nothing to create a community. They do nothing other than send milquetoasty protest letters and collect money for ridiculous political lobbying. In my opinion the JACL is similar to the NAACP, which is stuck in the past and has no future.

Scot Kamimae, Nisei-han

people of mixed race and mixed ethnicity to mark themselves as such. The count made a difference. Behind the Chinese, the largest AAPI population, *hapa* made up the second-largest subgroup.

Hapa has become a common term for mixed-race Asians, and these days it's even used by non-Asians who are mixed race. *Hapa* is a Hawaiian word that means "part" or "mixed." Originally it had no racial or ethnic connotation. After the arrival of European and American plantation owners to Hawaii, the phrase *hapa haole* was used to describe Hawaiians who intermarried with the landowners. (*haole* is Hawaiian for "foreigner"). The later Japanese laborers who came to Hawaii in the late 1800s adopted the term *hapa*. (Japanese also use the more pejorative *hafu,* or "half.") Today, the word *hapa* includes AfroAsians, Eurasians, Latin Asians, Native Asians, and mixed AAPIs.

According to the census, almost a third of JAs are *hapa* (30.6 percent). The numbers are a reflection not only of the post-internment assimilation process, but also of the fact that many JAs are the children of postwar marriages between American GIs and Japanese women. This military attraction has continued for as long as U.S. forces have been stationed in Japan (I'm a result of this process, since my Hawaiian-born father met my Hokkaido-born mother while he was stationed in Japan during the Korean War). Although I'm not *hapa,* I share an important distinction with the *hapa* children of the U.S. military who were raised overseas on military bases in Japan or other countries: we grew up isolated from JA communities and didn't grow up with JA friends and support groups within the JA Buddhist or Christian churches, and we didn't have extended families to celebrate holidays and special events.

In addition, there's a new wave of Japanese immigrants creating a different set of Issei, Nisei, and Sansei dynamics. The Shin Issei are Japanese who have arrived in American more recently than the first generation more than a century ago. They have come for school, for work, or on diplomatic assignment and stayed in the United States. I fit into this category also, since my family first moved to the States in 1966. Yet I feel as American as any kid raised here. For a child of a Shin Issei family, being Japanese is a fresher experience than it is for a JA kid the same age from a Sansei or Yonsei family. The American melting pot has room for the entire spectrum of JAs, from the *hapa* to those who have roots here stretching back decades.

America isn't the same as it was when it was founded, and the JA community isn't the same as it was when the first immigrants stepped off their boats in Honolulu or San Francisco and formed associations with other Japanese from the same prefecture. JAs share a cultural background, but they vary in ways those first immigrants could hardly imagine. We don't just come from Hiroshima or Kumamoto, or share backgrounds as carpenters, farmers, or fishermen. Now, we span ethnicities, sexual orientations and preferences, economic classes, and educational achievements.

It's harder to categorize us, except to say that we share those deep roots that we can be proud of and hand down to the generations that will follow us.

Photo by Erin Yoshimura.

Four generations of JA women. This photo of Erin Yoshimura, right, and her mother, grandmother, and great-grandmother was taken in the mid-1960s.

Pan-Asian, not pan-Oriental

For many younger JAs, their identity is less connected to Japan than it is to the larger mass of Asia. The United States is a perfect hothouse environment for cross-cultural pollination—the Japanese and Chinese may be the oldest Asian immigrant communities here, but over the past several decades a host of other Asians have made an impact. Young Yonsei and Gosei in many parts of the country (but, as usual, predominantly on the West Coast) attend school with Vietnamese, Cambodian, and Hmong kids. There has been a flood of Asian Indians coming to America since the technology and Internet boom of the 1990s. More Chinese, Filipinos, and Koreans have arrived in this country to find a better life. More recent immigration means more connection to the root culture. Fewer Japanese immigrants are moving to the United States, reflected in the fact that according to the 1990 Census only 52 percent of people of Japanese descent could speak Japanese. In contrast, 93 percent of people of Vietnamese descent could speak Vietnamese.

Such strong ties have brought new waves of pan-Asian culture, and young JAs—along with other Americans—have eagerly explored fresh ethnic cuisines such as Vietnamese and Thai with such cutting-edge menu items as *boba* tea and *pho*, the Vietnamese noodle soup.

We might have Japanese food with non-Japanese friends at a sushi bar, or eat traditional dishes when we get together with family for special occasions, but we don't always take stock of ourselves as Japanese Americans. What we are—and what other Americans treat us as—is simply Asian.

We've come to a crucial place in our journey as Americans. We're

Beyond JA

In many ways, I feel like I'm my own race—the "Sansei and Later" generation. On many subjects I don't clearly relate with a lot of Nisei elders, I'm not a new immigrant, I'm not a Japanese citizen, and I'm not blonde and blue-eyed. I'm an island with my own unique memories and experiences.

Scott Takeda, Yonsei

WORDS & PHRASES

yogore

Dirt or filth. "Don't touch that—*yogore*."

This shirt from Nikkei Traditions says it all.

Disadvantages of being JA

One rarely feels that one "belongs"—and of course one feels left out of many discussions about racial issues and the like. Also, given the atrocities done by the Japanese in recent history, I always feel awkward among Asians (especially older generation Asians), since I worry they will resent me. Among Japanese people, there's a vague feeling that one is probably still considered an outsider, even if one has a Japanese passport. Hence, one just doesn't fit.

Eri Izawa, postwar Nisei

yasui

Inexpensive. "That's all that cost? Wow, that's *yasui*."

beginning to embrace the fact that we're part of a larger population with whom we share many attributes and values, even as we accept and celebrate the diversity and uniqueness of each others' traditions.

JAs are part of the Asian "melting pot" within the larger American society. We participate in pan-Asian celebrations such as Dragon Boat Festivals, and hang out and dine in emerging, hip, urban pan-Asian districts such as Sawtelle in Los Angeles. Sawtelle is a model for the evolving role of JA communities in a pan-Asian world. It's a long-established JA area that has recently become a hotbed of pan-Asian businesses. Dozens of Japanese, Korean, Thai, and Vietnamese restaurants lie within a few short blocks, squeezed in among the Japanese gift shops and family-owned flower shops and nurseries. (One of my favorite stores in this district is Giant Robot, a cutting-edge pop culture shop featuring anime, J-pop music, toys, and books.) Everywhere you look, there are young Asians of all ethnicities enjoying the fruits of this colorful, diverse neighborhood.

Along with pan-Asian businesses, we're now able to see more AAPI role models. And it's not just the familiar faces of politicians and the few Hollywood stars who've been part of the AAPI experience (George Takei boldly went where no man had gone before, but few have been able to follow his path). New additions to the constellation of Asian stars include musicians such as Asian opera singers, virtuoso instrumentalists, and rock bassist James Iha, formerly of Smashing Pumpkins. Todd Park Mohr of Big Head Todd and the Monsters is Korean American. So is comedian Margaret Cho, one of the few AAPIs speaking out about the issues facing AAPIs.

That fact is, we can find strength and support as Asians in America because we'll always be seen as outsiders. The majority of Americans will probably continue to lump us together. Asians are Asians. We all look alike, right? And, Orientals are all inscrutable, anyway.

Rugs are Oriental; we're Asian

I grew up in a time when "Oriental" was commonly used, and it generally meant Chinese or Japanese, the two main Asian cultures that most Americans had any knowledge of before the Korean and

Vietnam wars. Nowadays, when someone uses the term "Oriental," I try to gently correct them.

The rule is simple: "Oriental" is a word for inanimate objects from Asia, not for people. If you're describing people from Asia, use the word "Asian." Or better yet, take the time to delve beyond the gross racial distinction and find out what country or heritage people are from. Asia is an awfully big place.

There's a natural inclination to simplify the world and file people within broad categories. But few people would without thought lump Italians and Swedes or French and English together culturally and ethnically just because they all happen to be Europeans. For some reason, it seems easier to assume that all Asians think alike and act alike just because we have a few physical characteristics in common.

No one calls Eastern Europeans "Occidentals." Today, "Oriental" is considered by most Asians to be a derogatory term because it reflects centuries of a Western-centric view of the world, a view that assumes that civilization and knowledge flowed from Europe to the rest of the world. The cultures of Asia, of course, in particular China, are much older and were refined long before Europeans wandered into other continents.

In addition, the word "Oriental" is confusing because it's used to describe the Middle East as well as the Far East (two more phrases that indicate geographic locale relative to Europe). Hence, rugs from Persia are today still called "Oriental rugs." At the same time, a Vietnamese shop owner might put a sign reading "Oriental groceries" above his door. That brings me to another point. These changing terms for ethnic groups in the United States are sometimes evolving even within the ethnic groups themselves, not just with Americans at large. Many Asians, especially older Asians, still use "Oriental" to describe themselves. Partly, that's because for years that's what they were called, and how we were referred to on legal and official forms. In fact, my memory of U.S. government forms includes the choice of checking off my race as "Mongoloid," as if all Asians had roots in Mongolia. My childhood memories may be fuzzy, but I'm sure glad that term didn't stick around.

The rise of Yellow Power

"Mongoloid" definitely does not fly in the post–Yellow Power era.

The Yellow Power movement was an aftershock of the Civil Rights movement fought by the African American community. In fact, one of the founders of the radical Black Panther group was a Sansei,

"Jap"

I grew up with mostly inner-city kids in a school with mostly Hispanic, Black, and Asian populations. I had never been called "Jap" until I came to Seattle as a child. I was riding a city bus and some woman called me that and she was livid. I don't remember where I was going or any other circumstances about that incident. Then, I was called "Jap" in anger again during the gas shortage of the 1970s. It brought up a strong memory of my father telling me, "They might call you friend or be nice to you or whatever, but when the pressure is on and it is a matter of money or a job, they'll call you 'Jap.'"

Masaye Okano Nakagawa, Sansei

WORDS & PHRASES

mochiron

Of course. "Dad, *mochiron* I did my homework, otherwise I wouldn't be asking for the car keys."

Rejected by Asians

Aside from my mother's Japanese girlfriends, Asians never accepted me as Asian so I developed a strong Black identity. The irony is I grew up knowing more about Japanese culture than American-born Japanese. Japanese, after all, was my first language and I had a constant instructor (Mom) imploring me to pronounce the words correctly. The Asians I knew as a child when we lived on military bases were all married to either Black or Caucasian men so they were different; nonjudgmental about race and culture. We had an ideal environment as long as we were in a military dependents' community where over half the kids were mixed or an ethnicity other than Caucasian. Once we moved to an all-white neighborhood, the disaster began. The only Asians I knew were my Mom's Japanese girlfriends and they were all immigrants married to Americans. Otherwise, the one Japanese family who owned the Fuji Ten Cent Store in Tacoma would sneer at us whenever we shopped there.

Yayoi Lena Winfrey, *hapa* Issei

WORDS & PHRASES

henna

Strange, different. "What do you mean you don't want to be an engineer? What kind of *henna* career are you going to have?"

Richard Aoki, who was born in an internment camp but raised in Oakland's black ghettos. The Yellow Power Movement was officially born in 1969 when a radical East Coast Asian group formed, calling itself I Wor Kuen in tribute to the Chinese Boxers who rebelled against colonial British rule. The group in the early 1970s moved to the West Coast and merged with San Francisco's Red Guards, an Asian group connected with the Panthers. Like many radical movements, the Yellow Power Movement inspired many people outside its core membership, which splintered and ultimately dissipated along with the other "Power" movements.

The movement combined a passion for civil rights with an awareness of the value of cultural roots. The radical era planted the seed for establishing Asian studies programs in schools across the country; and it increased interest in preserving ethnic enclaves such as Chinatowns and Japantowns and in fighting to save them from urban renewal and redevelopment. The rise of Asian-American theater, the start of artists such as the JA band Hiroshima, and the establishment of a plethora of AAPI social services organizations and civil rights groups (the Organization of Chinese Americans, OCA, was formed in 1973) can also be traced back to this era.

The movement also helped assure close ties between AAPI organizations. For instance, JACL and OCA are closely allied, and many chapters of both organizations not only have overlapping memberships but also cosponsor events with each other.

More recently, the sense of unity between AAPI communities has resulted in an organization called the 80-20 Initiative, a national nonpartisan Political Action Committee dedicated to Asian American issues. The group is based on the concept that Asian communities might be small and relatively powerless individually, but when united as a pan-Asian bloc AAPIs can have a tangible impact on national politics.

During the 2012 presidential election cycle, the media made much of the demographic power of the Hispanic vote. But Asian Americans have also become a force to be reckoned with. According to the 2010 Census, Asians as a whole are the fastest-growing ethnic group in the United States, thanks to immigration, and can swing elections in parts of the country where the population includes large Asian communities. More and more Asian Americans are running for public office in those communities, too, which brings visibility and inspires the next generation of Asian Americans to enter politics. Hawaii just elected its second-ever JA governor, David Ige, for instance, in 2014. He was the first candidate to ever beat an incumbent governor of Hawaii, fellow Democrat Neil Abercrombie, in a primary, and he went on to defeat Republican and Independent opponents in the general election.

Asian Americans have also found their collective voice thanks to the Internet, blogging, and social media, and they are finally starting to find meaty roles in Hollywood, in movies and on television. The future is bright for Asians in America, and Japanese Americans are enjoying the attention too.

A better tomorrow for AAPIs on screen

One of the heartening signs for the Asian Pacific American community is the increasing awareness of films made by AAPIs and starring AAPIs that capture our experience. I'm not talking just documentaries, or films about Asians by non-Asians, or martial arts movies, or even foreign films from Asia. I'm talking about the authentic expression of Asian Americans.

Better Luck Tomorrow, the 2002 independently produced film written and directed by Justin Lin, showcased a cast of young Asian actors playing the part of Asian high schoolers who take that stereotype of the Asian straight-A student and turn it upside down. The students in the film find their lives to be empty and unsatisfying and turn to crime and, eventually, violence.

In recent years, other AAPI films have been making the rounds of Asian film festivals: *Green Dragon*, about the first wave of Vietnamese immigrants to arrive in the United States; *The Debut*, about the generational conflicts within a Filipino American family; and *Charlotte Sometimes*, a film about relationships between four Asian American friends.

Japanese American filmmaker/playwright/actor Lane Nishikawa has filmed the first two parts of a trilogy of movies. The first film, *When We Were Warriors*, an adaptation of a play he wrote, is about the fifty-year friendship between a Nisei soldier and the Jewish concentration camp survivor he freed at the end of World War II. The second in the series is *Forgotten Valor*, which was funded by the California Civil Liberties Public Education Program. The short film is a beautifully written and directed gem about a Nisei veteran (played by Nishikawa) who disappears when it's announced that a group of 442nd vets' wartime medals will be upgraded to the Medal of Honor. The third part

Family members remember JA veterans every Memorial Day in services like this one in Denver.

Being the "model minority"

For me, the very thing that makes us this "model minority" is also one of things that I regret about being Japanese American. Why is it that Italian or Irish Americans still proudly wave the flag of their ancestors eight generations after leaving those countries while only three or four generations later, many Japanese Americans my age know little or nothing about the culture that their parents and grandparents grew up in? Because of this need to assimilate and be accepted into the mainstream, Japanese Americans even a generation removed from immigration become more American than the Americans.

Lisa Sasaki, Yonsei

of the trilogy, *Only the Brave*, released in 2006, is about the famous rescue of the Texas "Lost Battalion" by the Nisei 442nd Regimental Combat Team/100th Battalion. This film crosses the generation gap because among its cast of young JAs it features one of the most famous of JA actors, Pat Morita, in a role.

The creativity of AAPI filmmakers is finally getting its due. It's only a matter of time before a Japanese American filmmaker or actor finds commercial success and opens the floodgates for the many Asians who've worked in obscurity for years.

An apology at last

The most important result of the Yellow Power movement, especially for JAs, was the effort that ultimately gained a national apology and reparations for Japanese Americans from the U.S. government for internment during World War II. The Redress movement combined the ethnic solidarity of the civil rights era with the Vietnam/Watergate mistrust of government to question the legality, and even the necessity, of internment. Once historian Michi Weglyn's *Years of Infamy* was published in 1976, proving that there had been no "military necessity" for internment, there was a raging debate within the JA community about whether to demand redress from the government. Veterans groups fought against it, claiming it was unpatriotic; many JAs who had been interned opposed it for the same reason they'd kept silent about it for decades: they didn't want to relive those years.

The JACL during its 1970 biennial convention in Chicago, passed a resolution calling for recognition of, and reparations for, the injustice of internment. Groups such as the National Coalition for Redress and Reparations were formed. On February 19, 1976, President Gerald Ford signed Proclamation 4417, which called internment a "national mistake." It was another step closer to redress. In 1980, thanks to the leading efforts of legislators such as Congressman Norman Mineta and Senator Daniel Inouye, Congress established the Commission on Wartime Relocation and Internment of Civilians to take testimony from survivors about their wartime experiences and to study the causes of internment. It wasn't until 1988 that President Ronald Reagan signed the Civil Liberties Act of 1988, establishing a $20,000 reparations payment for internees and their descendants. The bill also included a formal apology from the U.S. government.

Our work's not done

Unfortunately, even though JAs have won redress and AAPIs as a whole are uniting and working toward a shared future, racism against AAPIs continues in America. In the early 1980s, Vincent Chin, a Chinese American, was beaten to death in Detroit by two unemployed autoworkers who assumed he was Japanese. A number of Asian students have been shot in the past two decades, hate crimes against Asians are on the upswing according to groups like the National Asian Pacific American Legal Consortium and the Asian Pacific American Legal Center of Southern California, and stereotypes of Asians remain a seemingly inescapable part of American pop culture.

Offensive racial stereotypes still persist. Every year, Asians continue to be the butt of both unintended and intended slurs: the clothing chain Abercrombie & Fitch sold a line of tee-shirts emblazoned with buck-toothed, queue-haired caricatures of Asians that harkened back to the coolie era of the 1800s; a Halloween costume maker sold a kung fu spoof with slanty eyes and, of course, buck teeth. If these types of caricatures were of African Americans, the outraged response would be loud and swift. It's even acceptable for major sports stars to make fun of Asians. Shaquille O'Neal in 2002 made a comment about a Chinese NBA player, imitating the "ching-chong Chinaman" sound that many of us grew up hearing, and there wasn't much of a controversy about it.

Even in 2003, Congressman Howard Coble of North Carolina said on a radio talk show, when asked his thoughts about interning Middle Eastern people in the wake of the 9/11 attacks, that he thought the wartime internment of Japanese Americans had been the right thing to do. Asian organizations including the JACL and OCA, as well as Arab organizations, protested, but unlike fellow Republican Trent Lott, who was removed from his leadership position in Congress for making a comment that seemed to support anti-Black sentiments, there was no other backlash against Coble. In 2004, the JACL got Coble to admit that he had been mistaken in his thinking about internment.

The Asian community is still largely invisible and mostly silent. It'll take time and much hard work by the younger generations of JAs and other Asians who are still finding their voice before the mainstream culture will heed our presence.

Courtesy Erin Yoshimura.

JAs showed their patriotism before, during, and after World War II.

Who I am

I don't consider myself JA. I consider myself a Black woman with a Japanese mother.

Yayoi Lena Winfrey, *hapa* Issei

garra-garra

A rattling sound, as in "What's all the *garra-garra* when you start the car?"

Building bridges in a post-9/11 world

The number of hate crimes against Asian Pacific Americans increased after the terrorist attacks of September 11, 2001. Organizations attribute much of the greater than 20 percent increase in hate crimes to the climate of fear caused by the attacks. One of the first such attacks was the shooting death of a South Asian man who worked at a gas station. According to the Asian Pacific American Legal Center, this was one of the first "bias murders" related to the September 11 attacks. Even before the terrorist attacks, hate crimes against Asians was on the rise, but 9/11 unleashed a wave of attacks specifically targeting South Asians and Sikhs, who were mistaken for Middle Easterners (Sikhs wear turbans, a common stereotype of Middle Easterners).

The post-9/11 backlash has led to coalitions between Asian American groups and Middle Eastern and Arab groups. At a 2002 "All Camp Summit" sponsored by the Japanese American National Museum, the keynote speech was given by the head of an Arab American civil rights group. During that summit, John Tateishi, the executive director of the Japanese American Citizens League, the country's largest and oldest Asian American civil rights organization, described how he had fielded calls in the wake of the terror attacks from panicked Nisei who were concerned that Arab Americans might be rounded up and interned as Japanese Americans had been after the bombing of Pearl Harbor. The JACL has also been active in fighting the federal government against the USA Patriot Act of 2001, the antiterrorism legislation passed immediately after 9/11 that has, among other things, allowed men of Middle Eastern heritage to be imprisoned for months without charges or a trial.

Many of the JAs interviewed for the book *Nisei Voices: Japanese American Students of the 1930s—Then & Now* (Hirohata Design, 2003) also expressed concern for the treatment of Muslims and Arab Americans in the wake of 9/11, and hoped that the injustice of internment wouldn't be committed again.

The United Response Collaborative, a group funded by The California Endowment, was formed after the 9/11 attacks by San Francisco Arab, Muslim, South Asian, Asian American, and other civil rights organizations to jointly work together to address backlash hate violence and discrimination. Similar bridges have been built in the past few years across the country, and JAs have been involved in many of them because of the memory of what happened to Japanese Americans.

These pan-ethnic alliances have continued since the attacks, with student groups promoting discussions that include Asian Pacific

American and Middle Eastern perspectives. In 2002, a coalition of almost two hundred organizations and individuals including many Asian and Arab American groups called for a National Day of Solidarity with Muslim, Arab, and South Asian Immigrants. In November 2003, the University of California at Davis sponsored a panel discussion, "The War at Home: Detentions, Deportations, and Dissent," featuring Cambodian, Palestinian, Pakistani, and African American speakers.

Many Day of Remembrance events within JA communities make clear the similarities between the treatment of people of Middle Eastern descent today and the Japanese American community sixty years ago.

So, as we move forward into the future, the past hasn't been forgotten. And Japanese Americans are making sure that their history—both the injustice of internment and the ultimate triumph of the JA experience—is an integral thread of the American fabric.

Being JA is a blessing

Being able to look from both the inside and the outside of two distinctly different cultures, both of which are known throughout the world, has been an incredible blessing and opportunity. I pray that perhaps I and others like me may be able to build bridges of understanding that will help disparate societies, cultures, and nations better understand each other—and perhaps most importantly, understand the need for understanding.

Eri Izawa, postwar Nisei

Staying Informed, Staying Connected

If you care at all about Japan, you won't find very much news—good or bad—about the country in mainstream U.S. media. Even with our cable-driven 24/7 news cycle, there doesn't seem to be enough time to turn the spotlight on news from other countries. Unless something big (usually a natural disaster or big political news) happens, mainstream American media won't report on the day-to-day news of Japan.

The best U.S. sources for Japan news include the *New York Times* and *CNN*. *The Wall Street Journal*, the Business Insider Web site, and Bloomberg also do a good job covering Japanese news, although not surprisingly they focus on business stories. In England, the *Guardian* and the *Independent* newspapers as well as the BBC seem to pay closer attention to Japan than most American media.

For daily or tailored information about Japan, explore the resources in this chapter. Many of the groups and organizations listed here either have Web sites or are themselves Web sites, and there are now so many sites about Japan, Japanese culture, and Japanese Americans that only a sampling can be presented here.

I also maintain lists of links to Web sites and blogs on my **Nikkei View** blog, www.nikkeiview.com—click on the "Nikkeiview Links" tab at the top of the page. You can also find many of these companies and Web sites on Facebook with a social media presence—just search for them on Facebook!

THE INTERNET

Fortunately, you can get Japan news direct from Japan over the Internet. The web has become a reliable source of all sorts of news, information, and opinions from and about Japan—in English or Japanese, so take the time to surf and search for your own favorite resources. And although the algorithms aren't quite fine-tuned yet, you can even look at Japanese web pages and translate them into English ... albeit sometimes nonsensical English.

The same is true of English to Japanese translations using **Google Translate** When I write letters or emails to people in Japan in English and then copy and paste the Japanese from Google Translate, I've received some quizzical responses in return because of the odd translations. Okay, so technology isn't perfect, yet. You can find plenty of English-language information about Japan on the web, though. (For more on Google Translate, see the chapter "Language.")

One simple way, if you're truly serious about keeping up with news about Japan, is to use **Google Alerts**. Alerts allow you to set up emails that you receive as stories happen or once a day (your option) about any keywords of your choice. You can set up just one Google Alert about "Japan" or separate ones—like I have—for "Japan," "Japanese," "Japan travel," "Tokyo" … you get the idea. Just go to www.google.com/alerts and follow the instructions. If you end up getting too many emails with too many links to stories you don't care about, try fine-tuning your keywords or delete the alert altogether. You'll receive email alerts in real time, so if something big happens in Japan, you'll know about it right away.

When big news happens in the middle of the night, though, you may have to wait until the morning when you check your email to see your alerts.

That's what happened late in the night of March 11, 2011: I happened to see an email alert when I couldn't sleep and read about a big earthquake in Japan. I immediately turned on CNN and watched the live coverage, horrified at the site of the tsunami captured on video, roaring over fields and roads and effortlessly knocking down buildings, pushing cars and boats and debris along at high speeds across the landscape of northeast Japan.

After the initial wave of coverage, the American cable channels moved on to other stories. That's when I began exploring alternatives and found individual bloggers in Japan passing along live updates about the devastation caused by the tsunami, including people who were following coverage in Japanese media and translating it and passing along information in English for the rest of the world. A simple web search for "Japan tsunami news" was all it took to find these sources.

I also found **NHK World** (http://www3.nhk.or.jp/nhkworld/) online, the English-language version of the Japanese equivalent to America's public television. NHK World was my ultimate source for ongoing news. After watching NHK World online and keeping CNN on the television I noticed that CNN was using a lot of video footage that had first aired on NHK. Even today, NHK World has a special section, "Japan Beyond 3.11—Stories of Recovery," that tells an amazing array of stories about everything from Tohoku students studying in Paris to a transcript of a story the network aired about "Convenience Stores in the Disaster Areas."

NHK World may be available on your cable or satellite dish programming. It's not part of the list of channels available through my cable provider, but I watch it whenever I'm traveling if it's on the list of channels provided by the hotel. I've also seen the Japanese version of NHK, which is what my mother watches all day, available in hotels, especially on the West Coast. I stare at it hoping that hearing nonstop Japanese will somehow soak into my brain and activate dormant language cells. I can usually pick out a lot of English words in the news broadcasts— "pop music" and "top 40" jumped out at me one day when I was at my mom's house. But so far, I'm not so sure that having NHK on nonstop has helped me be a better Japanese speaker.

In the days and weeks that followed the earthquake in Japan, **YouTube** became a primary source for amateur video footage of the destruction caused by the tsunami, with dozens of horrifying clips shot by people who'd climbed to high ground, chronicling the rushing water and debris going by.

The 2011 disaster has for me become a "proof of concept" of how you can follow news about Japan using the Internet as a tool.

NEWSPAPERS

Unlike in the United States, where newspaper circulation has dropped so much that many papers have cut their staff, Japan is still a newspaper-friendly country, boasting several national newspapers with huge readership, in addition to local newspapers throughout the country. National newspapers in Japan with English Web sites are the *Mainichi Shimbun* (http://mainichi.jp/english/), *Asahi Shimbun* (http://www.asahi.com/english/), and *Yomiuri Shimbun* (http://the-japan-news.com/).

English Web sites are also available that cover news of Japan. *The Japan Times* (http://www.japantimes.co.jp/) was launched in 1897 and is the country's oldest English-language newspaper. Japan Today is a newer, online-only English-language news source that launched in 2000 (http://www.japantoday.com). It features original reporting as well as translations of articles from other Japanese media. Both Japan Today and *The Japan Times* also offer international news, using wire service reports such as Associated Press.

Kyodo News is Japan's version of the Associated Press, a wire service with reporters filing stories from all over Japan, covering a variety of beats. Kyodo has a Web site with English versions of its stories at http://english.kyodonews.jp/. Unfortunately, there's a subscription fee of 3,500 yen every month.

Some sites merely compile news stories from legitimate news sites and present them as their own, but several notable Web sites present a unique view of Japanese news, and certainly Japanese culture.

Kotaku is a gamer-oriented Web site that covers edgy, youth-oriented Japanese culture. Its Japan news section (http://kotaku.com/tag/japan) covers the latest Japanese video- and computer-game news as well as news about cats on TV news programs, unusual Japanese pizzas, and the latest oddball offerings at Japanese fast-food chains.

RocketNews24 (http://en.rocketnews24.com) is another youth-oriented source about Japan (and China and Korea), with a mix of news stories and features on wacky Japanese food, fashion, music, and other pop culture.

MAGAZINES

Magazines in Japan are mostly in Japanese, but a few are published in English. *Metropolis* (http://metropolisjapan.com) is an edgy culture magazine that has some news but mostly concentrates on feature and entertainment stories. *Metropolis* is distributed in Tokyo, Chiba, and Yokohama every two weeks.

Japan Monthly Web Magazine (http://japan-magazine.jnto.go.jp) is issued monthly by the Japan National Tourism Organization, and its Web site includes a treasure trove of feature stories for visitors to the country including sections on food, shopping, and seasonal, traditional, and other destinations.

Kyoto Journal (http://www.kyotojournal.org) began in the late 1980s as a print magazine published by a volunteer-driven nonprofit organization, but more recently has become an online showcase for feature stories, commentary, and art (including graphics and photography) in English. The organization still publishes occasional special print editions, but readers can easily get lost in the Web site's depth of content. The journal covers not just Kyoto, where its offices are located, but stories from throughout Japan and Asia. The magazine has won awards for its design and is now available via subscription as a downloadable PDF file. The Web site features a portion of the content available in the digital magazine.

And if you're interested in Japan-related events in Southern California, there is no more complete source of information than editor Shige Higashi's *Cultural News* (http://www.culturalnews.com/), a Web site that gathers together every event of interest in the Los Angeles area. Japanese American events are noted, but Higashi's passion is for "Japanese art and culture," and that's primarily what he focuses on.

BLOGS

Japan-related blogs are thriving and offer an endless variety of subtopics to explore. You can find blogs about Japanese recipes, food-specific blogs, travel blogs, blogs about cities where the bloggers live, and so on. Many of these blogs are written by non-Japanese who are Japanophiles or who live, work, or study in Japan. You can find hundreds of Japan-related blogs through a site like the **Japan Blog List** (http://japan-bloglist.com), or just do a Google search for "Japan blogs" and you'll be rewarded with a lot of links to follow! Additional sites about Japan are listed below.

SOCIAL MEDIA

You can find Japan-related content online on **Facebook, Twitter, Tumblr, Instagram,** and **Pinterest** (warning: some of them may contain adult material). You'll find a lot of Japanese American content on the same networks too. Just type "Japan" into the Facebook search box and you'll get a mishmash of Japan-related pages, as well as pages for Japan America Societies, Japanese American Citizens League chapters,

and other organizations. You'll also find **JAJA** (Japanese Americans and Japanese in America), a loose-knit group that brings together Japanese nationals and JAs for cultural discussions, and **JapanCulture-NYC**, a group that focuses on the people and culture of the Japanese community in New York City. See also the listings under "JA/Nikkei/AAPI Sites & Blogs" below.

ORGANIZATIONS

Japanese American Citizens League

The Japanese American Citizens League is a membership organization whose mission is to secure and maintain the human and civil rights of Americans of Japanese ancestry and others victimized by injustice. The JACL also works to celebrate and preserve Japanese and JA culture. 1765 Sutter St., San Francisco, CA 94115, Tel.: (415) 921–5225, http://www.jacl.org.

Japanese American Museum of San Jose

This museum is housed in a small, lovely building built to evoke Japanese architecture, filled with an Informative history of San Jose's quiet Japantown neighborhood. The museum has permanent displays on the settling of Japanese in the South Bay area's farmlands and of course follows the community as it scattered to the wartime prison camps. A recommended stop if you're anywhere near San Jose's J-town. 535 North Fifth St., San Jose, CA 95112, Tel.: (408) 294-3138, http://www.jamsj.org.

Japanese American National Museum

The Japanese American National Museum is a resource for the history and culture of the JA experience, with permanent and temporary exhibits, a research center, and a media center that has produced award-winning documentaries. JANM has done a terrific job of appealing to future museum members with forward-looking exhibits such as artwork by rocker Mike Shinoda of Linkin Park, a mixed-race exhibit curated by Hapa Project's Kip Fulbeck, and a brilliant PR coup with a 40th-birthday exhibit for Hello Kitty, the cutest iconic Japanese image in the world. 100 North Central Ave., Los Angeles, CA 90012, Tel: (213) 625-0414, http://www.janm.org.

National Association of Japan-America Societies

The National Association of Japan-America Societies, Inc. is a private, nonprofit, nonpartisan organization that offers educational, cultural, and business programs about Japan and U.S.-Japan relations to the general public through its member Japan-America Societies. The Web site includes links to Japan-America Societies throughout the country. 1819 L St. NW, Suite 200, Washington, DC 20036, Tel.: (202) 429-5545, http://www.us-japan.org.

National Japanese American Historical Society

The National Japanese American Historical Society (NJAHS), founded in 1980 in San Francisco, is a nonprofit membership-supported organization dedicated to the preservation, promotion, and dissemination of materials relating to the history and culture of Japanese Americans. NJAHS specializes in traveling exhibitions, publications, videos, interactive multimedia, military and camp collections, and educational programs. NJAHS also operates a building at the Presidio of San Francisco, a former U.S. Army facility that's now a National Park. NJAHS's MIS Historic Learning Center at 640 Mason St. pays tribute to the Military Intelligence Service (MIS) language school, where Japanese Americans taught and learned Japanese during WWII. 1684 Post St., San Francisco, CA 94115, Tel.: (415) 921-5007, http://njahs.org.

Nikkei National Museum & Cultural Centre

Nikkei Centre is a multiuse facility in Burnaby, British Columbia. The Centre opened in 2000 and houses a Japanese Canadian cultural center, the Nikkei National Museum, a community center serving the neighborhood, and a Japanese Canadian garden. Its mandate is to promote a better understanding and appreciation by all Canadians of Japanese Canadian culture and heritage and an awareness by all Canadians of the contribution of Japanese Canadians to Canadian society. 6688 Southoaks Crescent, Burnaby BC V5E 4M7, Canada, Tel: 604.777.7000. http://centre.nikkei place.org/.

Northwest Nikkei Museum

Founded in 2003 by community leaders, the Japanese Cultural & Community Center of Washington (JCCCW) is dedicated to preserving, promoting, and sharing Japanese and Japanese American history, heritage, and culture. The center is located at the site of the original Seattle Japanese Language School, which was founded in 1902. The center's programs include the Northwest Nikkei Museum. Issei Legacy Site, 1414 South Weller St., Seattle, WA 98144, Tel: (206) 568-7114, https://jcccw.org/.

Oregon Nikkei Legacy Center & Japanese American History Museum

This is a small two-room museum that's jam-packed with information and artifacts in the main room's permanent exhibit and with art and multimedia temporary exhibits in the back room. It's located in what once was the Japanese neighborhood in Portland, now a hipster's paradise. 121 NW 2nd Ave., Portland, OR 97209, Tel.: (503) 224-1458, http://www.oregonnikkei.org.

U.S.-Japan Council

The U.S.-Japan Council was founded in 2009 by former Senator Daniel Inouye of Hawaii and his wife, Irene Hirano Inouye, the founding president and CEO of the Japanese American National Museum. The organization promotes the high-level role that Japanese Americans can play in strengthening U.S.-Japan relations by cultivating a national network of Japanese American leaders. The U.S.-Japan Council collaborates with other organizations and institutions to develop programs that allow Council Members to engage with their Japanese counterparts and leaders in the United States. The Council also runs the Tomodachi Initiative, which offers educational and cultural exchanges between young people of both Japan and the U.S. The Initiative grew out of the post–March 11, 2011, earthquake and tsunami that devastated the Tohoku region of Japan, when the U.S. military sent troops to aid in the recovery, dubbing the partnership with the Japanese Self-Defense Forces "Operation Tomodachi." 1819 L St. NW, Suite 200, Washington, DC 20036, (202) 223-6840, Tel.: http://www.usjapancouncil.org.

SITES ABOUT JAPAN

Donald Keene Center of Japanese Culture

A bit scholarly, but that's because this Web site is hosted by Columbia University. Founded in 1986 at Columbia, the Center is named for Professor Keene, an internationally renowned scholar, Columbia University teacher, and interpreter of Japanese literature and culture to the West. The Center is dedicated to advancing the understanding of Japan and its culture in the United States through university instruction, research, and public education. http://www.keenecenter.org.

The Gail Project

A cool collection of archival photographs of early Occupation-era Okinawa shot by Army captain Charles Eugene Gail. The photos were donated to the University of California Santa Cruz's McHenry Library, and the library has turned it into an ongoing project and traveling exhibit that gathers together the photos and oral histories of both U.S. personnel and Okinawan citizens to remember the history and create stronger relationships between Okinawa and the U.S. http://thegailproject.routes.ucsc.edu/.

J-Guide

A comprehensive list of links about Japan run by Stanford University's US-Asia Technology Management Center. It's a good starting place for Americans interested in finding out about Japan, Japanese cyber-culture, and Japanese Web servers. http://jguide.stanford.edu/.

Japan FAQ: Know Before You Go

An exhaustive and helpful list of answers to frequently asked questions about Japan, lovingly compiled by Robert Murphy with attention to facts but presented with a sense of humor. At the bottom of the long page are links to other sections he's gathered on topics such as "Manners & Etiquette," "Why Are Prices So Damn High in Japan?" and "The Japan Biker F.A.Q." http://www.thejapanfaq.com.

Japan-Guide.com

A handy online overview that includes broad categories with information and links to other sites. The History section is concise and complete. There's also a forum for communication, photo galleries with special historical exhibits including the 1923 Great Kanto Earthquake that destroyed Tokyo, and images from Japan's 1937 invasion of Shanghai. A great place to start your research and education about Japan. http://www.japan-guide.com/.

Japan Information Network
JIN is part of the Japan Center for Intercultural Communications (JCIC), an independent public interest association established in 1953 to introduce Japanese politics, economy, society, and culture to the rest of the world and enhance overseas understanding of Japan. The Web site is an index with links to other Web sites about Japan, divided into areas of "Opinions," "Facts" and (soon to come) "Business." http://nippon-jin.com/.

Japan Reference Page
The Japan Reference Page, a private and non-commercial site, is an extensive and well-organized directory covering online resources related to Japan. In the years since I've been linking to Web sites about Japan, there has been such an explosion of online resources that it's great to have a site such as this to help sort it all out. http://www.jref.com.

Japan Zone
A guide to Japan and Japanese culture aimed at the rest of the world, with travel information and sections for Japanese popular culture and Japanese etiquette. The site's a labor of love for Mark McBennett, a young Irishman who found himself working in Japan in the late 1980s and then married a Japanese woman and settled there. It's nicely organized with lots of informational text supporting relevant links to sites about each topic. http://www.japan-zone.com.

Keiko Schneider's Bookmarks
Keiko Schneider has a list of links about Japanese language and culture, with an emphasis on language studies. Schneider manages an extensive e-mail group, called the SenseiOnline Network, of Japanese-language teachers. http://www.sabotenweb.com/bookmarks.

JAPANESE CULTURE

Anime Cons
This is a handy site to see if there's an anime convention near you and when it's held. http://animecons.com.

Arudou Debito
"Arudou Debito" is the Japanized name of David Aldwinckle, a U.S.-born writer and teacher who has lived in Japan since the late 1980s and became a naturalized Japanese citizen in 2000. He now lives in Hokkaido with his Japanese wife and two daughters and is a tenured teacher at a university in Sapporo. He writes about issues of assimilation and bigotry in Japan, and he's an activist for a more multicultural Japan. A fascinating guy, with a lot to sift through at his Web site. http://www.debito.org.

The Asian Rare Books Home Page
Great for book freaks like me, and a helpful resource for research. http://www.asianrarebooks.net.

Atomic Bomb Museum
Moving and historically complete overview of the atomic bombings of Hiroshima and Nagasaki, with gut-wrenching photographs taken within days of the Hiroshima bombing. http://atomicbombmuseum.org/.

The Black Moon

A site based in Los Angeles that promotes the understanding and appreciation of traditional Japanese culture, art, and animation with news, reviews, and merchandise in an online marketplace. http://www.theblackmoon.com.

Crunchyroll

A Web site with free and premium access to a variety of latest anime, including anime that is streamed within hours of its original broadcast in Japan, with subtitles. http://www.crunchyroll.com.

Daily Zen

This isn't quite a Japan site, but it's close enough. You can get your daily dose of Zen Buddhist wisdom here. http://www.dailyzen.com.

Denver Taiko

Formed in 1977, Denver Taiko is one of the first *taiko* groups in the United States. The group is composed entirely of Sansei, Yonsei, and *hapa* Japanese Americans. You can use your Web browser to find many other American *taiko* groups online. http://denvertaiko.org.

Engrish.com

It's hard not to chuckle at how English is misappropriated in Japan for signs, slogans, packaging, and just about everything else. This site collects a lot of examples of English that just doesn't quite make . . . sense. http://engrish.com.

Ichoya Japanese Kimonos and Textiles

A Denver-based couple who collect Japanese textiles have put up this Web site to sell their wares from buying trips to Japan. http://www.ichoya.com.

J-ENT

This site has been covering Japanese entertainment in English since 1993, with coverage of J-pop, movies, and databases for Japanese drama and celebrities. http://j-entonline.com/.

Japan Photo Gallery

The home page says it all: It's a "Gaijin's view of modern Japan," by W. Dire Wolf. You can click from image to image (they're snapshots, but they do represent his view of modern Japan), or visit his other online content—including a lot of examples of "Shockwave" multimedia production in the "Get Shocked" section. There's lots and lots of stuff—and a lot of contemporary pop culture. http://www.wdirewolff.com/japangallery.htm.

Japan Ukiyo-e Museum

Ukiyo-e (which means "Art of the Floating World") is a beautiful woodcut print art developed in Japan about four hundred years ago that later greatly influenced the French Impressionists. You'll immediately recognize many of the most famous ukiyo-e works by such artists as Hiroshige and Utamaro, because they've become familiar symbols of Japan of the feudal era. This is a great Japanese site run by the Nagoya TV Server, broken down into categories (my favorite: "Demons and Ghosts by Yoshitoshi"). http://www.japan-ukiyoe-museum.com/collection_en/.

Japanese War Crimes

As horrible as the U.S. atomic bombings of Hiroshima and Nagasaki (not to mention the conventional firebombings of Tokyo and other cities) were, the government of Japan still has unresolved issues of its own. This site can be strident in its anti-Japanese sentiments, but the crimes documented here in gruesome detail (including many graphic photographs, such as victims of the Rape of Nanking) can't be denied. Not for the squeamish, but not to be forgotten or dismissed, either. http://www.centurychina.com/wiihist.

Jim Allen's Japanese Baseball Page

History, stats, trivia, and more about Japan's national pastime, from an American working on the *Yomiuri Shinbun* sports page. http://www2.gol.com/users/jallen/jimball.html.

Kabuki for Everyone

This is what the Web is perfect for! This site uses high tech to provide a great introduction to the Japanese theatrical tradition of Kabuki. Famed actor Ichimura Manjiro guides the viewer through text (translated into English), sound files, and even video clips of Kabuki performances. What a wonderful way to bridge the cultural gap! http://park.org/Japan/Kabuki/kabuki.html.

National Cherry Blossom Festival

The Web site for the annual celebration that commemorates the gift of 3,000 cherry trees from the city of Tokyo to the people of Washington, D.C., in 1912. http://www.nationalcherryblossomfestival.org.

Official Sanrio Web Site: Home of Hello Kitty!

The enduring popularity of the cute Hello Kitty image with little girls everywhere makes the manufacturer Sanrio one of the great pop culture bridges between Japan and the United States. This is the company's English-language home page for the now-forty-year-old icon of *kawaii* culture. http://www.sanrio.com.

Ramen Home Page

A Web site maintained by Matt Fischer exclusively focused on—you guessed it—ramen. I didn't know there could be so many recipes for the stuff. I wonder though if he's ever had real ramen, or if he has only had the dried instant stuff that college kids feed on. The site's not updated very often and isn't fancy, but it's a good start for ramen fans. http://mattfischer.com/ramen.

Rekihaku: National Museum of Japanese History

Rekihaku is an interuniversity research institute for Japanese history, archaeology, folklore, and museum studies. It doesn't cover recent history, but this is a nicely designed Web site, and it has evolved since the time I first bookmarked it in 1994. http://www.rekihaku.ac.jp/english/.

Roger and Marilyn's Photo Tour of Tokyo, Japan

An incredibly deep—though graphics heavy—site created by Roger and Marilyn Jesrani. Worth a visit, but it helps if you have a *fast* connection. http://www.artisandevelopers.com/web/tokyo.

Rolling Thunder Taiko Resource

A complete Web site for anyone who enjoys or plays *taiko* drums, an increasingly popular traditional Japanese instrument. The site has not been updated. http://www.taiko.com.

Stone Bridge Press

A California-based publisher of books about Japan, including English translations of Japanese literature, original fiction, and nonfiction books. Look especially for *Four Immigrants Manga*, a recently rediscovered manga that depicts the lives of four young Japanese men who came to San Francisco in the early twentieth century. http://www.stonebridge.com.

Tokyo Food Page / Kansai Food Page (Bento.com)

A nice site with recipes, a gallery of images of food in Tokyo, and a guide to restaurants. http://www.bento.com.

Ukiyo-e, Pictures of the Floating World

A terrific resource compiled by Hans Olof Johansson, who's obviously knowledgeable about *ukiyo-e*. There's a gallery, a Q&A about the art, a guide to other Web sites, and "The Floating World of Cyberspace," a very complete list of links to *ukiyo-e* artwork throughout the Net, organized alphabetically by artist and title. Take your time, and enjoy! http://www.ukiyo-e.se/.

GENEALOGY

Ancestry.com

This U.S.-based company has made researching genealogy pretty simple. I found immigration information about my grandfather, who left Japan for Hawaii in the early 1900s, with just a few clicks. http://www.ancestry.com.

Japan GenWeb

Combines helpful genealogy information with general information about Japan. http://www.rootsweb.com/~jpnwgw/.

Japanese American Family History Resources

A helpful Web site for researching your JA roots. http://www.carolynbrady.com/jagen-links.html.

Japanese American Genealogy Forum

The section on Genealogy.com featuring extensive discussion boards from people researching their Japanese family ancestry. http://genforum.genealogy.com/japan.

National Archives Genealogy Web site

The U.S. government's Web resource for researching your family history. http://www.archives.gov/research/genealogy/index.html.

Reenvisioning Japan

This fascinating Web site grew out of postcards, travel posters, and artifacts of twentieth-century Japan collected by Joanne Bernardi, Ph.D., Associate Professor of Japanese Studies/Film and Media Studies at the University of Rochester. One of the coolest sections is her archive of videos of and about Japan (some are pretty racist American depictions in cartoons and TV commercials), including a timeline of videos (not all are available for viewing) that begins with stock footage from 1900. http://humanities.lib.rochester.edu/rej/

HAPA ISSUES

Hafu the Film

This excellent and moving documentary follows a group of mixed-race Japanese in Japan, where they face issues different from those they might in the United States. http://hafufilm.com/en.

Halvsie.com

A Twitter account that shares news and information about mixed-race Japanese. "For, by, and about half Japanese people everywhere." http://twitter.com/halvsie.

Hapa-Palooza

Sounds great: Hapa-Palooza is a "celebration of mixed heritage and hybrid cultural identity" held every September in Vancouver, Canada. http://www.hapapalooza.com/.

The Hapa Project

Kip Fulbeck is a half Chinese, half Caucasian writer, comedian, academic, and certified lifeguard who has many mixed-race projects to his credit, including "The Hapa Project," a book and traveling exhibit of portraits of mixed-race people of all ages, with brief statements from them. http://kipfulbeck.com/the-hapa-project.

Hapa Voice

A very active Web site where people of mixed heritage can state their ethnicity and explain how their identities have shaped their lives. http://hapavoice.com.

INTERNMENT RESOURCES

Children of the Camps

The Web site for Satsuki and Kim Ina's powerful documentary film, showing how the trauma of internment still haunts the generation that spent its childhood behind barbed wire. http://www.children-of-the-camps.org.

Densho

A terrific Web site based in Seattle, that has taken the concept of oral history in the form of audio and video tape, and combined it with an archive of photos from institutions and personal collections, and put it all online. http://www.densho.org.

Exploring the Japanese American Internment through Film and the Internet

A project of the National Asian American Telecommunications Association, which presents the history of internment in words, pictures, and movie clips and then asks the question, "Could it happen again to another group of Americans?" http://caamedia.org/jainternment.

Japanese American Veterans' Association

A wonderful resource for celebrating and remembering the work of the 100th/442nd and their fighting in Europe, and also the thousands of JAs who served in less-heralded roles in the Pacific and in Japan during the Occupation. http://www.javadc.org.

Japanese Relocation during World War II—National Archives

The federal government's collection of materials and data from the internment years. You can research history here, or order copies of your family's records. http://www.archives.gov/research/alic/reference/military/japanese-internment.html.

Many Mountains

This site commemorates those who were imprisoned in a Justice Department camp near Santa Fe, New Mexico. There were Justice Department prison camps like this one in addition to the main internment camps where suspected Japanese leaders and sympathizers were held in isolation from their families in the internment camps. http://manymountains.org/.

Manzanar Ringo-en

Ray DeLea's Web site incorporates photos by Ansel Adams taken at Manzanar relocation camp. http://www.owensvalleyhistory.com/manzanar1/page10.html.

A More Perfect Union—Smithsonian Institution

The Smithsonian does an impeccable job of telling the story of internment in a multimedia Web site. The materials were drawn from an exhibit at the museum. http://americanhistory.si.edu/perfectunion/experience/.

Rabbit in the Moon

Emiko and Chizu Omori's companion Web site for their award-winning documentary about internment and the crisis it forced on members of the JA community over whether to accept the injustice or fight it. http://www.pbs.org/pov/pov1999/rabbitinthemoon/index.html.

Resisters.com

Frank Abe created this righteous Web site about the men who refused to serve in the U.S. military while interned, and the treatment they received not only from their country, but from the Japanese American community. Abe was instrumental in the moving documentary "Conscience and the Constitution," which is now available in a two-disc DVD set. http://www.resisters.com.

JA/NIKKEI/AAPI SITES & BLOGS

8 Asians

Commentary and pop culture insights from a group of writers who contribute to this blog. http://8asians.com.

80–20 Initiative

This organization was created to act as a political advocate for the AAPI community, with the idea that, as a group, AAPIs have more clout than they do as discrete communities. http://www.80-20initiative.net/.

Angry Asian Man

Angry Asian Man is a daily must-read for all Asian Americans. Blogger Phil Yu presents links to news about and involving Asian Americans and Pacific Islanders, from pop culture to breaking news stories. He's a bellwether of what matters to Asian Americans, and he's fearless about pointing out whenever something is racist toward AAPIs. http://angryasianman.com.

Association of Pan-American Nikkei

An organization of Latin American Nikkei. http://www.copani.org/en.html.

Disgrasian

Snarky commentary about and for Asian Americans, which is also included on Huffington Post. http://disgrasian.com.

Goldsea Asian American Super Site

This large site appeals to younger AAPIs with an emphasis on contemporary pan-Asian pop culture. http://www.goldsea.com.

Hyphen

A nonprofit magazine that publishes quarterly and has a constantly updated Web site. *Hyphen* provides smart, thoughtful commentary about Asian America from a team of volunteer writers, artists, photographers, and editors. http://hyphenmagazine.com.

Japanese Canadian History

The history of Japanese Canadians, a subject that's not well-known in the lower Forty-Eight. http://www.japanesecanadianhistory.net.

Japanese Canadian National Museum

More Japanese Canadian history. http://www.jcnm.ca/.

Model Minority.com

A lively collection of articles and messages posted by the site's community of users, mostly concentrating on current pop culture and pan-Asian political issues. http://modelminority.com.

National Association of Japanese Canadians

Another resource for Japanese Canadians. http://www.najc.ca/.

Nikkei Voice

A national Japanese Canadian newspaper, published ten times a year by the Board of Directors of Nikkei Research and Education Project of Ontario, Inc. I've been writing columns for *Nikkei Voice* since 2013. http://nikkeivoice. ca.

Tao Jones—Jeff Yang Blog on Wall Street Journal

Jeff Yang is a godfather to Asian American journalists and bloggers: he was the editor way back in the day of *A Magazine*, the first AAPI national publication, and is the author of numerous books on AAPI pop culture, and he currently serves as the "Tao Jones" blogger for the *Wall Street Journal*. Always a thoughtful and reliable commentator on Asian America. http://blogs.wsj.com/speakeasy/tag/tao-jones.

SHOPPING

Japan Culture Club Catalog on the Web

This very cool store sells Japanese items including antiques, collectibles, and even custom-made *hanko*, or signature stamps with your name in *kanji*. There's also a fun page where you can find out what year you were born using the Japanese imperial calendar, as well as the Chinese zodiac. http://japan-cc. com/catalog.htm.

Japanese American National Museum Shop

JANM has an excellent online shop with many of the items sold in its museum store, including a great collection of books and videos as well as gifts from toys to t-shirts. http://janmstore. com//.

Japanese Style

A U.S.-based online store that offers Japanese gifts, kimono, clothing, paper lanterns, sushi supplies, home décor, and garden supplies. http://www.japanesestyle.com/.

Japanorama

An e-commerce site for Japan-related books, music, movies, screensavers, software downloads, and more. http://www.japanorama. com.

Japan Ring

An online hub, owned by Japanorama, of links to Japan-related Web sites. http://hub. yourlocaltake.com/hub/japan.

Japan-Shop.com

A virtual mall of Japan-related retailers online, nicely organized and easy to navigate, though not exactly elegantly designed. http://www. japan-shop.com/.

JUN Gifts

An elegantly designed site that features products from the traditional (*furoshiki* wrapping scarves) to the modern (mouse pads with Japanese prints). http://jun-gifts.com.

Kasuri Dyeworks

This venerable dealer in exquisite traditional Japanese textiles operates online from a remote part of Wyoming after nearly thirty years as a much-admired retail shop in Berkeley. Offers an astounding array of kasuri, shibori, yukata, katazome, chirimen, rinzu, and many other types of fabric in cottons, silks, and wools. The Web site displays dozens of swatches, a great resource for designers and artists. http://www.kasuridyeworksfabric.com.

Kimono Source

Another Web site that sells kimono, *obi*, *haori*, and other traditional clothing. http://www.kimonosource.com/.

Kinokuniya

A Japanese-owned bookstore chain, Kinokuniya is a presence in both LA's Little Tokyo and San Francisco's Japantown. Each store features a large section of books in English about Japan and Nikkei subjects. http://www.kinokuniya.com/us/.

Kyoto Kimono

This site sells authentic Japanese vintage kimono, *obi*, fabrics, and unusual items from the markets and auction houses of Kyoto. http://www.kyotokimono.com/.

Marukai

This is the Web site of the giant discount warehouse with outlets in Gardena and other places. The Web site offers e-commerce deliveries for everything from groceries to furniture. http://www.marukaiestore.com/.

Nichi Bei Bussan

A San Francisco–based retailer founded in 1902 to sell Japanese goods. http://www.nbstore.com/.

Nikkei Traditions

A store based in San Jose's wonderful little Japantown, founded by JAs to sell items of JA culture—modernized clothing with Japanese flourishes, books and CDs by JAs (and Hawaiians), and food and crafts by JAs. One of my favorite stops whenever I'm in the Bay Area. http://www.nikkeitraditions.com/.

Uwajimaya

A Seattle institution that's survived World War II and internment and is now at the heart of Seattle's International District. Uwajimaya is a family-owned Japanese grocery that in its main Seattle location is a hub for Asian businesses including Kinokuniya and a handful of great takeout restaurants. You can order groceries online through an "Instacart" service. But the company now has four locations in the Pacific Northwest, so go in person if you can. http://www.uwajimaya.com/.

TRAVEL TO JAPAN

Japan Exchange and Teaching (JET) Programme

Many young Americans get a great introduction to Japan by signing up as English teachers in the JET program, sponsored by the Japanese government. Embassy of Japan, JET Program Office, 2520 Massachusetts Ave., NW, Washington, D.C. 20008, Tel.: (202) 238–6772, http://www.jetprogramme.org.

Japan National Tourism Organization

Japanese government office whose sole purpose is to help promote tourism by foreigners in Japan, including making their trips as pain-free as possible. 10 Fl., Tokyo Kotsu Kaikan Bldg., 2–10–1, Yurakucho, Chiyoda-ku, Tokyo, Japan 100–0006, http://www.jnto.go.jp.

Japan Rail Pass

If you're thinking about traveling to Japan for a week or longer (who would go for less than a week?), the Japan Rail Pass, or JR Pass, is a must. It's a great deal cost-wise and can save you a lot of money if you're going to see various parts of the country. It will get you onto trains with just a wave of the pass at the ticket booths, including most Shinkansen bullet trains, and many of the standard Japan Rail lines. In Tokyo, the pass is handy for the JR Yamanote line that travels in a loop and stops at many key areas in the city, such as Akihabara, Shinjuku, Harajuku, and Tokyo Station. If the other lines you need to ride are run by JR, you can wave your pass to get on them as well. The pass is even good for the ferry boat to the island Miyajima south of Hiroshima to visit the famous Itsukushima Shrine. For Tokyo subways and the occasional other train lines, buy a Suica pass and avoid the sometimes stressful task of buying individual ride tickets. http://www.japan-rail-pass.com.

Manjiro Society for International Exchange

This innovative nonprofit organization hosts hundreds of people from Japan and the United States every year—alternating each year between Japan and the U.S.—who attend a "Grassroots Summit" as a way to build understanding between the two countries. The key to the summit is a few days spent during each event in homestays, seeing how regular families live in each country. 11227 South Shore Rd., Reston, VA 20190, Tel.: (703) 471–5466, http://manjiro.org.

BOOKS

American Patriots: MIS in the War against Japan, edited by Stanley L. Falk and Warren Tsuneishi, Japanese American Veterans of Washington, D.C., 1995. This is an oral history of veterans of the Military Intelligence Service, a group of JA soldiers who fought in the Pacific but whose stories are seldom told.

And Justice for All: An Oral History of the Japanese American Detention Camps, John Tateishi, University of Washington Press, 1984.

One of the first and best nationally published oral histories, these first-person accounts were collected by one of the leaders of the redress movement of the late 1970s and early 1980s. Tateishi today is executive director of the Japanese American Citizens League.

Baseball Saved Us, Ken Mochizuki, with illustrations by Dom Lee, Lee and Low, 1995. An evocative and educational children's book about how internment was made a little less horrible through the game of baseball.

Beacon Hill Boys, Ken Mochizuki, Scholastic Press, 2002. Mochizuki adds to his catalog of children's books with this semiautobiographical story aimed at a teenaged readership about a group of JA high school friends growing up in Seattle in the early 1970s.

Bon Odori Dancer, Karen Kawamoto McCoy, illustrated by Carolina Yao, Polychrome, 1998. A timeless children's book about how it's important to try your best even if you're a young JA struggling to learn traditional dance.

Cane Fires: The Anti-Japanese Movement in Hawaii, 1865–1945, Gary Y. Okihiro, Temple University Press, 1991. A serious study of racism against Japanese immigrants and their families in Hawaii.

Dear Miye: Letters Home from Japan 1939–1946, Mary Kimoto Tomita, Stanford University Press, 1995. A remarkable journal of one Kibei (a Nikkei who was sent to Japan for part of her education) who was stranded in Japan during World War II and went to work for the U.S. Occupation after the war.

Desert Exile: The Uprooting of a Japanese-American Family, Yoshiko Uchida, University of Washington Press, 1982. A touching personal memoir by author Yoshiko Uchida of her family's internment experience.

The Donald Richie Reader: 50 Years of Writing on Japan, Donald Richie, edited by Arturo Silva, Stone Bridge Press, 2001. This is a fine collection of essays by one of the pre-eminent American experts on Japan. Richie arrived in Japan during the U.S. Occupation following World War II and fell in love with the country and its culture. His passion, knowledge, and appreciation for all things Japan are obvious in every sentence, from his observations of a country in ruins to its regeneration.

Encyclopedia of Japanese American History: An A-to-Z Reference from 1868 to the Present, edited by Brian Niiya for the Japanese American National Museum, Checkmark Books, 1993. A terrific reference resource for any JA interested in the community's history with a chronology, as well as a large section with alphabetical entries. Updated in 2001.

Encyclopedia of Japanese Descendants in the Americas: An Illustrated History of the Nikkeis, edited by Akemi Kiku-mura-Yano for the Japanese American National Museum, AltaMira Press, 2002. A data-filled book that tells the story of Japanese immigration not only to the United States, but also country by country throughout North, Central, and South America. A great resource for learning about the population of Japanese Brazilians, from the earliest immigrants to today.

Executive Order 9066: The Internment of 110,000 Japanese Americans, Maisie and Richard Conrat, MIT Press, 1972. A pioneering book that has been reprinted a couple of times since its initial release, this is primarily a collection of powerful photographs of Japanese Americans taken during internment by Dorothea Lange and other photographers for the War Relocation Agency.

Farewell to Manzanar: A True Story of Japanese American Experience During and After the World War II Internment, Jeanne Houston and James D. Houston, Bantam, 1983. This is one of the best-known books about Japanese Americans, and for many readers their introduction to the facts of internment. The true story of Jeanne Wakatsuki Houston's years spent as a child in Manzanar has been a staple in schools for years.

Fish Head Soup and Other Plays, Philip Kan Gotanda, University of Washington Press, 1991. The first collection of the work of the most prominent Japanese American playwright. The four plays in this book explore relationships between Issei, Nisei, and Sansei, with the dark memory of internment looming in the background. Another collection, *No More Cherry Blossoms*, from the same publisher, was released in 2005.

Flowers from Mariko, Rick Noguchi and Deneen Jenkins, Lee and Low, 2001. A touching children's book not about internment, but the period immediately after the war, when a JA family struggles to re-establish its life on the West Coast and a flower business that was lost because of internment.

The Four Immigrants Manga: A Japanese Experience in San Francisco, 1904–1924, Henry (Yoshitaka) Kiyama, translated by Frederik L. Schodt, Stone Bridge Press, 1999. A snapshot of what life was like for early Japanese immigrants, who become houseboys or farm laborers while they saved money and educated themselves. But this isn't a typical history—the story's told in the form of manga, or comics. Kiyama was a talented young artist when he came to America, but he returned to Japan in 1924. This book was rediscovered years later and translated for this enlightening and entertaining edition.

From Our Side of the Fence: Growing Up in America's Concentration Camps, edited by Brian Komei Dempster for the Japanese Cultural and Community Center of Northern California, Kearney Street Workshop, 2001. This book grew out of a writing workshop that coaxed Nisei to write down their memories of growing up and the internment years; the stories were so successful they were compiled into a moving, emotionally gripping book.

Grandfather's Journey, Allen Say, Houghton Mifflin/Walter Lorraine Books, 1993. This Caldecott Award–winning children's book is a poignant story of how the author's grandfather loved both Japan and the United States, and how that split has affected the author.

Hiroshima in the Morning, Rahna Reiko Rizzuto, The Feminist Press at CUNY, 2010. Rizzuto's first book was *Why She Left Us*, a novel about a family tragically affected by JA internment. This one is her nonfiction memoir of a 2001 trip to Japan, paid for by a fellowship from the National Endowment for the Arts to research the stories of Hiroshima bomb survivors. The trip turns out to be a framework for her own search for identity and how it affects her marriage. She's a very fine writer, and this is an intense but satisfying read.

I Am an American: A True Story of Japanese Internment, Jerry Stanley, Crown Books for Young Readers, 1996. This book for grades 5–10 tells the true story of a Japanese American interned at Manzanar, and captures poignant details of the experience for young readers.

The Issei: The World of the First Generation of Japanese Immigrants, 1885–1924, Yuji Ichioka, The Free Press, 1988. A scholarly and fascinating history of the earliest immigrants to the United States and the obstacles they faced in establishing their lives.

Issei and Nisei: The Settling of Japanese America, Ronald Takaki, Chelsea House Publishers, 1994. The renowned author and JA historian covers the first waves of Japanese immigration and the coming of age of the Nisei generation in this compact book, based on his more exhaustive history of all AAPIs, *Strangers from a Different Shore*.

Jan Ken Po: The World of Hawaii's Japanese Americans, Dennis Ogawa, University of Hawaii Press, 1973. This book gives some context and insight into why and how JAs from Hawaii are different from mainland JAs.

J-Boys: Kazuo's World, Tokyo, 1965, Shogo Oketani, Stone Bridge Press, 2011. *J-Boys* wonderfully captures the sense of place of Tokyo in the mid-1960s, a time when I was about the same age as this book's main character, Kazuo. Oketani lived through that era and remembers details that bring the setting and situations to life.

Jet Black and the Ninja Wind, Leza Lowitz and Shogo Oketani, Tuttle, 2013. This is a thoroughly enjoyable young adult action thriller about a Japanese American teenager who discovers she's a descendant of a ninja clan and travels from New Mexico to Japan to fulfill her family destiny. Lowitz and Oketani, who are married and live in Japan, capture the cultural nuances of both America and Japan and, though a bit fantastic, make the characters and storyline believable.

Kids Explore America's Japanese American Heritage, Westridge Young Writers Workshop, John Muir Publications, 1994. A hard-to-find small volume written and illustrated by young JAs in Colorado, which covers JA culture and shows how even as youngsters they were interested in preserving their Japanese roots.

Last Witnesses: Reflections on the Wartime Internment of Japanese Americans, edited by Erica Harth, Palgrave, 2001. A thoughtful, thought-provoking collection of essays, commentaries, and memoirs by former internees, descendants of internees, and even non-Japanese who worked in internment camps.

Nikkei Donburi: A Japanese American Cultural Survival Guide, Chris Aihara, Polychrome, 1998. A fun, lively book aimed at JA kids that includes some history, a lot of culture, and a lot of hands-on group projects.

Nisei: The Quiet Americans, Bill Hosokawa, University Press of Colorado, 2002. Originally published in 1969, this was the first major historical account of the Japanese American experience, and the first book that taught me about internment when I read it in high school.

Nisei Voices: Japanese American Students, Then and Now, edited by Joyce Hirohata and Paul Hirohata, Hirohata Design, 2003. Joyce Hirohata, a Sansei, came across her grandfather's self-published book from the 1930s, in which he collected valedictorian speeches by the first wave of Nisei students in California's public schools. When she realized that most of these students, who were optimistic and patriotic about their status as American citizens, in a few years had to face internment, Joyce Hirohata tracked down the former students or family and friends and republished their speeches along with their life stories, from before and during the war to today.

No-No Boy, John Okada, University of Washington Press, 1980. Okada's powerful novel was his only major accomplishment. Because it addressed the sensitive issue of refusing to serve in the United States military while imprisoned in an internment camp, Okada and the book were generally shunned for years after its 1950s publication.

Obasan, Joy Kogawa, Anchor, 1993. This well-written historical novel about Japanese Canadian internment is by a gifted JC Nisei; the book has become a standard in internment literature.

Out of the Frying Pan: Reflections of a Japanese American, Bill Hosokawa, University Press of Colorado, 1998. Hosokawa is a veteran journalist and author of *Nisei,* the first history of his generation, who wrote a column called "Out of the Frying Pan" for decades for the Pacific Citizen, the newspaper of the JACL. Here he recalls his life as a narrative for the JA experience in a series of often funny, always observant stories.

The Red Kimono: A Novel, Jan Morrill, University of Arkansas Press, 2013. Jan Morrill is an Arkansas-based JA who tells a compelling story of the Japanese American internment through well researched and finely observed details about both prewar life on the West Coast as well as the experience of imprisonment in Rowher Relocation Camp in Arkansas.

The Rice Room: Growing up Chinese American from Number Two Son to Rock 'n' Roll, Ben Fong-Torres, Plume, 1995. Although this is the story of a Chinese American growing up in San Francisco, it shares many of the struggles and triumphs of Japanese Americans; there's plenty to identify with, and to learn from. Besides, Fong-Torres is a terrific writer and the book's a joy to read.

Secret Asian Man: The Daily Days, Tak Toyoshima, Perfect Paperback, 2009. Toyoshima is a Boston-based JA cartoonist whose "Secret Asian Man" character has been published in an alternative weekly since 1999. This book compiles the daily cartoons he drew for a syndication service, and is a fine introduction to his work and wit. He's like a blogger who captures his life with images as well as words, and his semi-autobiographical commentaries capture the rising voice of AAPIs.

Snow Falling on Cedars, David Guterson, Vintage, 1995. The bestselling novel was turned into a somewhat confusing, if beautiful, movie. It tells the story of a small Japanese community in the Northwest and the repercussions from internment that still divide the community in the 1950s.

Spy Catchers of the U.S. Army in the War with Japan, Duval A. Edwards, Red Apple Publishing, 1994. Most histories of JAs in the military focus on the 100th Battalion/442nd Regimental Combat Team, the heroic soldiers who fought in Europe. Less known—in fact, their story was kept secret for decades under the veil of national security—but equally heroic were the JAs who fought in the Pacific against the

Japanese, as translators, intelligence gatherers, and as postwar facilitators of peace during the Occupation. This book tells the story of the men who were in the Counter Intelligence Corps.

Strangers from a Different Shore: A History of Asian Americans, Ronald Takaki, Penguin Books, 1989. A well-researched, engagingly told history of all Asian immigrant communities in the United States. It places the JA story in a larger context, making clear how we're all tied together with other Asian Americans.

Summer of the Big Bachi, Naomi Hirahara, Random House 2004. This was the first In a series of books by Edgar Award–winning mystery author Naomi Hirahara, starring an unlikely sleuth, Mas Arai. Mas is a sort-of retired cranky old LA gardener who has a knack of stumbling into murders and other mysteries that need solving. All of the Mas Arai books are fun to read and accurately and fondly (Hirahara's father was also a gardener) evoke the Japanese American community of southern California. Hirahara has retired Arai and launched a new mystery series starring a Japanese American LAPD bicycle cop, Ellie Rush, with her 2014 debut, "Murder on Bamboo Lane."

Topaz Moon: Chiura Obata's Art of the Internment, text by Kimi Kodani Hill, Heyday Books, 2000. There are other books showing the art of Chiura Obata, an exceptionally talented and influential San Francisco area artist who was interned at Topaz in Utah. This book explores the range of works, from drawings to watercolors, many of them displaying his roots in Japanese calligraphy and brush painting, that he created while incarcerated.

To the Stars: The Autobiography of George Takei, Star Trek's Mr. Sulu, George Takei, Pocket Books, 1994. Yes, a lot of the book's about the *Star Trek* years (which is pretty cool if you're into the series) but the early part of the book is a fascinating tale of his childhood, growing up in California and being interned in Arkansas.

Tule Lake, E. T. Miyakawa, House by the Sea, 2002. Originally published in 1980, this novel focuses on JAs who resisted the injustice of internment and were sent to the one camp for "troublemakers," Tule Lake, which became notorious as the most violent of all the camps.

Why She Left Us, Rahna Reiko Rizzuto, Harper Collins, 1999. Rizzuto's first novel reveals a family tragedy through the eyes of four members of a JA family that is still haunted by internment today.

Years of Infamy, Michi Weglyn, Morrow Quill Paperbacks, 1976. A landmark book, which exhaustively researched and reported the racism and economic exploitation that led to internment—not national security or the safety of people of Japanese descent.

FILMS AND VIDEOS

Children of the Camps, produced by Dr. Satsuki Ina. This emotionally intense documentary follows a group of Nisei who had been children during World War II on a retreat with Dr. Satsuki Ina, who explores the long-term effects of trauma on people who were interned when they were young.

Come See the Paradise, directed by Alan Parker, 1992. Starring Dennis Quaid and Tamlyn Tomita, this film deals with internment through the plot of an interracial romance.

Conscience and the Constitution, Frank Abe. The story of the Fair Play Committee, a group of JAs interned at Heart Mountain in Wyoming who refused to be drafted into the United States military. They were branded traitors and ostracized not only by their country but by their community.

Forgotten Valor, directed by Lane Nishikawa, 2001. The second part of a trilogy by filmmaker/actor Lane Nishikawa about the 100th Battalion/442nd Regimental Combat Team, this short film stars Soon-Tek Oh as the commander of the World War II regiment, which is finally getting its medals upgraded to the Medal of Honor, fifty years after the end of the war. But one of its members has cracked under the post-traumatic stress and disappeared, and it's up to the colonel to find his lost soldier.

Go for Broke, directed by Robert Pirosh, 1951. An early Hollywood depiction of the 100th Battalion/442nd Regimental Combat Team, the all-Nisei group that fought in Europe. The film stars Van Johnson and is, not surprisingly, told from the perspective of Caucasians, although it's remarkably sensitive to issues of racial stereotypes.

Looking Like the Enemy, Japanese American National Museum. This documentary interviews JA veterans about their experiences serving in the military during World War II, the Korean War, and the Vietnam War, and how their race affected their service.

Moving Memories, Japanese American National Museum. George Takei introduces this fascinating and tragic collection of home movies taken by Japanese Americans before World War II—when their lives were filled with promise.

Only the Brave, a full-length feature released in 2006, is a drama about the rescue of the Texas "Lost Battalion" by the 100th Battalion/442nd Regimental Combat Team starring actors such as Tamlyn Tomita, Jason Scott Lee, Mark Dacascos, Pat Morita, and Nishikawa himself.

Picture Bride, directed by Kayo Hatta, 1995. Starring Youki Kudoh and Tamlyn Tomita, this film tells the not uncommon story of a Japanese woman who marries a man who is already in Hawaii, only to find when she arrives that the man is much older, less attractive, and less successful than she had been led to believe.

Rabbit in the Moon, Emiko Omori. This powerful documentary, which has been shown on PBS, showed that not all Japanese and Japanese Americans submissively went to internment camps.

Something Strong Within, Japanese American National Museum. This short video is a powerful, haunting collection of home movies—mostly shot surreptitiously—taken within internment camps of the day-to-day lives of incarcerated Japanese Americans. For many viewers, this is the first introduction to the reality of the experience, and it's presented simply, without narration.

Toyo Miyatake: Infinite Shades of Gray, Japanese American National Museum. This beautifully directed, award-winning short documentary tells the life and shows the work of a renowned photographer who chronicled the evolution of Los Angeles's Little Tokyo District over decades, and how internment affected his creativity.

Uncommon Courage: Patriotism and Civil Liberties, Bridge Media, Inc. A documentary about the JA soldiers who fought in the Pacific as part of the Military Intelligence Service.

Words, Weavings and Songs, Japanese American National Museum. Wakako Yamauchi, Momo Nagano, and Mary Nomura survived internment as teenagers with their art, music, and literature. This documentary shows how art can help people in the direst of circumstances.

Afterword

Since the first edition of this book was published in 2004, Japan has slipped from its long-held position as the number-two economy in the world to third place behind China. China is expected to overtake the United States soon and become the number-one economy in the world. The U.S. has been making an "Asian Pivot" under the presidency of Barack Obama, with varying degrees of success, and Japan has remained America's most ardent and critically important ally in Asia.

Japan is reaching out to the world and to the U.S. in particular with its "Cool Japan" charm offensive, which highlights not just the traditional culture that has drawn attention from across the Pacific to Japan, but the contemporary pop culture—anime, J-pop, food, fashion—that has helped spark interest in Japan today. It's worth noting that the "Hello Kitty" exhibit that opened in 2014 at the Japanese American National Museum smashed attendance records. China may be economically mightier, but Japan still has powerful cultural clout.

The U.S.-Japan Council (USJC) was formed in 2009 with offices in Washington, D.C., Los Angeles, and Tokyo. Headed by Irene Hirano-Inouye, the former President and CEO of the Japanese American National Museum, the USJC is an organization formed and led by Japanese Americans to build stronger ties between the United States and Japan. The group focuses on a Tomodachi ("Friendship") initiative that grew out of the relief efforts following the 2011 Tohoku earthquake and tsunami to promote young Japanese American leaders and scholars, as well as an annual Japanese American Leadership Delegation that sends leaders from business, government, academic, nonprofit, and cultural fields to Japan to meet with political, business, and cultural leaders there. Such a program, which is welcomed by all levels of the Japanese government, wouldn't exist if the ties that bind us together weren't strong.

TOMODACHI

The U.S.-Japan Council's logo for its Friendship initiative to help Fukushima earthquake recovery.

Even the ongoing controversy over the continued placement of United States military bases in Okinawa reflects how critical Japan still is to American security. I'm not sure how the base issue will play out, but all of the headlines show how, as Japanese Americans, the two sides of our heritage are inextricably linked together. Even the most nonchalant "banana" (like I was once accused of being ... by my future wife!) has a dormant Japanese core that can come to life with a little prodding, maybe by a book like this, or certainly, a trip to Japan.

As JAs, we should embrace the duality of our identities. We can be both Japanese and American and celebrate the richness of our eastern roots as well as our Western leaves and branches.

Since the first edition of this book was published so much has happened with technology, the Internet, and social media that allow us to move easily, seamlessly, back and forth between our two cultures. It's almost as if we can immerse ourselves in one side or the other and adjust our Japanese-ness or American-ness moment by moment, in real time, if we choose.

I choose to be a Japanese American, equal parts of both, and then an Asian American. And I'm proud to be who I am.

G.A.

Index

9/11, 157
80-20 Initiative, 154, 174
442nd Regimental Combat Team/100th Battalion, 30, 53, 103, 155, 156, 173, 181, 182, 183

AAPI, 7, 8, 94, 99, 105, 149–59, 174
alien land laws, 24, 25
All-American Girl, 105
All Camp Summit, 32, 158
Angry Asian Man, 96, 97, 174, 187
anime, 85, 85–88, 86, 87, 88, 99, 102, 111, 152, 169, 170, 185
Aoki, Hiroaki "Rocky," 60, 60–61
APA, 8
archiving. *See* preserving your family's legacy
Asakawa, Glenn, 42, 45
Asian American, 7, 8, 31, 95, 96–97, 103, 105, 107, 109, 149–59, 154, 155, 158, 174, 175, 186

Asian Americans and Pacific Islanders. *See* AAPI
Asian American Theater Company, 104
Astroboy, 85
atomic bomb, 39, 90, 104, 169
avant-garde JA artists, 111
azuki beans, 69, 70, 115

banana, 9, 10, 12, 185
baseball, 93, 94–95, 95, 109, 171, 177
Baseball Saved Us, 109
Beacon Hill Boys, 109
Benihana of Tokyo, 60
benjo, 14, 22, 74, 84, 126
Benkyo-Do, 114
Better Luck Tomorrow, 104, 155
bilingual household, 75–76
blogging, 96
books of interest to JAs, 177–81
bowing, 50, 51
bunka shishu (embroidery), 41
butsudan, 54

California Japanese American Community Leadership Council, 120
calligraphy, 114
Camp Amache, 15, 29
camps, 21, 22, 27–32, 33–34, 36, 98, 109, 117, 118, 124, 126, 130, 166, 173, 180, 182, 183. *See also* internment
celebrations of JA families, 52–54
Chan, Charlie, 103
Chan, Jackie, 103
chanoyu, 42
Charlotte Sometimes, 104, 155
chawan mushi, 61
Cherry Blossom festival, 40, 45, 53, 57, 171
Children of the Camps, 28, 34, 173, 182
Chinese Exclusion Act, 22, 23
Chinese immigration, 21
Chin, Vincent, 157
Cho, Margaret, 105, 106, 152
chopsticks, 55–57, 66
Christianity, 46, 120, 124

churches and the JA community, 120, 143
Cibo Matto, 111
Civil Liberties Act of 1988, 26, 33, 156
Clavell, James, 93
"Cool Japan," 185
crafts, 38–42
Cultural News, 166
customs and traditions, 47–58

Days of Waiting, 104
death, rituals regarding, 54–56
demographics, 8, 122–23, 149–50, 154–55
Densho, 15, 173
Denver, 15, 29, 31, 34, 42, 44, 45, 50, 52, 53, 54, 55, 61, 62, 70, 84, 87, 96, 113, 115, 118, 119, 121, 122, 143, 155, 170
dragon boat, 87, 111, 152
Dreams Come True, 99

Endo, Mitsuye, 31
enryo, 52, 54, 74, 106
etiquette, 21, 56–57, 119, 168, 169
Executive Order 9066, 32, 178

family history, 13, 125–35, 172
Farewell to Manzanar, 107, 178
films, Japanese in, 102–4
food, 59–72, 83–84
Forgotten Valor, 155, 182
Four Immigrants Manga, The, 49, 171, 178
Fresh Off the Boat, 106, 107
furoshiki, 52, 175
Furutani, Dale, 109

gagaku, 44

gaijin, 44, 50
gaman, 28, 58, 75, 84, 132
games, 36–38
gassho, 54
geisha, 84, 85
genealogy sites, 172
genkan, 47, 48, 144
"Gentleman's Agreement", 24
geta, 47, 48, 49, 88, 126
Giant Robot, 111, 152
gift-giving, 51–52
Godzilla, 89, 89–90, 90, 94
Go for Broke!,, 30
go (game), 37
gohan, 54, 59, 65
Gold Mountain, 21
Google Alerts, 164
Google Translate, 79, 80, 163, 164
Gosei, 13, 16, 29, 34, 104, 119, 135, 143, 149, 151, 156
Gotanda, Philip Kan, 104, 110, 178
Grannis, Kina, 101

hagoita, 40
hakujin, 98, 141
hanafuda, 36
hanami, 53
hapa, 19, 150
hapa, use of, 8, 19, 78, 150, 172–73
hapa haole, 150
Hapa Project, 167, 173
hapa-related sites, 172–73
happi, 48, 142
Hawaii, 11, 12, 20, 21, 23, 27, 28, 30, 33, 35, 45, 61, 67, 68, 80, 105, 114, 122, 126, 128, 129, 150, 154, 168, 172, 177, 179, 183
Hawaii Five-0, 105–6
Hello Kitty, 86, 114, 167, 171, 185

Hill, Judith, 100–101
Hina Matsuri, 40, 46, 53, 120
Hirabayashi, Gordon, 31, 33
hiragana, 11, 73, 77, 79, 91
Hirahara, Naomi, 108, 109, 181
Hirohito, Emperor, 90, 127
Hiroshima (band), 100
hoji, 54
Hokubei Mainichi, 121
Hollywood, 7, 87, 89, 93, 102, 103, 105, 152, 155, 182
Hongo, Garrett Kaoru, 110
Hosokawa, Bill, 14, 37, 180
Houston, Jeanne Wakatsuki, 107, 178
Huang, Eddie, 106, 107
ikebana, 41, 41–42, 42, 44, 45

IMI (app), 80
immigrant, 13, 14, 19–27, 20, 21, 22, 23, 24, 25, 26, 29, 35, 36, 37, 38, 41, 45, 48, 49, 60, 96, 106, 108, 113, 117, 119, 123, 127, 129, 150, 151, 154, 155, 177, 178, 179
Immigration Act of 1924, 24–25, 26
immigration records, 129
Ina, Satsuki, 15, 28, 34, 173, 182
instant noodles, 64–65
Internet, 95–97, 163–65
Internet and JAs, 95–97
internment, 12, 13, 24, 26, 27, 28, 29, 30, 31, 32, 33, 34, 39, 53, 58, 62, 69, 71, 75, 76, 77, 84, 97, 100, 104, 107, 108, 109, 110, 113, 117, 118, 119, 123, 124, 126, 129, 129–30, 130, 131, 135, 149, 150,

154, 156, 157, 158, 159,
173, 174, 176, 177, 178,
179, 180, 181, 182, 183
internment resources, 173–74
Ishikawa, Travis, 95

JA food specialties, 67–68
JA/Nikkei/AAPI sites and
blogs, 174–75
Jan ken pon, 36
JANM. *See* Japanese American
National Museum (JANM)
Japan-America Grassroots
Summit, 140–41
Japan Blog List, 166
Japanese American Citizens
League {JACL), 28, 31, 32,
33, 77, 121, 122, 150, 154,
156, 157, 158, 166, 180
Japanese American Museum of
San Jose, 117, 166
Japanese American National
Museum (JANM), 15, 32,
100, 116, 117, 128, 129,
130, 131, 158, 166, 168,
175, 178, 182, 183, 185
Japanese Canadian National
Museum, 124, 174
Japanese Canadians, 12, 29,
110, 122, 124, 167, 174,
175
Japanese Cultural and
Community Center of
Northern California
(JCCCNC), 114–15, 116
Japanese culture sites, 169
Japanese dolls, 40–41
"Japanese lite", 85
Japanese used in English,
91–92
Japan Exchange and Teaching
Programme (JET), 139–40,
176
Japan in Hollywood films,
93–94

Japan Monthly Web Magazine,
165
Japan Rail Pass, 176
Japan-related shopping sites,
175–76
Japan-related Web sites,
168–69
Japan Times, 165
Japantown. *See* Nihonmachi
Jerome (camp), 30, 32
Jodo Shinshu, 44, 45, 46
J-pop, 7, 98–102, 99, 100,
152, 170, 185

Kadohata, Cynthia, 109
kamidana, 54, 55
kanji, 64, 73, 78, 79, 91, 92,
141, 144, 175
katakana, 11, 41, 73, 77, 79,
91, 92, 114, 141
Kibei, 25, 30, 177
kimekomi, 40
Kiyama, Henry Yoshitake, 49
Kogawa, Joy, 110, 180
Konda, Cynthia, 80
Korematsu, Fred, 31, 33
koseki tohon, 127, 127–29,
128, 129
Kotaku, 165
K-pop, 7
Kyodo News, 165
Kyoto Journal, 165

language, 73–80, 137, 143
language barrier, 49, 79, 98,
139, 143, 144
learning Japanese, 77–80
Lee, Bruce, 90, 93, 103, 105
Lin, Justin, 155
literature, JA authors of,
106–10
Little Tokyo, 15, 70, 71, 109,
111, 113, 114, 116, 117,
118, 119, 120, 176, 183
Little Tokyo Service Center

(LTSC), 116

Maggie Q, 105
mah jong, 36, 37
Mako, 103
maneki neko, 56
manga, 85, 88, 111, 171, 179
Manjiro Society, 140, 177
Many Mountains, 130, 173
Manzanar, 32, 33, 107, 119,
173, 178, 179
martial arts, 29, 45, 50, 93,
103, 155
matcha, 115
matsuri, 45, 53
Meiko, 101
Memoirs of a Geisha, 83, 84,
93
Metropolis, 165
Miki, Roy, 110
Military Intelligence Service,
30, 122, 167, 177, 183
minyo folk dance, 48
Misaka, Wataru, 95
Miyakawa, E. T., 07–8
Miyazaki, Hayao, 86, 87
Mochi, 68–70
mochitsuki, 47, 119, 120, 132
Mochizuki, Ken, 15, 109, 177
Morita, Pat, 103, 156, 183
Morrill, Jan, 108, 180
mottainai, 74, 78, 115
Mura, David, 110

Nakahama, Manjiro, 22, 140
Nakamura, Goh, 101
National Association of Japan-
America Societies, 167
National Association of
Japanese Canadians, 124,
175
National Japanese American
Historical Society (NJAHS),
117, 167
newspapers for JAs, 121

New Year, 33, 42, 51, 56, 57, 65, 68, 69, 70, 72, 75, 121, 132

New York City, 11, 60–61, 73, 99, 100, 101, 105, 108, 111, 114, 110, 166

NHK World, 164

Nichi Bei Times, 121

NigaHiga (Ryan Higa), 97

Nihongo, 9, 12, 28, 44, 62, 73, 73–80, 77, 80, 120, 137, 138

Nihonmachi, 21, 49, 60, 113–20, 114, 117, 118, 119, 120

Nihonmachi, decline of, 117–20

Niijima, Jo, 46

Nikkei, 11, 48, 63, 73, 77, 98, 108, 120, 121, 122, 122–23, 124, 132, 137, 152, 167, 174, 175, 176, 177, 180, 188, 189

Nikkei Family Magazine, 121

Nikkei Heritage, 117, 121–22

Nikkei National Museum & Cultural Centre, 167

Nikkei Traditions, 114, 115, 132, 152, 176

Nikkei Voice, 175

Nisei, 9, 11, 13, 14, 15, 19, 24, 25, 26, 27, 29, 30, 31, 32, 33, 34, 36, 37, 38, 40, 41, 45, 46, 49, 50, 51, 56, 57, 59, 61, 62, 64, 69, 73, 76, 77, 78, 79, 80, 83, 84, 85, 86, 89, 92, 94, 95, 96, 98, 99, 101, 107, 115, 117, 118, 119, 120, 122, 123, 124, 127, 128, 130, 135, 138, 140, 142, 143, 145, 150, 151, 152, 155, 156, 158, 159, 178, 179, 180, 182

Nishikawa, Lane, 103, 110, 155, 182

Nomo, Hideo, 95

No-No Boys, 9, 11, 29, 32, 107, 108, 180

Northwest Nikkei, 121

Northwest Nikkei Museum, 167

obon, 33, 38, 40, 45, 48, 51, 55, 101, 119, 120, 123

obutsudan, 54, 55, 57

Oh, Sandra, 105

Okada, John, 107, 180

Okazaki, Stephen, 104

okoden, 54

omiyage, 51, 52, 145

omusubi, 67, 91

onigiri, 67, 69, 70

Only the Brave, 155, 183

Oregon Nikkei Legacy Center & Japanese American History Museum, 167

"Oriental," 153

Origami, 38–40

osechi ryori, 69

oshogatsu, 33, 69, 101, 106

otoshidama, 57, 69

Otsuka, Julie, 109

Oya, Katsuji, 124

Pacific Citizen, 121, 180

pan-Asian culture, 151–53

Pearl Harbor, 8, 9, 12, 27, 29, 30, 31, 42, 108, 110, 158

Perry, Matthew, 22

Peruvian Japanese, 29, 123

photo albums, 125, 133, 134

Pink Lady, 98

Pizzicato Five, 99

Pokémon, 85, 86, 87

preserving your family's legacy, 133–35

racism, 10, 11, 21, 23, 24, 28, 49, 63, 91, 95, 103, 110, 111, 114, 116, 124, 142, 157, 177, 182

Rafu Shimpo, 121

ramen, 64, 64–65, 65, 171

recipes, 71–72

redress, 33–34, 123, 156–57

rice, 65–67

Rizzuto, Rahna Reiko, 108, 179, 182

RocketNews24, 165

Rocky Mountain Jiho, 15, 96, 121

Rohwer, 27, 32

Rokusei, 13, 104, 143, 149

ryokan, 139

Saberi, Roxana, 108

Sadako and the thousand cranes, 39

San Francisco, 21, 22, 23, 30, 44, 46, 49, 63, 67, 68, 95, 101, 102, 104, 108, 109, 113, 114, 115, 117, 118, 119, 120, 121, 129, 150, 154, 158, 167, 171, 176, 178, 181

San Jose, 114, 117, 118, 120, 132, 166, 176, 188

Sansei, 11, 13, 20, 23, 27, 29, 31, 34, 35, 42, 43, 44, 45, 46, 48, 53, 54, 55, 56, 60, 63, 65, 67, 68, 69, 70, 73, 74, 75, 77, 78, 80, 85, 87, 88, 91, 93, 94, 95, 97, 100, 104, 108, 110, 111, 113, 114, 115, 116, 118, 119, 120, 121, 122, 123, 127, 131, 132, 137, 138, 141, 142, 143, 144, 149, 150, 151, 153, 158, 170, 178, 180

Sawtelle, 111, 152

scrapbooks, 125–35

Seattle, 98, 102, 104, 109, 114, 118, 119, 121, 134, 150, 153, 167, 173, 176,

177

"Secret Asian Man," 15, 110, 111, 181

seiza, 50

sensei, 43, 50

shakuhachi, 44, 80, 98

shamisen, 43, 80, 98

Shichi-Go-San, 52

shikataganai, 28, 58, 60, 75, 76

Shin Issei, 13, 57, 74, 128, 150

Shinoda, Mike, 100

Shinran Shonin, 45

shodo, 41, 44

Shonen Knife, 98, 99

soba, 64, 65, 69, 115, 121

Soko Hardware, 114

songs, 42–45

spirituality, 45–47

sports, 94–95

sukiyaki, 115, 116, 142

"Sukiyaki" (song), 98

sumo, 33, 46, 90, 94, 95, 120, 157, 171

sushi, 7, 14, 21, 56, 59, 60, 61, 62, 63, 64, 65, 66, 69, 83, 84, 99, 103, 111, 115, 142, 151, 175

Suzuki, Ichiro, 95

taiko, 42, 44, 45, 54, 80, 100, 156, 158, 170, 171

Takaki, Ronald, 15, 179, 181

taking off shoes indoors, 47–48

Tamlyn Tomita, 103

Tan, Amy, 37

Tango no Sekku (Boys Day), 53

tatami, 42, 47, 48, 102

Tateishi, John, 15, 144, 158, 177

television, Asian actors on, 104–6

teppan-yaki, 60

Tezuka, Osamu, 85–86

tips for traveling to Japan, 144–45

Tohoku earthquake and tsunami, 164, 168, 185

Tomita, Tamlyn, 103

Tomodachi Initiative, 185

Toyoshima, Tak, 15, 110, 111, 181

traditional songs and music, 42–45

traveling to Japan, 50–51, 137–45, 176–77

travel to Japan sites, 176–77

Tule Lake, 29, 46, 107, 108, 182

Uchida, Yoshiko, 107, 177, 178

udon, 59, 64, 65, 115, 142

United Response Collaborative, 158

Uno, Edison, 33

U.S.-Japan Council, 168, 185

values, Japanese, 57–58

war brides, 83

Weglyn, Michi, 15, 33, 156, 182

When We Were Warriors, 155

World War II, 8, 12, 13, 25, 26, 27, 28, 29, 32, 33, 48, 58, 68, 83, 86, 88, 103, 114, 118, 120, 122, 123, 124, 129, 138, 140, 150, 155, 156, 157, 173, 176, 177, 178, 182, 183

Yagi, Curt, 101

Yamada, Mitsuye, 110

Yamagata, Rachael, 101

Yang, Jeff, 175

Yasui, Minoru, 31, 33

Years of Infamy, 33, 156, 182

Yellow Journalism, 23

"Yellow Peril," 119

"Yellow Power" movement, 33, 100, 107, 119, 153, 153–55, 154, 156

"yellowface," 103

Yonsei, 12, 13, 21, 26, 28, 29, 30, 33, 34, 39, 42, 47, 57, 58, 59, 66, 70, 72, 75, 77, 92, 99, 100, 103, 105, 106, 107, 108, 122, 125, 133, 137, 138, 140, 143, 149, 150, 151, 155, 156, 170

yukata, 48, 57, 175

Yu, Phil, 15, 96, 97, 174

zori, 48

GIL ASAKAWA is a Sansei (third generation) Japanese American who was born in Tokyo and moved to the U.S. when he was eight years old. He is a journalist, blogger, digital media expert and speaker on Japanese and Asian American topics. He blogs at www.nikkeiview.com and can be found on Facebook, Twitter, Instagram and other social media sites. He is active in the Japanese American and Asian American communities and lives in Arvada, Colorado with his wife Erin Yoshimura and their two cats Rufus and Hobbes.